Enduring Images

From the trauma of war to lifelong healing

Paul Fazekas

authorHOUSE®

AuthorHouse™
1663 Liberty Drive
Bloomington, IN 47403
www.authorhouse.com
Phone: 1-800-839-8640

First published by AuthorHouse 3/29/2010

ISBN: 978-1-4389-4487-6 (sc)
ISBN: 978-1-4389-4486-9 (hc)

Printed in the United States of America
Bloomington, Indiana

This book is printed on acid-free paper.

Dedication

To the memory of those who never returned home from the war into the waiting arms of their loved ones. And to those who cherish them in their hearts.

Introduction

The writing of this book over the span of five years has been a difficult undertaking. Many times I simply had to stop because of painful memories that were surfacing. On one occasion, I was absent from the keyboard for nearly a year. However, it was always on my mind and I was resolved to return as many times as necessary until the book was completed. Emotionally and spiritually, writing this book had an uncanny parallel to my actual combat tour in Vietnam. This time around, however, the pain was part of the healing process.

The book is divided into three separate sections. Part I, *A Rude Awakening,* deals with the sudden and unexpected manner in which the reality of my past connection with Vietnam was thrust upon me. This was not unlike the manner in which we experienced combat in Southeast Asia—days or weeks of calm punctuated by moments of terror. One day I was engaged in my profession treating patients with mental and emotional problems when, in an unguarded moment, I was "ambushed" by a telephone call that emotionally derailed me for the next six months. This flood of emotions propelled me to reach out to a number of people to help tame the inner turmoil and begin the healing process in earnest. Never in my wildest dreams did I envision the path upon which God would lead me in this sacred journey. Now, nearly six years later, I realize that this is not the end point, but only the end of the beginning. I had much to deal with following such a rude awakening.

Part II, *Vietnam: The Beginning,* deals with being drafted at age nineteen, becoming a soldier, and embarking upon a combat tour for which nothing could have possibly prepared me. Although I address some combat situations, this section is really more about the psychological impact that war has on the individual soul. Making matters worse, was the unpopular and controversial nature of the war in the years 1969/70. By this time, talk of "victory" or "good cause" had been absent from the national vocabulary for a few years. My sole mission was to survive the one-year tour. I reluctantly even included a chapter on my drug use in order to be as forthright as possible about what it was like for me while I was there. If I wanted to heal, then glossing over some areas in half measures would not suffice. This second part is not meant to be an exhaustive recounting of my combat tour, but highlights of some of the issues that had surfaced. There are some things that I felt would be better left out, albeit not ignored. I have admitted to God, to myself and to others the exact nature of these events and was blessed by the relief and healing that followed.

Part III, *Reflections: The Human Cost of War,* is a collection of vignettes that cover topics historically considered byproducts of war, long after the guns have been silenced. It is about the private burdens carried by those who have survived. My heartfelt concern is for combat veterans and their families, as well as for family members who spend an entire lifetime grieving for loved ones who died in service to their country. Our great nation has a moral responsibility to care for those who have borne the scars of war and we should never forget those who failed to return home alive. In the same manner that God "hates sin, but loves the sinner," we need to "hate war, but love the warrior."

Contents

PART III—Reflections: The Human Cost of War

PART I

A Rude Awakening

February 2002

The month of February in Buffalo, New York, is typically a cold one, with considerable snow and wind. The holidays, which usually bring a measure of excitement and anticipation for many of us, are now little more than a memory. We are in the doldrums of winter. Those susceptible to seasonal affective disorder, otherwise known as the "winter blues," are in the midst of these troubling episodes. Birds and squirrels are surviving off the kindness of people who routinely replenish the bird feeders. Deer in the outlying areas struggle; their herds are brutally, but naturally, thinning.

February is a particularly meaningful month for me; it was the month I left for Vietnam in 1970 and returned one year later, resolved to leave that part of my life in the jungles of Southeast Asia, buried along with the surrealistic memories of the most unpopular and controversial war in American history. February is also when I first experienced the bitter taste of combat, just over two weeks after my arrival. Ironically, it was the same month, thirty-two years later, when I received a telephone call that ushered in another defining moment in my life. I am convinced beyond a doubt that it was a telephone call orchestrated by divine providence. This was no random or circumstantial event. Even the manner in which I responded to the call, as well as the subsequent developments, was subject to God's all-encompassing grace.

It was early one Friday afternoon in February 2002, as I parked my car on a side street near the psychiatric clinic where I was scheduled to work on that day. Since the car was still warm, I decided to sit there and check my voice mail. The only message was from a woman with a deep Texas accent calling about a Vietnam veteran whose name was initially unfamiliar to me. As a clinical psychologist and nurse practitioner, I evaluated and counseled many veterans over the years. Occasionally I would hear from one of them requesting documentation about the treatment they received from me, usually for a disability claim. I decided to return the call, primarily so that I wouldn't have to do it at a later time. I wanted to get it off my mind and focus on the patients who were scheduled to see me later that day.

On the other end of the line was Peggy Barstow, a representative from a veterans' center in San Antonio. She asked me if I knew a Vietnam veteran by the name of Ray Wyatt Cage who she had recently interviewed. I pride myself on remembering names, but this one did not jog any memories. I told her that I had no recall of a former patient by that name. She quickly clarified that he was not a former patient but someone who claimed to have served with me in Vietnam in 1970. Following a brief pause, she further noted that he claimed he was with me when our squad was ambushed and "some soldiers were killed and wounded."

Despite the fact that the temperature in my car had dropped and more closely approximated the cold reading on the other side of my windshield, I found myself sweating. My hands began to tremble and my stomach was quivering. Without any warning, I was transported in my mind's eye back to Vietnam.

It was my first mission with the First Air Cavalry Division. Our company had made a combat air assault the previous day. A brief firefight had erupted within an hour after we were dropped off by helicopters and surprised some enemy soldiers in a clearing near a creek bed. Several of them were hit, but their comrades swiftly retrieved them and they seemingly vanished into the jungle. Cobra gunship air strikes were called in later that afternoon in the direction that the enemy soldiers were seen heading. But on this second day we were making preparations to proceed with our stated mission—to *search and destroy* an enemy bunker complex. We knew that they were waiting for us, but we couldn't see them. I was the third soldier in the point squad that was leading the attack for our company of about one hundred troopers. I didn't remember the names of the two men up ahead, but the one directly in front of me was my squad leader. We were contending with dense jungle foliage and visibility was limited. I remember hearing a loud explosion, followed by screaming and automatic weapons fire. To this day, I don't know for certain if I was knocked to the ground from the blast or dropped on my own accord.

In the heat of the moment, while we were engaged in the firefight, I didn't realize that the point man was killed instantly and my squad leader was mortally wounded. A few men behind me were wounded and yelling for a medic. The medic somehow managed to get up front toward our position and tend to the two stricken soldiers just ahead of me. He yelled for help and I made my way to him. We carried the squad leader to a safer area. Since the whole company was behind us, our main fear was that we would get caught in crossfire as they approached the enemy position. We moved my squad leader toward the base of a large tree, which offered a measure of protection. It was then I noticed that he suffered from a gaping neck wound and was bleeding profusely. It all happened in an instant. We tried in vain to stop the bleeding.

The medic attended to some of the others who were crying for help while I remained with my squad leader. I knew he was dying. He would return when the medevac helicopter arrived to pick up the wounded. My squad leader's last words were of concern about his family, his wife in particular. He was not afraid for himself. I held him when he took his last breath. By now the firing had stopped and we were engaged in the grim task of assessing our casualties, wondering who would be next to die such a gruesome death a half a world away from home.

What I failed to realize at the time I was sitting in my parked car was that I was experiencing a fully-fledged flashback characteristic of posttraumatic stress disorder (PTSD). Here I was the guy who treated others for the disorder over the years, most of them Vietnam veterans. How could this be happening to me? Why now, over a mere telephone call about something that happened in the distant past? Why didn't these intense feelings surface twenty years ago while I was listening to combat stories by Vietnam veteran patients? By now, Peggy seemed to sense that I was shaken and asked if I was all right. I noted that I was just "a bit surprised"—apparently I was still too much of a man to admit that I had been shivering and was emotionally derailed by this totally unexpected telephone call.

Since the soldier's name did not strike a familiar chord, I was especially curious how my name had come up. Apparently there were some inconsistencies in his military service records and she was calling me to verify his tour in Vietnam. One of the names he provided to her was our platoon medic, who lives about ten miles from my home. It had been nearly twenty years since we had any contact with one another. However, the medic and the soldier in question maintained sporadic contact with each other over the years. In fact, the former provided her with the spelling of my last name which she used to obtain the listing and telephone number for my office in the Yellow Pages.

Because the significance of the soldier's name still eluded me, I called the former medic later that day to help fill in the blanks. He reminded me that we simply referred to our squad member as "Cage" and that he was our M-60 machine gunner. Things were now starting to sound familiar. After a few phone calls and e-mail exchanges, the gaps in memory were finally closing. As it turned out some months later, Ray Cage was not only in Vietnam but was also twice decorated for valor. One of those medals was for his actions as our machine gunner on that fateful morning. The more we talked, the more it became apparent that we all had some unfinished business to deal with concerning the events that transpired that day, as well as many others during our one-year tour. Ray provided the first names of the two soldiers who died on that day in February 1970. At least now I had the names to go along with the repressed images that had haunted my psyche for such a long time and in so many untold ways. As I found out, our medic had been saying "good night" to Bill and Jim every evening for the past thirty-two years.

A Long Time Coming

The next several weeks were emotionally draining, to say the least. Images, memories, and myriad feelings had an unsettling effect on me. We exchanged numerous phone calls over the course of those first few days. Several other men from our old unit were also included. Finally, we had the exact date of the ambush. More importantly, we also had the full names of the two men who died that day—Corporal James Waulk, Jr., and Sergeant William Wood, both from Ohio. We reviewed the events of that day many times, each of us sharing from his particular perspective about the deadly ambush. In sum, we knew for certain that two soldiers had died on February 20, 1970, in Phuc Long province in South Vietnam, near the Cambodian border. We believe that at least four or five more were wounded, one of whom may have died in the hospital. Our squad, with only three men left, was reintegrated into the remaining three squads in the platoon.

I really can't say how often I thought about it, but every once in a while I would wonder about the family Bill Wood left behind that day. I do know, as the years went by, that my thoughts were heading more frequently in that direction. Perhaps as we get older, we begin to realize that time is running out on the things we hoped to accomplish. I even had vague intentions of "someday" initiating a full-scale search to contact them. I didn't realize then, as I do now, that I was emotionally frozen and could not manage the first step of this journey. In order to contact them, I had to begin to deal with the impact this traumatic event had on me. I always felt in my soul that my life and Bill's death were sealed together—I was still holding him. What happened that day, as well as other events in the next eleven months in Vietnam, would have a profound effect on the rest of my life.

Even as I write these words, I'm still in awe at how these events have unfolded for me. Without a doubt, this was far from the vague, feeble inklings I could muster to bring some measure of closure to my relationship with Bill. Timing was everything. But it was not my timing that mattered. It was God who was at work all along, waiting for the right moment to initiate His plan. I would have my part, but I would need to rest assured and trust in taking the path He was placing before me.

Bill Wood's hometown was Alliance, Ohio. Like many small towns, one doesn't have to make too many phone calls before obtaining the desired information. Bill was my first squad leader, but I spent less than a week with him before he was killed. I vividly recall him instructing me to stay close to him as he took me under his wing. Everyone had a great deal of respect for him. I knew he was married and had a family that he was worried about; he told me that much shortly before he died. But I knew nothing else about him, until now.

Her name was Mrs. Beulah Wood and she was eighty years old. She was his mother. Moreover, my contact informed me that Mrs. Wood had experienced serious health problems over the years, requiring numerous surgeries and hospitalizations. Her husband had died some years ago and she was living alone near her daughter in a seniors' apartment complex. I immediately resolved that this would be the end of the road. After all, I was finally talking about Vietnam and, although emotionally draining, the cathartic effect of commiserating with my army buddies continued to rearrange my inner life in ways I couldn't comprehend. Maybe that was enough. I certainly had enough internal material to process, which was already occupying many of my waking moments. My sleeping habits, which had been problematic for over thirty years, were starting to worsen and I was starting to have difficulty focusing at work. Those closest to me sensed I was troubled.

I decided that proceeding by calling Bill's mother was probably a bad idea for her as well as for me. Yet, I was in tremendous turmoil. How is it that the person who knew him the least could be in this position? The last thing I wanted to do was cause any further distress to a woman who lost her son thirty-two years ago and was elderly and in poor health. I decided to ask my wife, Donna, if she were in Mrs.

Wood's place, would she want to hear from someone who was with her son when he died. Without hesitation, her answer was a soft-spoken, definitive "Yes." This answer came from someone well qualified to speak on the subject. She was not only a clinical social worker but, more importantly, she was also my soul mate. We had been married for nearly thirty years. She knew firsthand how Vietnam had affected my life and our relationship. She immediately perceived a fortuitous opportunity for her husband's emotional healing—it had been a long time coming. The next step was a call to my best friend and confidant, Bill Stott. I first met Rev. Dr. Michael W. R. "Bill" Stott when I was twenty-one years old. I believe God placed him in my path at just the right time. I had returned from Vietnam less than a year before we had met. He had been a mentor, friend, and brother in Christ for over thirty years. I greatly valued his opinion and called him soon after I spoke with my wife. His answer was the same, as I knew it would be. It was not surprising coming from a man who, during World War II, pushed his way through the crowd as an eleven-year-old boy to shake the hand of Colonel Jimmy Doolittle when he visited Buffalo to a hero's welcome. Bill affirmed, rather emphatically I might add, that this was a blessed opportunity to provide some closure for both Bill's mother and me. The die had been cast; I decided to make the call the following Sunday, around seven in the evening.

I sat by the telephone for some time, contemplating how I would approach an eighty-year-old woman who was in poor health about the loss of her son thirty-two years earlier. Several avenues of thought ran through my mind. She might just think that I'm some kind of con artist—you know, the ones they profile on *20/20* or *Sixty Minutes*—trying a new gimmick to bilk an old lady out of her life savings. Unbelievable as it might seem, this potential scenario was more appealing than the one to follow. After all, in that scenario, she would just hang up and that would be the end of it. What I really feared was inducing some sort of medical crisis, like heart failure or a complete emotional breakdown if she believed me and allowed me to share about holding her son while he died in my arms. The phone rang about three times and she answered, "Hello?"

I simply responded with, "Hello, is this Mrs. Wood?"

She said, "Yes."

I said, "My name is Dr. Paul Fazekas and I am from Hamburg, New York, which is near Buffalo. I need to know if I have the right person, so please, I need to ask you if you had a son named Bill who was killed in Vietnam."

After a brief period of silence, she answered with a soft, resolute "Yes."

I said, "I wanted to let you know that I was with your son when he died. I was holding him in my arms. Please let me know if you want me to continue about what happened that day."

She said, "Please go on."

I shared the details about the events of that day in February and that we knew for certain that Bill's close friend, James Waulk, who also was from Ohio, was killed next to him. There were some wounded and maybe another soldier who died later in the hospital. I told her that since I was the newest member of the squad, Bill was looking out for me and I was right behind him, just as he instructed. Finally, I told her that he suffered from a massive neck wound from a rocket-propelled grenade (RPG) that was fired directly at us. I told her that both our medic and I worked frantically but there was nothing that could have been done to save his life. I told her that he was not afraid and that he died about five or ten minutes after he was wounded. The only concerns he voiced were about his family. I told her that I was with him when he took his last breath.

After a brief pause, she said, "I'm so thankful that you called me ... you made my day." She went on to inform me that the official report from the Army was that he walked into a booby trap and was killed at night. She was still upset to think that he was alone in the dark when he died. The cruel fact that he was killed twelve thousand miles from home remained unchanged but knowing that it was during the daylight and that he was with someone when he died seemed to make all the difference in the world to her. She also told me that her son's widow, Bonnie, remarried about four years after his death. Bonnie was devastated by the loss and grieved for a long time. Mrs. Wood noted she was the one who encouraged Bonnie to begin dating again. They were still very close and maintained regular contact with one another. She then asked me a question that caught me totally off guard: "Would you like to come and visit me and the rest of the family so we can have a reunion? We have a community room in our building that can hold a lot of people." I was now on automatic pilot, emotionally drained, not thinking very clearly … I said, "Yes."

She was going to share the news with her family and I told her that I would call her back within a few weeks. No words can describe how I felt when I got off the phone. I had just spoken with the mother of the man who died in my arms thirty-two years before. Connecting with Bill's family was something I had periodically thought about doing but had never actually considered how to take the first meaningful step. Besides, that was long ago and I convinced myself that his family properly grieved his death and went on with their lives like scores before them. But here she was, Bill Wood's living, breathing mother—the woman who brought him into the world and was there when he took his first breath. And then there was me, the one who was there when he breathed his last. I realized beyond a shadow of a doubt that this three-way meeting between us was no coincidence; it was a phenomenon that transcended the expanse of time. I was thoroughly convinced that God Himself orchestrated this encounter. Something else was emerging: I was now beginning to learn about the man who had died. Initially, I had known him for less than a week and couldn't even recall his first name. But now I was beginning to learn about his personal life. We would all become much better acquainted in the weeks ahead.

Preparation

A few days later, I followed up my phone conversation with a letter to Mrs. Wood. My hope was that she would have something concrete to share with her family. I took the additional step of placing it on my official office stationery, which would add some legitimacy for the rest of the family. The contents of the letter were as follows:

March 06, 2002

Dear Mrs. Wood,

It was truly an honor to speak with you the other evening. My heart was deeply moved. It has been an eventful few weeks as I have been speaking with five members of our old platoon after nearly thirty-two years. We all served with your son Bill in D Company, 1st Battalion, 12th Regiment, of the First Cavalry Division (Airmobile). I would consider it an honor to visit you and your family and share my memories and healing with you. I knew Bill for only about a week. I was the new soldier in the squad and Bill was training me. As I mentioned to you over the phone, Bill lived for about ten minutes after he was wounded, and I held him and talked with him the entire time. He died in my arms and was not afraid. During his last moments, he was talking about his loved ones. His words left a deep impression on my soul. It is a great privilege to know what a fine man he was with each person I have spoken to over the past few weeks.

Please feel free to give my address and phone number to members of your family. Let them know that I would welcome the opportunity to have them contact me. I will call you in a few weeks and let you know more about out visit in the near future.

God Bless You,

Paul

About a week later I received a phone call from a man who identified himself as Sam Rhodes, a close friend of the family and especially of Mrs. Wood. He reiterated her strong desire to meet with me but added that the rest of the family was ambivalent about an upcoming visit. My sudden bursting on the scene, out of nowhere, was creating some painful reminders for them about the death of their brother Bill so many years ago. However, Sam made it clear that he was mainly there for Mrs. Wood who he endearingly referred to as "Beulah." She wanted very much to meet me and was excited to have heard from me in the first place. He also confirmed that she had numerous health problems, but her spirit remained undaunted.

I could immediately sense that Sam was a kind and gentle man. Soft spoken, he was very protective of Beulah. He asked if I would be comfortable describing the circumstances around Bill's death. Since I felt safe and sensed a certain kinship with him already, I went over the details. I also mentioned that I had been in contact with our medic and machine gunner the past few weeks as we reviewed the events of that fateful day.

The machine gunner and I were in the point squad as we approached the enemy bunker near a clearing in the thick jungle. We heard a loud explosion, followed by automatic weapons fire. Adding to the confusion was the fact that the rocket that hit some of the men also set off the smoke grenades that were strapped on their rucksacks. The resulting purple and yellow smoke, which was used to guide the helicopter gunships, was clouding our vision. We were returning fire at the North Vietnamese but feared hitting our own men. It all added to the surrealism of combat in the dense jungle foliage. I told him that the point man was killed instantly, as he took the brunt of the rocket. Bill was directly behind him and was hit in the neck with shrapnel. Although I was only about eight or ten feet behind Bill, I was unharmed. The medic who ran up to the front risked his life as he was temporarily caught between our return fire and the enemy. I found out later that he was decorated for valor for his actions.

We could hear screaming from the wounded on both sides during and after the firefight. After the enemy disengaged and pulled back, our lieutenant, who by now was with us and brought some reinforcements from the rest of the platoon, gave the order to cease firing. We then carried Bill to a safer area, which the rest of company had secured while we waited for the medevac to arrive. It was there that Bill died in my arms, while the medic left momentarily to meet the helicopter which was hovering about sixty feet above the dense jungle canopy. Since there was no place for it to land, a jungle penetrator was lowered for him through the layers of branches. We put him in it and watched as they slowly lifted his lifeless body into the sky. The wounded were carried out in like manner.

I told him that the few of us who remained were integrated into other squads in the platoon. We pounded the enemy position with machine guns, grenade launchers, and light antitank weapons. Later we called in Cobra gunships and air strikes. With late afternoon approaching, we set up night defensive perimeter (NDP). I remembered that, as shaken up as I still was, I was thirsty and hungry.

As I sat down to eat that evening, my friend Larry Toczek approached me. Larry and I trained together in Fort Gordon and came to Vietnam on the same flight. He happened to be in the squad that was immediately behind us and asked me to fill him in on the details of the ambush. It's ironic that soldiers only a short distance from you can only guess what is occurring with their fellow troopers a mere hundred feet away. You can't see each other and you can't see the enemy. You try to remember the general direction of the rest of the platoon in order to avoid fratricide. Larry remembered hearing a lot of shooting and screaming—there is always screaming during a firefight. Apparently, they were pinned down behind us but withheld their fire in order to avoid hitting us. He told me the grim news that he was helping to carry Jim Waulk's body in a poncho because they didn't have time to have it evacuated with the wounded, as the medevacs did not want to take any unnecessary risks. It was pitch dark later that night when it was my turn to pull guard duty at the listening post. The silence during that hour was deafening; everything seemed to be moving in the darkness. I felt like a blind man who can sense the slightest vibrations of sound and motion around him. After I was relieved, I plunged into a deep sleep from total exhaustion.

Sam was a good listener and seemed to appreciate what I was saying. This was important to me. Afterwards, he shared that he was a Vietnam veteran as well. He was a professional soldier who was in the Army for twenty years, including two tours in Vietnam. He also shared that everyone was wondering about my legitimacy, so he took the liberty of doing a preliminary background check on my identity. He verified my professional credentials. He then related that a personal contact confirmed I was on the company roster for that particular mission when Bill Wood was killed. He also informed me Beulah had been suffering from a number of chronic medical problems and her health was quite poor. Interestingly, I don't recall asking about Bill's widow, with whom Mrs. Wood maintained regular contact. I was caught up in an emotional roller coaster ride that was showing no signs of slowing down.

During the ensuing days, I was seriously beginning to consider declining her invitation of making the trip to Alliance. Even under the best-case scenario that I could conjure up in my mind, I was feeling intensely ambivalent about the visit. Not unlike my tour in Vietnam, I was beginning to find myself in an emotional quagmire with no readily discernable exit strategy. I needed help. Once again, I contacted my closest friend, Bill Stott. To him, the matter was quite simple—go. He reminded me about this unusual window of opportunity, which would be of great benefit to at least two people—Beulah and me. At that point, I was starting to believe that some measure of good might be achieved from the tragedy that occurred decades ago, twelve thousand miles away. He then shared a story about himself when he was a young minister in Buffalo around 1960.

A nineteen-year-old Romanian-born young man had been convicted of murder. He dumped his victim's body in the Niagara River, which runs parallel along the western side of the city, bordering Canada on the far side. His family was indigent and could not afford funeral services after he was executed at Sing Sing in downstate New York. He was given a public funeral when his body was returned to Buffalo. My friend Bill officiated at the wake and was accompanied by his own father for moral support. He described the scene as his father approached the casket and stood alongside the executed man's father who was weeping over the loss of his son. Before long, Bill's own father began to cry as he placed his arm around the grieving parent. He also remembered that the entire funeral was an economy job since the city was springing for the bill. Consequently, the funeral director had done a less than adequate work preparing the body for the viewing and my friend noticed some of the embalming fluid leaking into the young man's shirt collar. It all combined to make a remarkably tragic affair that much more difficult to bear. However, it was the conversation he had with his own father later that evening that struck a chord in my heart. His father told him that if he never again did a good thing the remainder of his life, then what he did for that family would suffice. He was telling his son that he was born and groomed by God for that very day. Obviously, this message was one he never forgot.

Needless to say, my friend continues to go on doing good for many people, myself included. His work hadn't ended that day. He then focused his attention on me and told me in no uncertain terms the same thing his father told him. This moment in time was appointed, as was the day Bill was killed in Vietnam. In a very real sense, this was the day I was born for. This opportunity eclipsed everything in my life for the time being. A short time later, I felt a growing sense of purpose, no less than the one that drives a salmon upstream to spawn, to complete his mission. It was no longer momentum, just gathering strength—a definite decision had been made. Only Beulah changing her mind would have prevented me from going forward.

For some reason, I felt that her decision had been made long ago and no power on earth would change her mind. The whole process was taking on an otherworldly dimension. I was caught up in a powerful current and swimming against it would only prove to be futile. The best thing I could do would be to allow it to take me on its predetermined course. I believe we all experience defining moments in our lives that are thrust upon us and the decision we make sets a series of dynamics in motion. Some of these opportunities may never present themselves again.

About a week later, I received another call from Sam to discuss the visit. It was at this juncture that he revealed his identity relative to the Wood family. He told me that he married Bonnie, Bill's widow, about four years after Bill's death. They had a daughter who was now in college. He had been warmly integrated into the family. Both he and Bonnie were close friends with Beulah and her other three children. He freely shared some additional background information on Bill Wood. Bill was the first born of four children. He was involved with the local youth groups and beloved by his community. The turnout for his funeral was the largest in the town's recent memory. He was raised in a Quaker church and was a devout Christian. During the Vietnam War, the military made errors in sending the wrong bodies to homes in America. Consequently, Beulah, in her grief, had five different individuals make a positive identification at the funeral home before she would view his body. The family was proud of his accomplishments as a civilian and soldier.

Although he was drafted, Bill was planning to make a career of his army service. They were especially proud that he successfully completed Non-Commissioned Officer School to prepare him as a squad leader, with the rank of sergeant, immediately upon his arrival in Vietnam in December 1969. His brother, Raymond, also became a career soldier and was the father of identical twin boys. One of them was named after Bill and was presently an officer completing his Army Ranger training. Beulah was beginning to worry again, as her grandson would soon be deployed to Afghanistan. How ironic that thirty-two years after her son was killed in Vietnam, she had to worry about her grandson going to another war, again half a world away. Once again, Sam kindly explained that there was still some considerable ambivalence about my upcoming visit, but Beulah remained undaunted in her desire to meet with me. In fact, she seemed to be getting more determined with each passing day. Both Sam and Bonnie would be there as well. The decision was made and the date was set. Donna would go with me.

All the while that I was struggling with the preparations for my visit, Ray Cage was making his own plans to visit Jim Waulk's family in another part of Ohio. Although Jim had died instantly, Ray was looking directly at him when the rocket-propelled grenade was fired into our squad. He felt his own bond of death with our fallen brother.

Alliance, Ohio

With my upcoming visit to Bill's mother and widow only a week away, I reread his obituary from the copy that had been faxed to me from the Alliance library. Unfortunately, the photograph was grainy and I couldn't make out his face. I was struggling in vain to recall what he looked like as I read the following words.

OBITUARY—ALLIANCE REVIEW, MONDAY, FEBRUARY 23, 1970

Was Outstanding Athlete

Sgt. William Wood, 22, Gives Life in Vietnam

The war in Vietnam has claimed the life of another Alliance man, Sgt. William Wood, 22, of 176 W. Cambridge St. He was killed in action Friday in Vietnam. Born in Alliance, May 7, 1947, he was a life resident of the area and a former star athlete for McKinley (Sebring) High School. Prior to entering the armed forces Dec. 3, 1968, he was an apprentice patternmaker at the American Steel Foundries. Sgt. Wood, a 1965 graduate of McKinley High School, was a four-year veteran of the Trojan football team. He played offensive guard and defensive end for the team and served as co-captain in his senior year. He also participated in track. During the football banquet in 1964, Sgt. Wood received recognition as the "most tenacious" player, an award rated as "unusual." It was given for his 100 percent cooperation in practice and in the games. Coach Chester Riffle of Sebring today commented, "He was one of the finest kids Sebring had."

After Sgt. Wood entered the service, he was selected as an outstanding advanced infantry trainee and presented an award for that distinction. He was chosen from among 2,700 men in the third advanced individual brigade.

Sgt. Wood, assigned to overseas duty in December, was a member of the Quaker Hill Friends Church. He is survived by his wife, Bonnie McPhearson Wood of the home; his parents, Mr. and Mrs. Homer Wood of Alliance; two brothers, Raymond and Larry; a sister, Sharon of Alliance; and his parents-in-law, Mr. and Mrs. William (Red) McPhearson of Alliance. Funeral services are pending at the Myers Funeral Home.

The more I thought about the ambush the harder it was to focus on any aspect of it. My mind was playing in slow motion with no sound and I was unable to feel that it belonged to me. Although I knew it happened, I seemed to be an outside observer. I don't remember shedding any tears or crying for Bill or any other soldier who died afterwards. It was a rather bizarre incident, but I did recall shedding some tears one time—or a least I think I did.

After another firefight a few months later, I was sitting in the grass about ten or fifteen feet from the bodies of American soldiers who were already zipped into individual body bags. There were about five or six of them, neatly lined up. I don't even remember what I was thinking about as I sat in the jungle clearing, smoking a cigarette and staring at them. At some point, I noticed that there was something odd about one of the body bags. It had a unique contour and overall configuration that set it apart from the others. I slowly approached it and gently began to feel along the sides of its unusual shape, apparently to satisfy my curiosity. It sounds macabre as I write these words, but I thought nothing of doing it at the time. I suddenly realized that I was feeling an unusually thin leg that was set in a horizontal position. I immediately realized what it was—a scout dog, a German shepherd that was assigned to our unit to sniff out booby traps and detect ambushes.

I became teary and choked up over the loss of this animal that hung around our platoon. I remembered how most of us had felt a special bond with him. We sympathized with his handler because he had to carry water and food for the both of them—and this dog could eat and drink. He was with us for only a short time. In fact, the last time I saw the dog was when we had just completed a mission and were waiting in a jungle clearing for a few hours to be extracted by helicopters. During this period, I was absolutely delighted to have caught a four-foot green tree python. It was a magnificent creature and quite tame, as it found a home comfortably wrapped around my arm. Compared to the run-of-the-mill garter snakes from Western New York, it was a real treat for an amateur herpetologist. When it finally came time to board the helicopter, I entered from one side with my new pet, and the dog and his handler jumped in from the opposite side. As we started lifting off, the dog began lunging toward the snake, restrained only by the leash from his handler. Sensing that this scene was only going to get worse, the door gunner in no uncertain terms told us that one party had to get out immediately. Since we were already about thirty feet off the ground, the answer was obvious. The snake made a safe landing in the elephant grass and, in all likelihood, it resumed its life of hunting parrots and small monkeys in the dense jungle canopy. However, I was unable to see how something like this would prepare me for my visit with Bill's mother. After all, it had occurred a long time ago.

My main concern now was how I would act when I finally met Beulah Wood. Since I placed a high premium on maintaining control, I feared that I would just politely go through the motions during the meeting. This scenario began to torment me. I envisioned recounting the critical details surrounding his death in a way that would be comparable to reading a newspaper account. I envied people who were more connected to their feelings, especially about events that had a major impact on their lives. I was feeling emotionally numb. The whole thing was beginning to take on a clinical dimension. I was going to help someone who had lost a son in the war, but somehow I was unable to emotionally enter into the traumatic experience that occurred thirty-two years ago. It was as if I sensed that someone else was there, but it didn't feel like it was me. The anxiety attack and surge of disturbing images that I experienced when Peggy first contacted me seemed to have been buried again. Yet, I knew they were there. If anything, I was getting more confused. I was beginning to develop a greater appreciation for the adage, "Let sleeping dogs lie." But I was in the present day and there was no turning back. Once again, I looked at the map. Alliance, Ohio, was about a four-hour drive from our house and the day was fast approaching.

It was Saturday morning, and Donna and I were having breakfast before we set out on the road to Alliance. The telephone rang and it was Sam, informing me that Beulah was in the hospital for a respiratory infection. She was rather weak and expected to stay for at least a week or two. He asked me if I still wanted to come. My answer was in the form of a question: "Does Beulah want me to come?" He said "Yes." By this time, I realized that our meeting was a matter of destiny. Its course was unalterable. It was agreed that he and Bonnie would meet us in a Burger King parking lot located in town. We would then all go together to the hospital. The drive down was somewhat of a blur. Donna continued to be a tremendous source of support. I got lost a few times but, true to form, I refused to stop and ask for directions. Unlike previous road trips however, Donna didn't even venture a comment, perhaps sensing that there is a time to refrain from a wife's sacred rite of admonishing her husband on the road.

It was an eerie feeling, passing through the town. I was now starting to relate to a person who once lived here but didn't return from the war. I felt unsettled while an inner connection was emerging. I was feeling something after all. We soon pulled into the parking lot and made the telephone call to Sam and Bonnie to meet us there as planned. They arrived in a dark green Chevy Suburban and made me feel at ease from the start with their warmth and graciousness. After a few moments talking about our trip and reviewing my somewhat circuitous route, Bonnie headed for the rear of their car. She gathered a fairly good-sized picture frame and carefully approached me with it. She gently turned it toward me. I immediately recognized who it was as she said, "This is Bill."

There he was in a clear, color photograph, probably taken in Bien Hoa, where fresh First Cavalry troopers spent the first few weeks upon their arrival in Vietnam. Superimposed off to one side and above his head was a smaller picture of Bonnie—the effect being that she was always on his mind. I had had one taken just like it when I arrived there a few months later, probably by the same Korean merchant who was operating his studio out of a parked trailer. Finally, I now had a face to go with the name. Bill was now starting to feel real to me. Temporarily dazed, I began to wonder how Bonnie could be so lovely and poised when her husband was killed in Vietnam. I didn't realize at that moment that I was the one in a time warp. She had been grieving his loss for many years. In my own way, I was just beginning to acknowledge what he meant to me.

I vividly remember getting back into our car to follow them to the hospital. Before I turned the ignition, Donna looked toward me and said spontaneously, "I love her," referring to Bonnie. We arrived at the hospital, and Sam informed me that Bill's youngest brother, Larry, who was twelve years old when Bill was killed, would be waiting for us in the room with his mother. He was the same age as my brother Robe when I was in Vietnam. We entered Beulah's hospital room, where she was awaiting our arrival. Sam immediately introduced us and I gently shook her hand. Sam took the lead and guided our conversation. It was readily apparent that they were a close-knit family who loved each other very much. Immediately, I felt at ease and listened as Sam and Beulah bantered back and forth about the growing size of her medical chart and the number of times she had been admitted to the hospital over the years. At some point Bill's name came up and Bonnie and Larry joined in with some comments.

I recall handing Beulah a photo of Bill kneeling as he was preparing a C ration meal in a jungle clearing. I also provided her with several additional pictures, which included me and other members of our squad who were present the day he was killed. Although she had a nasal cannula for oxygenation and an intravenous hookup, she was a woman who was at peace. She possessed a sweet spirit that seemed to radiate, "It is well, it is well with my soul." She humorously mentioned the first time that her son Bill met Bonnie and came home to tell her, "Mom, I met a beautiful redhead today, and I'm going after her." We all seemed to be having a friendly social visit when Sam gently said, "Beulah, would you like Paul to tell you what happened to Bill?" She turned toward me with her loving eyes and said, "Yes, I would."

I approached the side of her hospital bed, sat on the edge, and reached out to hold her hand. I have to defer to my wife to recount what took place next. All I can remember for certain is that I started to tell the story and suddenly began to weep uncontrollably. I don't recall much of anything else, except for holding her hand. Donna tells me that I provided a fairly detailed account of the ambush scene and our frantic efforts to save Bill's life. This bedside scene that I thought lasted only a few moments apparently lasted for about twenty minutes. Donna was hardly prepared to see me cry and the flood of tears took her by surprise. It was all pure emotion and remains a blur to me to this day. She remembers the maternal look in Beulah's eyes as I wept like a child.

Even as we talk about it today, nearly four years later, Donna thinks that Beulah's primary motivation for going through this entire ordeal was for my sake. Her female intuition sensed that this fine woman had been at peace about the loss of her son for a long time. I was the one still carrying the full burden and the last one to realize it. Soon afterwards, a nurse came in to do a finger stick to measure Beulah's blood glucose level. The nurse reached for the hand I was holding and I reluctantly let go. She commented how blanched Beulah's fingers were, apparently from my holding on so tightly for such a long time. The nurse had to settle for using the other hand to obtain the needed sample. I believe we then resumed holding hands, but I consciously employed a much gentler grip. I was still concerned about cutting off the blood supply and asked her if she would like me to let go of her hand. She looked at me with a gentle smile and said, "It's been a long time since a man held my hand, and I'm not about to let go now." This was just the right thing to say to help us all regain our sense of equilibrium, especially mine which was really askew, to say the least.

Beulah delighted in talking about the grandsons who were identical twins. She said of the one named Bill with a proud, gentle smile, "He looks just like him." He was an Army Infantry officer who was just completing his Ranger training and awaiting deployment to Afghanistan. She was very proud of him and his wife, who was also an officer, but she was worried about him. She very much wanted to return to her apartment, and we talked about a future visit that some of the other family members might also be able to attend. We had been there for several hours and our time to say good-bye was approaching. The nurse was kind enough to allow us this extended period of time for much-needed privacy. It all went by quickly. I then asked if we could pray before we left and the suggestion was unanimously affirmed.

We stood in a circle around Beulah's hospital bed and held hands. We thanked God for the opportunity He provided in bringing us together on this day, which was appointed before any of us was born. We prayed for the rest of the family and for God's protection of Beulah's grandson, who would soon enter the danger zone of combat like his uncle before him. My wife and I each gave her a hug and a kiss as we parted. In a sense, I had been connected to this remarkable woman for a long time. She was there for her son's first moments of life and I was there when he took his last breath. The thought of such irony catapulted me for a moment into the realm of the mystery of life. Truly, not a single one of us knows what is in store in the moments ahead, let alone tomorrow, next week, or next year. I was reminded of the words of Jesus, "The very number of hairs on your head is numbered ... you don't have the power to turn even one hair black or white." In such rare, unexpected moments, when my inner balance has been shaken to its very foundation, His gentle reminder about my powerlessness in all things resonates within the core of my being.

Sam had anticipated that I would wish to visit Bill's grave at the cemetery. We accompanied him and Bonnie in their car, while Larry, Bill's youngest brother, followed us in his pickup. As best as I can remember, the cemetery was located near the center of town. More feelings began to well up in me as we approached his grave. We all stopped on the path that passed about fifty feet from where he was buried. Thirty-two years ago we were going down a jungle path together. True, we were soldiers sent to a foreign land and our intention was to kill the enemy on that day, as it was every other day. It was a "search and destroy" mission, but we were not killers at heart, of that I'm sure. We would much rather have been in the safety of our homes, in the company of our loved ones. By that point in the war, the only reason we were there was to complete our tour and survive the best way we knew how. On that day of death, he had nine months remaining on his tour in Vietnam and I had over eleven. Neither of us knew what was about to occur in the next few moments.

The switch from intense fear to pure terror was close at hand. A loud explosion, gunfire, screaming and it was all over. Both of us knew that he was dying. I could see it in his eyes and, undoubtedly, he saw the validation in mine. He was not afraid. During his last moments, he was thinking about others. It is said that a man dies in much the same manner as he lived. Until a few weeks ago, I knew only how he died. I was now learning how he lived. He loved God and cared about others; it was as simple as that. While my mother would once again embrace her son, his had buried him. Why it wasn't the other way I truly don't know. I can say with certainty that up until that time, he had lived his life in a far more upright manner than I had chosen to live mine. It wasn't fair, and yet it wouldn't have been any more fair if I had been the one who was killed. Fairness has nothing to do with war; it has nothing to do with life as we know it either. Emotions follow their own logic— enter survival guilt, the "why him and not me?"

I approached his grave alone, while the rest of the group stayed on the path. I knelt down and felt him in my heart. He had always been there; I just hadn't realized it. I don't remember what I said, or even if I said anything at all. It wasn't about words; it was about presence. We were connected in a special way, brothers forever. His gravestone read:

SGT. WILLIAM W. WOOD
MAY 7, 1947
FEB. 20, 1970

BELOVED HUSBAND OF BONNIE
CO. D 1ST BN. 1ST CAV. DIV.

I was beginning to recognize that in some way this was all part of me. Unwittingly, I had been trying to disconnect myself from that day for a long time. It was time to embrace Bill and what had happened. A sense of peace was ever so slowly and imperceptibly beginning to filter into my soul. In a mysterious sort of way, I felt that I was coming home. Bill came home in a coffin. I came home alone as well when my tour was up. It felt as though we were now home together. More about it, I can't really explain. I was bathed in his presence and feeling whatever emotions were surfacing at this appointed time.

I then asked if I could take a picture of Bill's grave to send to some other soldiers who served with us. A few photos later, we were ready to leave the cemetery. It was getting close to dinnertime and Sam suggested we go to a steak house for a meal. Since it was Saturday afternoon, the main eateries all seemed to have lengthy waiting lines and we ended up in a Pizza Hut. As we were seated around the table, I overheard Bonnie and Donna sharing their views on diet and exercise. The two of them bonded instantly. Sam, Larry, and I had our own discussion—about an assortment of things that guys usually talk about. I had a brief moment alone with Bonnie as we were getting our jackets on the way out. I approached her and said that I was sorry that I waited so long to make this trip here, but I was glad that I had finally come. She said, "I'm glad you came ... I'm sure Bill wanted you to come too ... he would understand that you would come when you were ready. He would have done the same."

The last stop was the Sub Shop. Sam and Bonnie owned and operated this establishment that specialized in submarine sandwiches and related items, all neatly listed on their extensive menu. It was here that Bonnie wanted to show me some of Bill's personal items that she had prepared for my visit. It was a quaint, charming little place and we had it all to ourselves. Sam asked us to place an order for a submarine sandwich for our trip home. We sat around one of the tables and Bonnie brought out what looked like a shoebox. She carefully lifted out Bill's medals and accompanying paperwork. She mentioned that he wrote faithfully and often, but the last batch of his letters had not reached her until after he was killed. She then passed me the letter she received from our company commander, Captain White, describing the manner of his death. It was only a paragraph or two in length, but the one thing I remember was that it stated that his death was the result of stepping on a landmine. This was an obvious error that I later related to two other soldiers who were present with us that day. The old saying, "The first casualty in war is truth," apparently applies to all aspects of war, except perhaps whether one returns home alive. I continue to hear about such mistakes as our nation is at war in Iraq and Afghanistan. Most notable are the circumstances surrounding the death of Pat Tillman, who gave up a promising career in the NFL to enlist in the army following the 9/11 terrorist attack on the World Trade Center.

She then handed me a small container, which I slowly opened. It was Bill's Purple Heart. I remember that it felt cold, like his gravestone.

I held it and caressed it, like it was part of him. How powerful is our sense of touch. For some unexplained reason, I needed to feel the cold hardness of his gravestone and now the equally lifeless metal. It was a sort of confirmation that he was gone. Even more so, perhaps, it reaffirmed that he was once here and alive. He was no longer a vague, dreamlike, surrealistic image derived from a moment of terror, confusing me for so many years within the very depths of my soul. *He felt real.*

Homecoming

It was a long ride home. I was grateful that Donna was with me, as she was a much-needed source of comfort. It rained heavily all the way to Hamburg. Midway home we stopped at a rest area to feast on the greatest submarine sandwiches ever made, compliments of Sam and Bonnie Rhodes. I called some of my army buddies the following day to share my visit to Alliance with them. I also sent them some photographs of Bill's gravesite. The whole experience was disorienting and soothing at the same time (quite frankly, I'm still processing it emotionally, six years later). My mind kept going over the scene where I was holding Beulah's hand in the hospital. In a mysterious sort of way, I felt as if I was Bill for a moment in time.

The more thought I gave to the matter, the more I felt an eerie kinship with all of the soldiers who died and never had a chance to say good-bye to their mothers. Beulah was the universal mother who wasn't able to embrace her son one last time. I would sit by myself for extended periods in a trance-like state, just allowing the experience to filter through my being. It felt like there was a deep reservoir of feelings that had been tapped. Images of soldiers from all wars who paid the ultimate sacrifice began to occupy my mind. They had no homecoming, except to be grieved and buried by their families. We were all so young.

But then I started wondering, how and where does all this end for those who have been left behind with such a devastating loss? Invariably, they have to go on with their lives. How would my mother and family have continued without me if I had not returned? How would my family and friends have remembered me? To date, I have been blessed with thirty-five additional years more than the over fifty-eight thousand who were killed in Vietnam. Each and every one of them was a son, brother, father, or husband to someone at home, anxiously awaiting their return. Many were also a friend, fiancé, nephew, uncle, and neighbor. Such was the stream of consciousness that was my lot for the month following my visit to Alliance, Ohio.

Then one day I received a telephone call from Sam. This had been the first contact with Bill's family since our visit a few months earlier. He informed me that Beulah was in the hospital again, never having recovered from her last illness. However, this time her condition was deteriorating rapidly. She was not expected to live much longer and she wanted very much to talk to me again. She had hoped to do this at a later date when she was in better health, during the return visit that we discussed. She wanted me to call her at the hospital and Sam gave me the number.

Someone answered the phone and held it to her ear while we talked. I could tell that she was somewhat disoriented and possibly delirious, yet she remembered who I was when she answered, "You came to visit me with your wife, Donna." Her speech was a bit slurred, most likely from the analgesics. Our conversation was short, as her voice and stream of consciousness seemed to fade-in and fade-out. I asked her if she wanted me to pray with her and she immediately said, "Yes, I do," reminiscent of the first time I called her and asked if she wanted me to continue with the story of how her son died. I don't remember what I said exactly. I believe that it was a simple prayer, asking primarily for God's presence and His peace that "passes all understanding" to be with her at that hour. I said a few other things before we said our good-byes, but I don't recall any of them. Maybe what was said was not as important as what I felt.

Words could hardly describe the resonance within my soul when the call ended. God was present and I was the one who felt the peace that passes understanding. The next morning Sam called to tell me that she died peacefully later that day. I cannot describe my thoughts or emotions at that moment. There was a gentle calm and surrender of my all to God's glory. I was awestruck by how He put all of us in contact to accomplish this work. All I had to do was say yes and He did the rest. But even my ability to say yes was by His grace. I am mystified as

I write these words and reflect on God's perfect plan. I never could in my wildest dreams or imaginings have orchestrated such an ending or, as it turned out, a beginning. I recall someone once saying, "God may not seem to be there when you expect Him, but He's always on time." Thirty-two years after Bill died in my arms, I was able to pray with his mother during her final hours on this earth. I began to wonder what she might have wanted to say to me at a later date in private. But it was not to be. Not in this life anyway. For the remainder of that day it seemed like I was walking around in a fog. Mother and son were both now gone, yet I felt an eternal connection with them. The whole timing of my involvement in their lives, as brief as it was, seemed other-worldly. I felt in my heart that they were finally reunited.

I received a letter from Sam about a month later. Included in the envelope was the following letter addressed to Donna and me from Sharon, Bill's only sister. I will treasure it all the days of my life.

Dear Paul and Donna,

I am Sharon, Beulah's daughter. Mom is at peace now; she is no longer in pain. Mom can see, walk, and talk to my dad and two brothers. Mom was able to close the book on her life because you brought her a message from God. Mom finally knew for sure about my brother Bill, and it gave her the satisfaction that once and for all Bill came home thirty-two years ago. I would never want you to think I could ever blame you for my Mom's decline in health. I can't count the times I prayed to God: "Please let her come home from the hospital just one more time." The last six months Mom was in a lot of pain. Mom didn't want to go to a nursing home. I think she realized she wasn't able to come back to her apartment. I believe she finally stopped fighting.

Mom enjoyed the visit, and I am glad she was able to talk with you and Donna. I am sorry now I didn't meet with you two, but I didn't want to hear about Bill after he was wounded. I am a firm believer that God looks at things in a way that, as a human, I or we will never understand here on earth. I also believe God knew how much pain Mom was in; he decided to take her home. God sent you to tell Mom it was okay, Bill was with God, and they were waiting on her in heaven.

At the hospital that night she was uneasy—my husband, Bill, prayed with her. The nurses gave mom two injections of pain medication. Mom was still not settled. I said to her, "Mom, do you want me to pray with you?" She nodded her head yes. I asked God to let Mom feel his presence and his peace in her. Mom soon quieted down, and then she was gone.

Mom cared for people; once she met the two of you, that was just two more people for her to care about and love. I want to thank you and Donna for a long-awaited peace you brought into my mother's life. May God always keep the two of you in his heart.

Blessings and peace unto you.

Sincerely,

Sharon K. Main

P.S. Thank you for holding my brother in your arms and for all these years in your heart.

Beloved John

The painful memories of Vietnam were left buried for many years before I met with Bill's family. I avoided association with anything that might stir things up. Although fleeting thoughts about friends who died would periodically surface, I was effective in immediately dismissing them. Then, around 1996, I read a piece in the newspaper about the *Moving Vietnam Memorial Wall* being displayed at Mount Calvary Cemetery in Buffalo during the month of May. I went specifically to see if I could locate two names on the wall, John Gmack and Richard Timmons.

It was a beautiful, sunny day and only a handful of people were present for this solemn occasion. Since I did not care for crowds, it was the perfect opportunity to meet again with my friends. Although I had vague recollections of the faces of those who were killed in combat in my presence, I could not recall a single name. However, it was different with John Gmack and Richard Timmons. They were part of the original "five of us" that spent more than two months together in Advanced Infantry Training in Fort Gordon, Georgia. The other three, Larry Toczak, John Meisenbach, and I, returned home alive. Even though I was not present when they died, I could picture their faces, especially their boyish smiles. After all this time, they were still only eighteen and nineteen years old to me. They never grew older.

It was a tender moment when I finally located their names on *The Wall*. I don't remember any tears, but I was deeply moved. I began to reminisce about an incident during our infantry training when a group of us sat down and ordered a pitcher of beer. No sooner was it placed on the table than John pulled his dentures out and tossed them into the pitcher. Richard Timmons was also present to enjoy the raucous laugh-

32

ter with the rest of us; we were so young and full of life. I stayed there for only a short while. I could handle only so much at any given time, as this "moving memorial" had the potential to overwhelm me. I was still protecting myself, as I had been for many years. It would be another six years before I received the telephone call from Peggy Barstow that would force me to confront the pain of Bill Wood's death and the rest of the inner turmoil from the war, including grieving for the loss of these two best friends from Wisconsin. God in His infinite wisdom was setting the stage for a much-needed healing. Although a measure of healing had been taking place for some time, the visit to the wall was the first direct confrontation I had with the ghosts of Vietnam.

All bets were off after my visit with Bill Wood's family in Ohio in 2002. I was now in the "flight into health" mode, a concept in psychiatry where the patient becomes activated to the point of hypomania, following a long period in the doldrums of depression. One of the items on my agenda was to see who else I could contact from that otherworldly dimension of my past life. I soon discovered the Vietnam Memorial on the Internet. One could readily find someone who was on the wall by submitting some identifying information. I plugged in John Gmack's name and accessed his Web page, which provided the following:

JOHN ROBERT GMACK

CPL—E4—Army—Regular
1st Cav Division (AMBL)
Eighteen years old, single, Caucasian, male
Born on July 20, 1951
From Green Bay, Wisconsin
His tour of duty began on Feb. 06, 1970
Casualty was on May 28, 1970
Cambodia
Non-hostile, ground casualty
Accidental self-destruction
Body was recovered
Religion: Roman Catholic
Panel 10 W—Line 114

Once again, thirty-three years later, I was confronted with the mysterious circumstances of John's death. I didn't have much time to think about it the first time I heard about it while in Vietnam; besides, it didn't seem to matter since he was dead. But now several different scenarios were racing through my mind as I noticed the smaller inscription "Personal Comments or Pictures—Click Here" near the center of the page. This was the section where anyone who cared to leave a note or photograph regarding the fallen soldier was encouraged to share his/her thoughts for all to read. It is here that personal memories are shared and the loss is felt. The first one was from Kathy Wagner, a friend of John's sister. She wrote:

> Back at Franklin Jr. High School, while eating lunch with my friend, Nancy, she had a blank, hollow stare, something ripping her heart apart, a stare that revealed shock and pain, and a look I will never forget. She had just received news that her brother, John, had been killed in Vietnam, something about a land mine. I had only met John once. I could not imagine what pain my friend's family was enduring. We were at that age of in between understanding of what this war was all about, if at all. Now, it really hit home! My thoughts and prayers for continuing comfort go out to this wonderful family!
> Friday, November 08, 2002

Here was a scene in a junior high lunchroom, undoubtedly teeming with life, where the hollow presence of death was leaving its mark. One cannot help but focus on this scene in the heartland of America where a young girl's heart was breaking as a close friend was witnessing it. This was the human part of the ripple effect of the "I regret to inform you …" letter that was initially presented to the next of kin. It is a profoundly sad moment in time that will be etched in the memory of the loved ones left behind. My emotions were already in turmoil, but the next entry, by John's mother, Mrs. Gertrude Gmack, was as shocking as it was revealing. It was entitled "Untrue Information."

Your information lists the cause of death as accidental self-destruction. John was ordered to tie in ACTIVATED land mines with three other men in the rain and dark of night. One of the men tripped the mines, and they lost their lives.

Friday, August 30, 2002

So this is how John died. Her description was short and to the point—nothing but the facts. His mother wrote it as she presented a clear and concise confirmation of the truth. My immediate reaction to the cause of death, listed as "accidental self-destruction," was anger over the possible causes readers might entertain, as I did, for how he died. Perhaps she initially felt that as well, but later chose her words carefully; an angry or resentful response might have dishonored his name. I immediately realized that she was a woman of character. The final entry was by Philip Smith, a "distant cousin."

I first visited you in November of 1988 at the Wall in Washington DC, and then again more recently at the Moving Wall Memorial displayed in November at Flat Top Park in West Richland, Washington. To my knowledge we never met, but your sacrifice has been with me since the day we heard the news. When the phone call came I was only four years old, and I was spending time with my grandmother Edna at her house in Sturgeon Bay, Wisconsin. I can vividly recall that day because I had never before experienced Grandma crying. Grandma never cried until then, and I will remember this forever. I remember being terribly afraid of whatever made Grandma cry, and at the time I didn't understand what happened to you other than it was bad enough to make Grandma cry. Now I understand. May God bless you and your family and help comfort them.

Saturday, November 29, 2003

Here was a grown man who was deeply affected by his distant cousin's death when he was four years old. Many of us who were old enough at the time remember where we were when President John F. Kennedy was assassinated on November 23, 1963. It was a time and a place, not just an event. We mourned as a nation. But the news of death that daily trickled in during the Vietnam War affected only isolated pockets of friends and loved ones. Although millions of Americans were briefly saddened by the nightly casualty reports, it was the family with the empty chair at the dinner table that continued to feel the pain. The next step on my journey was obvious—I had to make contact with Mrs. Gertrude Gmack.

Trudy

I wrote a brief e-mail to Mrs. Gertrude Gmack in February 2004 and a week went by without a response. I thought that perhaps it was too painful for her to connect with someone who knew her son. At least I now knew how he died and that alone was more than worth the effort. Then one day, to my surprise and delight, I received the following response.

Dear Paul,

It was a surprise and joy to receive your note. Up until now the only person we received letters from was a brother of a medic who was killed in Nam in July 1970. The medic's name was Louis Crosby. Do you remember him? When were you in Vietnam? At the same time as John? John went there in February 1970, and was there until May. Regardless, it was nice to hear from you.

We would very much like to see the pictures you have. Do you remember the names of the guys? We have several snapshots that John sent home, but there are no names. It would be nice to put a name to the pictures. I realize it's been thirty-four years since these were taken, but if you could identify anyone, we'd be happy to send them to you ... if it's not too painful. If you can remember names, I received letters from Greg Carlson and Tom Csakany who were with John's unit shortly after John died. Much later, after hearing from Dan Crosby, a William Johnson wrote. He lives in Staten Island, New York. He was with A Co.

1/8 CAV. also. In a few of John's pictures he identified Dutch Boer and Duane Saddler.

Enough of pictures, tell us about you! It's hard to think that you guys would be fifty-three or more now! What are you doing job-wise? It is so sad that war left so many with broken spirits. I feel that, if John had come home, he would have had a hard time too. He walked point and was a radioman, which must have been stressful.

You mentioned that you visited a Web site. I can't remember which one related to John. Could you tell me exactly which one? I searched several and couldn't find the one that I had left a message on. If you're interested, there is a notation from Dan Crosby for his brother Louis too.

Again, thank you so much for writing. We think of John daily, and our children enjoy hearing from his friends too.

Fondly, Trudy Gmack

Well, so much for my theory about a mother not wanting to talk about her son because it was too painful. It wasn't the case with Beulah and certainly was not true for Trudy. For now, I was excited to have connected with John's mother. Maybe the fact that my own mother had died a few months earlier after a three-year struggle with lung cancer made this whole process more meaningful. It is difficult to lose a parent, especially a mother who raised three children by herself while maintaining a full-time job.

My father died in 1961, less than four years after we emigrated from Hungary to the United States. My mother hardly knew the language, yet she somehow managed to prevail. She was a most determined individual with a remarkable sense of humor. Only recently have I begun to appreciate the extent of her sacrifice and the tremendous hardship she endured. Hardly a day goes by that I don't think about her; reminders are everywhere. Nothing could have prepared me for her loss. Yet, intuitively I realize that this is the way it is supposed to be—a parent dies before her child.

War is an anomaly that cruelly reverses the order. Many parents may live for forty years plus after their children are killed in a war. This is an utter perversion of the human experience. It is made even worse because our wars have been fought on other continents for well over a hundred years and the loved one is thousands of miles from home when he dies. However, my brief encounters with Beulah made me aware that dying in the company of another soldier was comforting to the mother. I was beginning to realize Trudy appreciated me just for being John's friend.

I mailed her a letter that included a few pictures of John taken during our Advanced Infantry Training at Fort Gordon, Georgia. Sadly, one of the photographs included Richard Timmons who was also from Wisconsin. His family never saw him alive again either. I also included a patch that I obtained from the Vietnam Veterans of America Web site with the words "Brothers Forever" placed around a Vietnam Service Ribbon. One final thing—I just had to know why an eighteen-year-old needed to wear partial dentures; tossing them in our pitcher of beer still had me baffled after all these years. It wasn't long before she sent me a package and e-mailed another letter.

Hi Paul,

I am sending some of John's pictures along with a copy of a letter we received from one of his buddies after his death. We were relieved to receive an honest account of how he died. I am also sending an article that appeared in Life magazine about his unit in October. John was a radioman, so I am wondering if it was he who the captain was referring to. Or are there several radiomen in a unit? Perhaps you've already seen this article, but it does give you an idea about his fellow grunts.

We'll be looking forward to receiving your pictures. Be sure to identify them so I can put a name to a face.

You asked how John lost his teeth, or tooth, I should say. Well, when he was in high school, he went to a "beer bar," and supposedly he was in the section that wasn't selling beer to minors, and a fellow who had a crush on John's girlfriend came up to him and "popped" him in the mouth. He managed to retrieve his tooth before being taken to the hospital, hoping that they could "transplant" it, but they couldn't. Thus the bridge.

Another incident involving John happened when he was in eighth grade and had climbed a tall tree. I got a call from one of his friends saying that John had fallen twenty feet. All of our kids have had braces, so my first question was, "Did he ruin his teeth?" John had just had his braces removed, and I was just concerned that the teeth went with the fall. Not a very good mother, not asking if he was all right, but it turned out that he just broke an arm.

I admire your faith in God, and I'm sure it helped you get through the memories of Nam.

God bless you,
Trudy

Now I had the story behind the dentures, or bridge, or whatever. Regardless, it seemed like an awful lot of material to keep a single tooth in place. No surprise that beer was involved in the initial incident which resulted in the "replacement" that found its way into our pitcher. Anyway, one of the things I needed to clarify with her was that, although we were both in the First Air Cavalry Division, we ended up in two different regiments. Our units operated in the same general area, but we never met in the jungle and our companies were never on the main base camp at the same time. I happened to meet a soldier from John's unit around July in Song Be, our main base camp, while our unit was reassembling to move to another area. This soldier also trained with us at Fort Gordon, but I can't remember his name. However, I was able to recognize him in several of the photos Mrs. Gmack sent me. He was recovering from some minor wounds that he sustained in a firefight. I met him near an old trailer that was used as a PX, where we indulged ourselves in Coca Cola and canned Vienna sausages. I do remember very clearly that he told me John had been killed, and he had heard from someone else that Timmons had also died while serving with the 101st Airborne Division. Out of the original five of us, I knew for sure that only Toczak and I were alive. We didn't hear from Miesenbach until I arrived in Fort Hood, Texas, some fourteen months later.

I received another e-mail after she received the pictures that I sent her. I deeply appreciated her sharing about John and it was becoming quite apparent that we both needed to talk about him.

Hi Paul,

The pictures were wonderful! It is good to become acquainted with the names and faces. I will be sending copies of John's snaps when I purchase photo paper. It does make a difference, although John's pictures were thirty-four years old already!

I noticed on your pictures that none of the fellows was smoking except our son. I think he picked up this habit way back when he was in Catholic high school. It was an all boys' school, which he wanted to go to because his friends were all going there. I was shocked one day as I entered the back door to find cigarette butts about an inch or more thick covering the entryway. Shocked, because I really didn't approve of my kids smoking and also because the administration would allow the build-up of butts in the doorway. I guess I didn't regret his going there, though, because he enjoyed playing hockey for them, was in the band, and eventually met his girlfriend on a ski bus. I later established a hockey award in his name and donated monies from the donations for a scholarship.

The fellow named Storm must have been in John's unit. He wrote about how Storm had been wounded in the hand on March 22, lost two fingers, and was "smiling all over the place" at the airport on the 29th on his way home.

Thanks again for the pictures and the article on you. I'm proud of you … you have done so much with your life! Tell me about yourself. Do you have any siblings? I looked at the map to find Hamburg, and it looks like you're not far from Niagara Falls. We took the whole family, minus the little one, to New York for the World's Fair. I think the kids enjoyed the "big city."

Love, Trudy

It was a real delight to have this ongoing dialogue with such a warm person who seemed to have a great sense of humor coupled with a direct, honest approach to life. We established a mutually enjoyable relationship over the next few months. Another e-mail was soon to follow.

Hi Paul,

Please pardon my very late thank you for first, the Brothers patch. When a soldier dies, the army delivers a "shadow box" with all the medals the soldier earned. I've had this frame hanging in our den, so I moved some medals around and added the patch. John would have been proud of it! Second, thank you for the photo pages. I fully intended to get out and buy some, but never did. Anyway, we are using them and will have copies sent to you very soon. When I say we, I guess I mean Jill, because she is doing the copying. I'm not computer literate, and my computer is about four years old, so she's doing her best to get sharper copies out to you. Most of the pictures have John on, because I thought you might be more interested in him than guys you don't know. I've put a few notes on the back of some of them.

I'm sorry to hear of your mother's passing. Our lost loved ones occupy some of our thoughts each day, don't they? Two of my sisters have died in the past four years, along with two brothers-in-law. There were five girls in our family (no boys), and the two youngest have left us. I'm next in line, up the ladder, so we'll see. I'm not sure what arrangement God has "up there," but I'm hoping John has been able to "connect" with them, along with his grandparents.

Where does Larry Toczek come from? You seem to have a close relationship with him. In one of John's letters after first arriving in Vietnam, he wrote that he was there with four guys he ran around with in AIT and made life pretty good being there with you. I'm glad you guys went over with him.

I hope we didn't screw up your photo sheets too much, and they are what you wanted.

Love, Trudy

P.S. Please call me Trudy... My mom had the worst taste in naming us girls. Lorraine, Bernice, Gertrude, Bonita, and Mildred! I think I got the worst deal, and for years I preferred to go under Mrs. Robert, but then my office buddies decided that Trudy (the end of Gertrude) should be my name. When I go to things like class reunions, several say they don't know what to call me anymore, for I had been Gert, Gerty, and now Trudy.

Vietnam 1970

It wasn't until I began treating Vietnam veterans around 1983 that I began to realize for the first time that there were two distinct wars. Veterans who served prior to the Tet Offensive in 1968 seemed to have a commitment to winning while they were there; they even had some pride in their service, though they felt let down by their country later on. Post-1968 was an entirely different story, for several reasons. First, we had no commitment to winning, as we were already gearing up for Vietnamization which meant we were gradually transferring the military operations over to the South Vietnamese government. Second, our nation, including my friends, either didn't care or had a negative attitude toward our being there any longer.

By 1969 and 1970, this national scene was even worse. When we were drafted, our nation was already resigned to our involvement in Vietnam as a hopeless cause. The peace movement, along with Vietnam Veterans Against the War, was already in full swing. We were frequently referred to as "baby killers," a term that surfaced after the My Lai incident in 1968. I remember seeing the movie *We Were Soldiers Once …and Young* several years ago about soldiers of the 7th regiment of the First Air Cavalry Division in 1965. I was in the 12th regiment of this same division five years later. Absent of any *esprit de corps*, our unit bore little resemblance to the one depicted in the film. Unlike the earlier version of the First Cavalry, which trained for an extended period together as a fighting unit while stationed on American soil, we arrived in a piecemeal fashion, plugging up the vacancies that were created by those trickling home due to being wounded, killed, or having completed their tour. We didn't even have the illusion that we could win or that we were giving our lives toward a worthy cause. Our assigned task was to survive for twelve months and then return to a nation that didn't want us there in the first place. Never before in the history of our nation had soldiers endured such demoralizing circumstances.

One of the items sent to me by Mrs. Gmack was a copy of an article that appeared in the October 23, 1970, edition of *Life Magazine* entitled, "You Can't Just Hand out Orders: A Company Commander in Vietnam Confronts the New-style Draftees." It was an in-depth analysis of an infantry unit in Vietnam dealing with the daily life-and-death issues that confronted its troops as the war was supposedly winding down. It was almost a mirror image of our company, which operated in the same area and at the same time. Tragically, it was the unit John Gmack served with when he was killed five months before the article was published. It accurately depicted the war during our time in Vietnam.

For seventeen days at a time through monsoon rains and tropical heat, the men of Alpha Company, 1st Air Cavalry Airmobile, hunt NVA soldiers and supply caches close to the Cambodian border. Stealthing through the bamboo-thicketed hills, they have the same air of acquired professionalism as drafted GIs of past wars. They look the same, even smell the same: a drab green centipede of men in soiled fatigues with the same boy-man faces under the bobbing steel helmet brims.

In reality, the 118 men of Alpha are quite different. They are the microcosm of an Army in evolution, an Army trying to adjust to the winding down war in Vietnam. Old ideas of dress, behavior, discipline, and rank no longer apply. Virtually no draftee wants to be fighting in Vietnam anyway, and in return for his reluctant participation, he demands, and gets, personal freedoms that would have driven a MacArthur or a Patton apoplectic. It is an Army in which all questions—including "Why?"—are permissible. Alpha company seethes with problems, but it has not fallen into chaos. Much of the reason is that a special kind of relationship, a new one in the Army, exists between the "grunts"—liberated, educated, aware draftees—and their youthful commander, Captain Brian Utermahlen, West Point class of 1968.

Utermahlen's continuing problem is to find an effective compromise between his own professional dedication and his draftees' frank disinterest in anything that might cost an American life. Nothing could suit them better than President Nixon's recent proposal for a cease fire in place, for Alpha Company has no desire to go on fighting. Grunt logic argues that since the U.S. has decided not to go out and win the war, there's no sense in being the last one to die. Followed to its conclusion and multiplied by every infantry company in Vietnam, this sort of logic—and the new permissiveness—has unquestionably affected the whole Army's combat efficiency. It is no longer the pliant and instantly responsive instrument of the past. Many officers frankly doubt that they could get their men to fight another costly battle such as the 1969 assault on Hamburger Hill that took eighty-four lives.

This article triggered conflicting emotions for me. The good news was that the war was indeed winding down but only because 16,589 U.S. troops were killed in 1968, the costliest year of the war in terms of American lives. The causality rates dramatically improved in 1969, with 11,614 killed. By 1970, the U.S. soldiers killed numbered a three-year low, at 6,083. The breakdown of American dead for that year was: Army 4,972; Marine Corps 691; Air Force 201; and Navy 219. Although a dramatic statistical improvement to be sure, an average of 116 Americans were still being killed on a weekly basis throughout the entire year of 1970; the vast majority of them were draftees in the Army.

Unfortunately, the First Air Cavalry Division was still in the mode of taking the offensive to the enemy. The article was quite accurate when referring to the unit "hunting" the North Vietnamese soldiers. To make matters worse, the First Air Cavalry Division invaded Cambodia with the 7th, 8th, 9th, and 12th regiments in May 1970. Much like the soldiers described in the article, our unit would have been content to remain in our relatively secure bunker complexes, watching the war wind down as we protected our perimeter. The North Vietnamese and the Viet Cong guerillas would have been happy to leave us alone; besides, they wanted to live just as much as we did and they would have welcomed the opportunity not to be hunted by our troops and ravaged by the Cobra gunships and air strikes we called in once they were discovered.

Tragically, every time we would discover them, it was at the cost of American lives in an ambush. Our unit of about one hundred soldiers would make a combat assault by helicopters to a targeted area, while gunships would be just ahead of us to "soften" the landing zone by strafing it with rockets and mini guns. I pitied anyone who happened to be in its line of fire. The enemy would rarely fire at us while we came in and jumped off the helicopters, for fear of incurring the wrath of the Cobras. After all, the enemy wasn't stupid. They would be content to wait until we would be stretched out in single file columns in dense jungle, and needed only a handful of men to effectively neutralize an entire company of airmobile infantrymen by ambushing the lead squad.

Over five years into the war and we were still employing largely conventional methods in fighting guerilla forces. Undoubtedly, this was the most frightening and demoralizing aspect of the war. It was like Russian roulette, as we took turns being the "bait" that would be used to spring their ambush so we might be able locate and hunt down a few of them. None of this made any sense, yet we were expected to continue until our time was up, whether that meant being killed, wounded, or completing our one-year tour of duty. As night arrived in the jungle, it was our turn to set the ambushes. This would typically involve setting up "automatic ambushes" consisting of claymore mines and small ambush teams near trails. Most of the enemy was killed in this manner. It was stealthy, brutal warfare without any goal or honor. The only thing that mattered to the Army was the body count, real or inflated. It was as if the number of enemy dead was the scorecard to justify being there. If you survived, you could then go home and live with the memories. No one wanted to hear about it and even close friends and relatives avoided broaching the subject. The company commander of the unit in the article quickly learned about the unusual pressures of commanding such an infantry unit.

Utermahlen has not always had Alpha's support. He relieved a very popular commanding officer. When he took over, he was half prepared for a vengeance grenade attack—a "fragging." "They told me horror stories about how bad the company was," Utermahlen remembers, "and there were signs around saying the colonel wasn't welcome. I thought, my God, I'm going to be fragged." He gingerly settled in, but found his position threatened from above by the colonel and from below by the grunts. "The colonel told me every time we had contact, we would report at least two confirmed kills. I said, 'I can't do that, sir.' It went against everything I ever believed in. Only a change in command (new colonel) saved me."

I now approached the part of the article that mentioned the circumstances around John Gmack's death on Memorial Day, 1970. Although his or any of the other soldiers' names who were accidentally killed were not mentioned, I'm quite positive that it was the incident in question. For one thing, John was a radio operator, as noted by his mother in one of her earlier emails to me.

The death of three of his men when they blundered into an ambush that had been set by other GIs was a crushing blow to Utermahlen, and it almost led to a no-confidence strike by the grunts. "I still think of it as my fault," he says, "and I fully expected to be relieved." A member of the company remembers, "Everybody I knew was pretty sore at him. The platoon the guys were from discussed not going back to the field." Utermahlen survived the immediate crisis … Since the death of his favorite radio operator, Utermahlen has often voiced his hate of the NVA. "Dammit," he will say, pounding his knee, "it's nice to kill gooks." Few, if any, of his draftee soldiers can work up such depth of feeling. Says Platoon Sergeant Curry, "I don't understand what makes him dislike gooks so bad he wants to kill them. He once said he had a desire to strangle a gook, and that sickened me."

I have no trouble empathizing with Captain Utermahlen. War generates hatred and revenge. It would appear that a large portion of his hatred was fueled by the deaths of the men under his charge, including one "favorite radio operator."

Since the bulk of the soldiers in my company and John's were composed primarily of draftees, the dynamics of these two units of the First Air Cavalry Division were indistinguishable. Some of the excerpts from the article, particularly the feelings of the infantrymen, led me to believe it was my company.

Pfc. Wayne Johnson, age twenty-one, from Kissimmee, Fla., has asked for a transfer out of infantry: "I don't like to kill. I hate the thing they believe in, but not the people themselves. Our business is killing, but my heart's not in it."

Perhaps half of Alpha's twenty-one blacks agree with the alienated view of Pfc. John Munn, a tall, somber soul brother. "I have my life to preserve," says Munn, "but I have nothing against that little man out there. They're fighting for what they believe in, and you can't knock that. I lie on my air mattress at night, and I say, 'What am I doing here?' I can imagine a war back in the world (United States) that I'd fight and wouldn't mind dying in—to keep your people free." Utermahlen quashed a court-martial against Munn after witnessing his bravery under fire.

"The colonel wants to make contact with the enemy, and so do I," says Utermahlen, "but the men flat out don't. It's frustrating, but I understand how they feel." Including himself, there are only five career soldiers in the company—"lifers," the draftees call them.

Joe Curry, aged twenty-five, is not one of them. He wears beads and a peace medallion and is one of Utermahlen's platoon sergeants. He was drafted out of an executive job and a prosperous home in Greenwich, Conn. "The object," Curry says, "is to spend your year without getting shot at, or if you do, to get the fewest people hurt. We don't try to frustrate the captain's attempts to kill gooks, but we don't put our hearts in it. If we did, we could kill a lot more. Supposedly, the mission comes first. I put the welfare of the men first." Pfc. Steve Wright says succinctly: "Two of them want to kill gooks, and the rest of us never want to see any again."

Curry's view finds a partial echo up the line: "We could kill a lot more enemy than we do," says Lt. Colonel Jack Galvin, CO of the battalion of which Alpha is a part, "but we'd have to pay for it, and I won't sacrifice anybody. I won't allow my companies to charge into a bunker area. I'd rather take some criticism." Utermahlem, for the most part, sees eye to eye with the colonel. "Charging up hills" he says happily, "has gone right out of fashion."

I read with particular interest about one of the men in Alpha who wanted to fight. I could never figure what drove a man to want to seek and kill another, seemingly just for the sake of it. It had been a well-known fact for some time that we were pulling out of Vietnam, so it made sense to avoid the enemy, thereby minimizing our own casualties. My life was important to me and I resented someone trying to shortchange my time on earth, especially for an unworthy and senseless cause.

One of Alpha's veteran second-tour soldiers is Sgt. Chris Manis, owner of a tigerish smile and a special favorite of Utermahlen for his skill and aggression. Manis saw heavy fighting in 1967–68: "We make a lot less contact now, and guys are a lot more afraid. I don't know why." For a time Manis led an elite recon squad popularly known as the "Crazy Eight," until draftee members balked at the discomfort and danger. The unit was dissolved.

And another one who seemed hell-bent on risking the lives of others for nothing:

Success depends on conscientious execution of patrols; many of the patrols are squad-size, and all nine squad leaders are draftees. Sgt. Jim Sgambati is a Silver Star holder: "They screw up the old man (Captain Utermahlen). They go out on a patrol and avoid the enemy."

Like Alpha Company, our unit had its share of soldiers who wanted to fight, for various reasons. One particular man, recently jilted by his wife, always volunteered to walk point and seemed to invite the enemy to take a shot at him and they readily obliged. Another soldier was noted for venturing off on his own, with the company commanders' blessing to "hunt for gooks" and add to the body count. Most of the time he returned with "proof" of his success. However, the vast majority of us hated being there, hated what we did, and would do almost anything to get out.

Interestingly, several of the pictures Mrs. Gmack sent me had the picture of a soldier posing with John who was his close friend—Pfc. Duane Sedler, who was on the primary picture of the article. She even penned his name on the back of the photo for identification. I was immediately struck by the quote in the Life article next to his picture: "Pfc. Duane Sedler holds the Bronze Star but refuses to go on an ambush: 'It's my life, and I'd like to keep it.'" I readily searched for the section that might provide more details about his position. It wasn't long before I found the following piece about him.

> Midway through the mission the spindle-legged figure of Pfc. Duane Sedler approaches Utermahlen. Sedler has already won a Bronze Star but now politely announces he must refuse an order to go out on a night ambush. Without rancor, Utermahlen tells him he will probably be court-martialed. Sedler, a California college dropout with gentle, deep-set eyes and sucked-in-cheeks, is obviously distressed: "Those small ambushes with people who don't know what they're doing are dangerous. It's my life, and I'd like to try to keep it." Sedler's friends are sympathetic. "Nobody owns anyone around here," says Pfc. Eugene Dillon. "If he doesn't want to go, it's up to him."

It was July 1970 and our unit, like Alpha Company, had returned from invading Cambodia. I was next to one of my friends when he was wounded during a mortar attack. Fortunately, he received only minor wounds and was given ten days to recover on our forward firebase camp. I discovered that he had been ordered back to the bush with the rest of us after using only seven of the ten days allotted by the medical officer for his recovery. But he refused to rejoin the company and was scheduled to be court-martialed within thirty days. During that time, he would remain in the base camp pulling guard duty on the bunkers, a far more appealing task than "humping the bush," carrying eighty pounds on your back while hunting NVA. This also presented an opportunity for me to extend my life a little longer.

I never really considered what a court-martial for refusing a direct order would ultimately mean to me. I lived as a creature of the moment that wanted to buy some time and live another day. In grunt time, thirty days was an eternity. Needing no further encouragement, I "willfully refused a direct order by an officer." Actually, my initial refusal was to our first sergeant; he then walked me to our company commander so the refusal could be witnessed and deemed official. So, my friend and I spent the next thirty days on our base guarding the perimeter while our unit returned to the jungle to hunt "gooks." Our platoon sergeant even agreed to be a character witness at our trial.

Apparently, we weren't the first ones scheduled for a court-martial; there was a backlog of combat refusal on the court docket. I was sentenced to six months in the army stockade, Long Bin Jail (LBJ, as it was infamously called). Since I was a high school dropout, I was given an opportunity to take my GED during my confinement. I was released after serving only forty-five days and given the option of being reassigned to another unit or given some sort of discharge from the army.

I'm still baffled that I made the choice to return to duty. Even though my life was at stake, somehow at the time I felt that the shame of not completing what I started would haunt me the rest of my days. Moreover, facing my family and friends as a quitter, even though they would have been supportive given the political climate regarding the war, was inconceivable to me. Apparently, those boyhood years of playing with toy soldiers made an indelible mark on my psyche. I was reassigned to the 11th Light Infantry Brigade of the Americal Division for my "second tour," which lasted nearly five more months. However, I first returned to my old unit to say good-bye to my friends. I even received a handshake and good wishes from the first sergeant whose order I initially refused.

The Americal Division operated in the northern region of the country. The first thing I noticed upon my arrival was that instead of the enemy referred to as "gooks," they were now called "dinks." I resumed going on combat air assaults and search-and-destroy missions. My new unit, Charlie Company, 4th Battalion, 3rd Infantry Regiment, was now engaged in platoon-sized operations consisting of about twenty-five men, so that we could cover more area hunting the enemy.

My last mission was with a five-man sniper team. Our job consisted of three men staking out ambush sites near the base of a tree while the two snipers would set up and pick their targets from their arboreal positions. We were inserted miles away from the rest of the unit. In a sense, I felt safer because such a small unit operated with a cloak of secrecy and had the element of surprise, but it also carried the risk of being annihilated if a much larger enemy force discovered us. The prevailing mind-set of the American policy was still fixated on the body count. Although I complied and obeyed orders and received a final rating of "excellent" as a rifleman by my new company commander, I vigorously protested going on every mission after my arrival at the new unit. My last few weeks in Vietnam were at Chu Lai, a large rear area noted for the TV series *China Beach*. My new job was a security guard. I was assigned to a latrine detail, which involved supervising two old Vietnamese men while they emptied and burned the contents of a fifty-five-gallon drum full of human excrement. It was an inglorious end to my nearly thirteen-month tour in Vietnam. I would return home, alive and in one piece, to fulfill the haunting lyrics of one of my favorite Beatle songs, "Boy, you're going to carry that weight, carry that weight a long time."

The following is a copy of the letter in its entirety that was sent to John Gmack's parents by a fellow soldier. It presents a vivid, eyewitness account concerning John's "accidental self-destruction" that Mrs. Gmack rightfully challenged and corrected on the Vietnam Memorial Web site. Moreover, the soldier also expressed his anger and frustration at being in a protracted and senseless war. His words echo the daily pain and fear of a grunt—the infantryman who sees death up close.

June 24, 1970

Mr. and Mrs. Gmack,

I'm one of the grunts from the second platoon of Alpha Company. I've been either in Vietnam or Cambodia for nine months now. We're in Cambodia right now. The last two days now the second platoon has made contact while on patrols. John and I got along quite well together, and I considered him one of my best friends. He was the only person in the platoon and one of three from Wisconsin (one of three in the Company). We went through bad times as well as the good times together. Up until the time I got wounded in Bu Gia Mop, I had spent a lot of time with him. I got out of the hospital a few weeks before we were combat assaulted into Cambodia, for our first mission. Now we're into our second mission in Cambodia, and I'm still going through the worst days of my life.

I really didn't know at first if I should tell you how he died because it was an ironic accident; but who has a better right to know than you? Here it is, exactly as it happened. That mission we were finding caches every day. On our seventh day we found an unusually large cache of NVA field gear. It took most of the day to uncover it and take an inventory of the items found. We were going to bring in engineers to blow a pad and extract the cache, but it was too late to get them in that day. To make sure the gooks didn't try taking it away before we got there the next morning, the 1st Platoon put up automatic ambush on the trail that led to it. An automatic ambush is several claymore mines on a trip wire. In the meantime the 3rd platoon moved about 150 meters out and found a suitable place to set up for the night. They called the rest of the company, but we had trouble finding them and walked eight hundred meters in a big circle before we found them. By that time, it was dark and raining, which just added to the confusion.

John's position was the next one to the left of mine. Two people from my squad went out to put out trip flares, and John went out with one other man from his position. To eliminate any gap a gook might walk through, the trip flares had to be tied in. Remember, it was 8:00 and already dark when we got there. The 4 men were walking toward each other when a man from our squad tripped the ambush. The blast was about 25–

30 feet from me, and it was absolutely deafening. Trees and bamboo were flying, and 3 big balls of fire and smoke rose above the treetops. Everyone was stunned at first and didn't know what it was for a while. I remembered they were out there putting out trips, so I grabbed my weapon and about 8 other guys and a couple of medics and went running out there in the dark to see what happened. This is the worst part; two of them we couldn't even find in the darkness. When the sun came up, we did find what was left of them. When we found John, he wasn't in bad shape—at least not that any of us or the medics could see. We called a medevac bird to take him out. In the jungles of Cambodia we had aerial illumination and strobe lights going, which is a bad thing to do in enemy-infested area, but when a life is at stake, the caution comes last. That morning word came over the radio that he had died in the early morning hours. This was hard to take, and it really hurt. I knew that I had lost my best friend, but then I wouldn't think about it and found myself not believing it. Since I've been here I have trouble believing it. Almost as though it's all a bad dream and some day I'll wake up and it'll all be over. But when the AK-47s start singing and the B-40 rockets start coming in, I know it's no dream.

Such is the life of the grunt. The people who are actually fighting this war; the people who search the dense jungles for the enemy and fight him face to face on his own ground. And what do we get for it? Quite a bit. We get our buddies killed and the chance to do it again tomorrow, and the next day for 364 days. When I stop to think about it, I wonder what's kept me alive and functioning all this time. But it's not over yet. At times I get so sick of seeing gooks, watching my buddies die, the mud and rain, the jungle and the bugs, that I feel like throwing down my weapon and quitting everything. Almost forgot. If I remember correctly, John did get to see the battalion surgeon about his jungle rot, but I can't recall if anything ever came of it. I haven't even had the time to write for six weeks now—to anyone—but I figured I just had to do this. I am *truly* sorry this had to happen, and I'm sorry for you people too. I hope I never have to see this type of thing again.

Sincerely,

Greg Carlson, 2nd Platoon

PART II

Vietnam: The Beginning

A Great Country (Boot Camp)

I was six years old when I immigrated to the United States with my parents and younger sister, Marti. We were fortunate to have escaped the war torn city of Budapest, the capital of Hungary. Russian tanks and soldiers were battling with Hungarian Freedom Fighters armed with only light weapons and Molotov cocktails. I vividly recall several scenes of Russian tanks that were set ablaze by homemade bombs tossed from building windows. However, the Hungarian Revolution of 1956 was finally crushed when the might of the Soviet Army was unleashed on the civilian rebels. Hungary, once again, was under communist rule. We made our escape across the Austrian border just ahead of the Russian troops. My family joined thousands of refugees at Camp Kilmer, a temporary shelter set up by the United States government. It was shortly before Christmas when I first heard a delightful but unfamiliar melody being played on a piano coming from the direction of the camp's community building. I immediately fell in love with the upbeat sound of none other than Jingle Bells! As we entered the building, we noticed that all of the children were on the stage area surrounding the lively gentleman who was playing the piano and teaching them to sing this most wonderful song. Needing no encouragement, I readily joined them in the festivities and maneuvered my way through the other children until I was standing right next to his shoulder. It wasn't until several years later that my mother informed me the piano player at our refugee camp was Vice President Richard Nixon. This man was the President of the United States when I was drafted into the U.S. Army. To his credit, he was a pretty good piano player.

The two historical events that I can recall during my first few years in America are the space orbit of the Russian sputnik and Hawaii becoming our fiftieth state. History was always one of my favorite subjects, along with biology and literature. I had the good fortune to live within walking distance of the Museum of Science, located within the Humboldt Park area in Buffalo. I spent countless mornings and afternoons staring through the pane glass windows at the three-dimensional exhibits covering a wide range of subject matter, including history, geology, wildlife biology, chemistry, archeology, and anthropology. In fact, I made it a point to arrive early and spend the first few hours of every Saturday morning visiting my favorite exhibits before I ventured off with my friends to play army. Since the museum strongly resembled a medieval fortification, it was also an ideal place to play "Knights and Vikings" around the outdoor walls, which were surrounded by well-manicured gardens. With garbage can lids as shields and sticks as swords, we intensely, and sometimes painfully, reenacted the old days of hand-to-hand combat. Twenty or twenty-five third grade boys engaged in banging each other's shield is a rather noisy enterprise. But it was great fun despite the beating my hand would take holding the "shield" up for protection while my adversary whacked away at it with a wooden "sword." When the combatants finally returned home for supper, I doubt there was a single trash can in the entire neighborhood that had a properly fitting cover.

Buffalo is exceedingly rich with ethnic and cultural diversity. I had the benefit of having friends from many different backgrounds, including Polish, Italian, Ukrainian, Irish, African American, Hispanic, and Jewish. But it wasn't until I started basic training in Fort Dix, New Jersey, that I came to realize the extent of American diversity. The first thing I noticed was the variety of dialects—all in the same barracks! I was in near disbelief when we received our first "lecture" from a drill instructor who happened to be from Ohio. Since Ohio borders New York and is about a hundred miles from Buffalo, one would not expect such a dramatic change in dialect. Even more bewildering was trying to understand someone from New York City—which is in my home state after all! It was amazing that people who lived nearby could sound so different, while residents of California and Wisconsin, both a considerable distance to be sure, sounded like they lived next door. Southerners were an entirely different matter. Our brothers from down south sounded like they were recently transported in a time machine from the Army of Northern Virginia—the pride of the Confederacy. It wasn't long, however, before I began to notice that their individual dialects were distinctive in their own right. It took some additional time before I fully accepted the fact that they were actually in the Union Army. In fact, as a group, they rarely questioned the authority of the instructors. It wasn't long before it dawned on me that most of the drill sergeants were also from the southern states. This made sense, since most of the Army and Marine Corps basic and infantry training was accomplished south of the Mason-Dixon Line.

One of the truly remarkable by-products of a draft is that it brings young men together from every walk of life. Most of us were nineteen years old, but that's where the similarity ended. Some were accomplished high school athletes, while others were close relatives of the Pillsbury doughboy. Some were articulate and very bright, while others struggled to complete full sentences. Some were born leaders; some could only follow orders, while others were fiercely defiant. Some would become officers, helicopter pilots, door gunners; others would go into artillery, military police, armor, communications, cooking, intelligence, quartermaster corps, etc. The rest would go on to advanced infantry training, where the need to replace the ongoing casualties was the greatest. Most would live, many would be wounded, and a sizeable number would die—much like preceding wars. But unlike World War II, we seemed to be missing a key ingredient—a cause. Yet, because our country called us up, we obeyed and reported for duty. To say that for the majority of us in August 1969 our hearts were not in it would minimize the intense ambivalence that most of us felt at the time. Besides our youth, being drafted was our common denominator. But despite our many differences, or perhaps because of them, it wasn't long before we were forged into a training unit as we sang in unison, "I wanna go to Vietnam, honey … I wanna go to Vietnam, babe … I wanna go to Vietnam, I wanna kill the Charlie Cong, oh honey, oh babe of mine," marching to cadence in the early morning light. I can't recall anyone who sincerely believed this in his heart. Most had no gung ho in their souls.

For many, it was the first time they ventured beyond county lines, let alone out of their home states. Marching, standing in line, pushups, sit ups, chin ups, running, eating, more marching, more running, verbal abuse (which provided comic relief for those not on the receiving end), and finally ... blessed sleep. All of our heads were shaved and we all wore the same olive drab garb. If you were overweight, you lost weight; if you were underweight, you gained the needed pounds. This was a truly remarkable nutritional feat, as we all ate the same "chow," and burned off roughly the same number of calories. After a while, we became sick of seeing nothing but other guys running around Fort Dix with the same shaven heads sprouting from the same green attire. This olive drab scene would be repeated during recreation time, whether on base or in the nearby "GI town," readily accessible by a short bus ride. Every day was jammed pack with activities and the endless lines that were formed for just about everything, including meals, toileting, telephone use, and inspections. We even waited in line to beat each other half to death with pugile sticks. We were slowly being absorbed into the "green machine," which has been in the business of turning raw recruits into soldiers, willingly or not so willingly, for over two hundred years.

It wasn't long before we were introduced to our weapon, an M-14 semi-automatic rifle. One was never, ever, to refer to it as "gun," "rifle," or anything other than "weapon." Even though the M-14 had been phased out and replaced by the smaller, lighter, and fully automatic M-16 some three years earlier, it was still the one we were trained on. Just as well, as things came full circle during the last few months of my tour in Vietnam. I readily traded my M-16 in for an M-14 with an attached bipod after someone from one of our platoons killed a tiger that tripped off an automatic ambush along a trail at night. It was a huge male specimen that was estimated to weigh around five hundred pounds. Quite frankly, I could not envision stopping a creature of this size and power with the smaller caliber weapon if one ever lunged at me from the dense foliage. The M-14 would have much more stopping power in this regard (fortunately, the only tiger that I would ever see resided in the Buffalo zoo). The bipod on the M-14 also allowed me to prop it up on the ground, like an M-60 machine gun, without worrying about getting dirt into the barrel or firing mechanism. Prior to the M-14, my only exposure to weapons consisted of a toy bow and arrow, various plastic peashooters, and of course the ever-popular wooden swords and garbage can covers. But this was the real thing. It looked and felt like a weapon. There was no pretense in its intended design. Using the same caliber ammunition as its bigger cousin, the M-60 machine gun, it was designed for only one purpose.

The simplicity of design and lack of pretense in the M-14 is something that was an inherent feature of the army as a whole. Similarly, the discipline and structure of boot camp made life more manageable. We were too busy with our daily training schedule to be concerned about the war itself. It was still something in the distant future. The class, racial, and geographic differences were things in the forgotten past. There were some who immediately took to the M-14, like a duck to water. With considerable hunting experience lining their résumés, they instinctively knew to squeeze the trigger, rather than jerk it like the rest of us.

We all missed our loved ones and lined up on Sunday afternoons to wait our turns to make brief telephone calls on the few available pay phones in our battalion area. There were times that I went through nearly a half a pack of cigarettes before my turn came up. While we waited we would make conversation with the men nearest to us. Without realizing it, we were forming altogether new families in a matter of weeks. Truly, "it was the best of times and the worst of times." We would seek familiar faces at mealtime and commiserate with our new family before lights out. We may have felt many things, but I never heard anyone say that he felt alone. We were there for each other.

How amazing that someone who was a complete stranger two weeks ago and lived a thousand miles away could become your best friend. I can recall many of their faces, but very few of their names. What lingers is the feeling of warmth I'm experiencing as I write these words. We responded when our nation called and were bonding with each other. We were all training to be soldiers. Hundreds of us were lined up in formation on the parade grounds on that final graduation day. How proudly we marched past Old Glory as we saluted, with "eyes right," in the direction of our brigade commander. The band was playing, "Stars and Stripes Forever." What a great country!

The Five of Us (Infantry Training)

I first met Larry Toczek, John Meisenbach, Richard Timmons, and John Gmack in October 1969 at Fort Gordon, Georgia. I had recently completed my eight weeks of basic combat training at Fort Dix, New Jersey, and was scheduled for ten weeks of advanced infantry training. Our housing was identical to the accommodations we had become all too familiar with in basic training—two-story "chicken coops." Once again, we were to spend the next several months in the same barracks used by soldiers during World War II. If it was good enough for them it would have to do for us twenty-five years later.

Strangely enough, we became quite fond of our Spartan dwelling, primarily because of the relationships we established with one another. It's really quite an amazing process how certain people are drawn to one another—a sort of gathering of the likeminded. I took an immediate liking to these four. Larry Toczek and John Meisenbach were from Orange County, California. They grew up together and were close friends. Richard Timmons was from Fond Du Lac, Wisconsin, while John Gmack came from Green Bay. John Gmack was the baby of this circle of best friends that I associated with, and our bunks were near each other's. He was only eighteen years old, while the rest of us were already a "mature" nineteen. He was energetic and had an infectious smile. A warm feeling comes over me as I reminisce about him and the times we shared. It was our youth and we were going off to war. One of the unique features of being a soldier is that you are never referred to by your first name—by anyone. Most of the time drill sergeants referred to us as "troop," "trainee," or "private" or a host of other names hardly worth repeating. During roll call or if the instructor liked you, your last name was invariably used. In that vein, we referred to each other by our surnames. It was almost as if our parents had never given us first names.

While we had been in basic training just a short time before, we still didn't know what type of specialty training we would receive. Those of us who had some type of special skill, profession or education had at least a fair chance of being assigned to an area that would capitalize on those abilities, since a modern army requires at least a dozen personnel to support one infantry soldier in the field. I believe I was the only one in my immediate group who was a high school drop out; the rest at least had a high school education. All that changed as we found ourselves in the most dreaded military occupational specialty—11B10 (Light Weapons Infantry). We were informed that, since World War II, only about 10 percent of the soldiers in the field comprised the infantry, but they made up 80 to 90 percent of the casualties. We started doing the math. A sizeable number of our company of about one hundred infantry trainees would be either killed or wounded. But that was still several months away, an eternity to a nineteen-year-old.

Our training was serious business, but it never prevented us from engaging in humorous escapades. My all-time favorite was when about six of us went to the canteen after a long day of training for some watered-down beer. Reportedly, the army beer had a lower alcohol content than civilians were being served off base. For someone who was used to the rather potent Canadian beer, this barely tolerable substitute was even more of a shock to the system. We seated ourselves at a table and ordered a pitcher of beer. No sooner was it placed in the center of the table than John extracted what appeared to be a set of dentures from his mouth and plunked it directly into the container. Stupefied, all we could do was watch the dentures gently sink to the bottom. Following a brief period of silence, and tempered by disbelief, we all burst into laughter. Needless to say, we ordered a replacement and carefully guarded it against another surprise attack from John's direction. He joyfully drank from his own pitcher, the dentures still clinging to the bottom like a freshwater clam. It was a memory I will always cherish.

Fort Gordon in late fall and winter seemed like an unlikely place to train for the jungles of Vietnam. This was highlighted by a photograph of me and another friend in full combat gear with our M-16s, wearing gloves and field jackets. Long-needle pine trees surrounded us and red clay was everywhere. These conditions could hardly simulate the tropical climate we were headed for a half a world away. Our two-story wooden barracks were heated by coal, and we were supposed to take turns feeding the furnace throughout the night. But for some reason, most likely as a form of punishment, a small, blond-haired trainee from one of the southern states seemed to have been awarded the job on an almost full-time basis. He gradually took on the appearance of a West Virginia coal miner. His infraction must have been fairly serious, as the rest of us would typically get extra guard duty or the hated kitchen patrol (KP) for not doing something "the army way."

Since our training period overlapped Christmas, we all went home for about a week. I believe we had only about three weeks of training left when we returned just after New Year's Day 1970. The weather became colder and we actually had some snow flurries. The poor guy manning the coal furnace had his work cut out for him. He trained with us during the day and spent many nights stoking the furnace in between the little sleep he managed to get next to the coal bin.

Our little group was closely bonded and we talked about all sorts of things—family, girlfriends, friends back home, etc. Vietnam was still an eternity away and we seemed to be rather flippant about the entire matter. We never seemed to be at a loss to find something to ridicule our instructors about. One of our drill sergeants was a large, muscular man with numerous patches and ribbons, a testimony to his warrior status and combat tours in Vietnam. Of course, we wouldn't even think of cracking a smile in his presence for fear that he would eat us alive or something worse. I can still recall being huddled around him while we were in our barracks as he was lecturing about something related to setting an ambush in dense jungle foliage. I believe he had an *Airborne Ranger* patch on his shoulder and another one that I distinctly remember with the inscription, *Jungle Expert*. The irony of it all was that it was snowing outside and we would be shipping off to Vietnam in a few weeks. It seemed that our group was collectively pondering the humor of the entire scenario. Most of all, I avoided any eye contact with John, as that would bring certain ruin to any semblance of the straight face I was struggling to maintain.

The day after graduation, we were all heading for home one last time before we went overseas. Most of us, perhaps all of us, hoped against hope that we might be the lucky ones to be stationed in Germany. But that pipedream was short-lived. The orders were clear. We were to report to Oakland Air Force Base to process for the "Republic of South Vietnam." The good news was that President Nixon had recently announced scheduled troop reduction as more of the direct combat operations were being handed over to the Army of the Republic of South Vietnam (ARVN). With a modicum of realism, we believed that perhaps we would wind up pulling guard duty in some relatively safe rear base. After all, the war for America was scheduled to wind down within the next year or two. Protests were at their peak and there was plenty of turmoil at home with race riots, hippies, drugs, campus unrest, Woodstock, etc. The war had been going on for over four years and had already claimed thirty-six thousand American lives. But it was far from over and it would go on for some more years; twenty-two thousand more American soldiers would die before it finally ended. Two of them, Richard Timmons and John Gmack, would be from the small circle of my best friends.

Augusta was the town near our base. A full two inches of snow fell within a twenty-four-hour period, creating near panic conditions and closing the airport. We found this amusing, as Richard and John were both from Wisconsin and I was from Buffalo—two inches of snow might raise an eyebrow in July, but in January it's referred to as a "trace of precipitation" or "a light dusting." We all were eager to get home and we devised a surefire plan. We called a local taxicab and offered him an exorbitant amount of money to drive us to the airport in Atlanta, some 150 miles away. He agreed, and we were on our way. Once there, we dispersed to our individual destinations. The five of us would meet again in Oakland just over a week later to process for Vietnam.

I left my home on 91 Clay Street in Buffalo in the pre-dawn hours of a snowy winter day in February 1970. I said goodbye to my mother, sister, and brother the night before. I stayed up to watch a late show movie, *Palm Springs Weekend*, starring Troy Donahue. That was the closest I had ever gotten to tropical weather since a group of us from the neighborhood went to Florida nearly a year earlier. In fact, the only one awake with me was our new Beagle puppy, "Cinders," who was following me around our small kitchen as I packed my duffel bag. She was a recent addition to our family. My mother, who was not known as an animal lover, finally acquiesced to the incessant pleading of my little brother, Robe, and allowed him to have a puppy. He succeeded where I had failed on numerous occasions over the years. She was comfortably bedded in a cardboard box in the kitchen area

I remember taking a measure of comfort that I would be once again united with my best friends within the next few days. I had known these four guys and a few others for just over two months, and we were already closer than brothers. I had many friends, and several close ones, in the neighborhood but this was different. We were embarking on a journey that was at once exciting and dangerous—just the right ingredients for teenage boys looking for an adventure. We heard a lot of stories and completed our infantry training, but nothing could have prepared us for Vietnam. It was another world, in another galaxy far away. We were drafted, and we were headed to fight an unpopular war that was already supposed to be winding down. There was no sense of a cause, victory, or fighting for anything right or noble. We were just supposed to survive a one-year tour.

The five of us, along with the rest of the company, met at Oakland Air Base. We spent a few days processing, which meant waiting in endless lines. It was here that I finally achieved the milestone of dozing off in a standing position. I had already accomplished sleeping while sitting a few months earlier. It still all seemed like we were headed to another camp or training event. Boarded on a commercial airliner, accompanied by pretty stewardesses, hardly compared to the massive troop movements we were accustomed to viewing in a typical war movie. We made a brief refueling stop in Hawaii and the Philippines and arrived in Bien Hoa, Vietnam, on February 6, 1970.

The intense heat and humidity had an immediate impact on us as soon as we stepped off the plane. This would be our lot for the next twelve months. We were loaded on buses and transported to our billets for the night. It was at this point that our little band was separated. John Meisenback was assigned to the First Infantry Division and the 101 Airborne Division picked up Richard Timmons. That was the last time I would see Richard; he was killed five months later. I would see John Meisenback again at Fort Hood in about fourteen months. Our band was down to three: John Gmack, Larry Toczek, and me. All three of us were assigned to the First Cavalry Division (Airmobile) in Bien Hoa, home of the "Sky Troopers," the name depicted in the black and yellow banner over the compound entrance.

For the next two weeks we would be attending "cherry school." This was a combination of jungle training (finally in tropical weather!), rappelling from helicopters, and various tactics used by the airmobile infantry. We were split up again after we completed our training. John was assigned to the 8th Regiment, while Larry and I ended up in the 12th Regiment. As luck would have it, Larry and I not only ended up in the same regiment (four hundred soldiers), but the same company, Delta (one hundred soldiers), and in the same platoon, 3rd (twenty-five soldiers). We bid John farewell. I can still recall his smile. Six months later, we would hear from another fellow trainee who also ended up in the 8th Regiment that both he and Richard Timmons were killed. Although they were in separate army divisions located in entirely different areas of operation, I can recall first hearing about their deaths while on a firebase as being under "unusual circumstances." How one died or lived by that time mattered very little to me. You were either dead or you were alive. There was nothing in between.

February 1970

Advanced Infantry Training at Fort Gordon, Georgia, during the winter of 1969 did very little to prepare us for the dramatic climate change that we would encounter as we first stepped off our civilian airliner in Bien Hoa, South Vietnam. This massive army and air force base housed tens of thousands of American military personnel and was fortified by well-placed bunker complexes. As new arrivals, a caravan of buses transported us to the processing and training center only a few miles away. It was early evening as our convoy made its way along the road toward our next destination. Both sides of the road were dotted with shanties, flimsy structures that would hardly do for a doghouse in my neighborhood—that is, if you cared about your pet. Yet, entire Vietnamese families were seated around fires near the entranceways, apparently having their evening meal.

It was at this very moment that I *smelled* Vietnam for the first time. It was like nothing I had ever experienced before or since. Olfactory receptors were awakened that I never knew existed. It was the first real assault on my senses and I had no idea how many more would follow in the next twelve months. Vietnam, after all, was a total sensory overload in the realms of sight, sound, smell, hearing, touch—all converging on a visceral intensity that rearranged me from the inside out. The next few weeks were pretty much an extension of advanced infantry school, except the climate more resembled Vietnam—because it *was* Vietnam. We would attend various training seminars on helicopter assaults, ambush techniques, rappelling off towers, etc., and return to our wooden barracks at dusk. Ironically, these wooden structures were more modern (toilets actually flushed most of the time) than what we were accustomed to at Fort Gordon. So how bad could Vietnam actually be, except for the weather, of course? It was all still part of one long training exercise, much like becoming glorified Eagle Scouts, with the exception of having loaded weapons during bunker guard duty with which we were expected to kill the enemy should he venture within range of our perimeter.

The day finally arrived when we completed "cherry school" (a "cherry" is an infantryman who has not yet experienced combat) and our group was herded into a most unusual-looking airplane waiting for us on the far end of the runway. It was a camouflage-painted, fixed-wing aircraft with twin engines, sporting an elegantly sleek body and an oversized tail fin. Assigned to the U.S. Air Force, the Caribou was a transport plane that would fly us to our new battalion headquarters in Song Be. Interestingly, these airplanes are still being utilized nearly forty years later to transport personnel and much-needed supplies to remote outposts near the North Pole.

Numbering about twenty men, we were seated along the two sides of the fuselage in the fashion of paratroopers—minus the parachutes. In civilian airliners, every measure is taken to muffle the noise of the engine in order to ensure that the passengers have an enjoyable ride. In the military, this notion is not even worthy of a consideration. One can hear every pitch sound that the engine makes, especially the changing of gears. The Caribou was a noisy aircraft. It wasn't so bad taxiing on to the runway, but the real adventure was about to start when the aircraft was finally ready for takeoff.

Without warning, the pilot revved up the engines until the entire aircraft began trembling like a mechanical contraption about to give up the ghost. Fortunately, there were no windows to peer through to see whether the rivets were actually coming loose from the incessant rattling. We were instructed by the crew chief to hold on to the cargo nets that were conveniently located directly behind us—for we were about to take off! But the plane remained stationary, as it continued shaking vigorously. Suddenly, the pilot released the brakes and the Caribou accelerated like a dragster on an abbreviated runway. This stage of the operation was very short-lived because, before we could adjust our senses (or our hand grips), he pointed the nose up at a sharp angle—and we were airborne! This was not the gradual and comfortable ascent that one is accustomed to in a civilian aircraft. This was more like the launching of a spacecraft. Once again, I could hear the engines straining at the task of having to climb at such a steep angle. The only thing I noticed was the fear in the facial contortions of the other infantrymen's faces, contrasted by the sadistic grin sported by the crew chief of this bizarre flying machine.

Mercifully, and not a moment too soon, we finally achieved altitude, and the plane went into level flight. But the *real* treat was just ahead. The crew chief informed us about twenty minutes into our flight that we were approaching Song Be and to prepare for landing—in short, hang on to the netting for dear life! The plane was so noisy that we had to pass the message by yelling it to the man next to us. Suddenly, and without a hint of warning, the unthinkable happened—the engine was no longer making that loud, disturbing noise, because it had been turned off! The sadistic smile once again returned to the crew chief's face. We were literally dropping out of the sky, and the only thing that could be heard was the windy sound the plane was making from the drastic descent. Ironically, my only source of comfort was that all-too-familiar sadistic grin, as I figured this guy knew his plane—that's why he was the crew chief in the first place. Unbeknownst to us at the time, this aircraft was especially designed for a very short runway. In this manner, it could take off and land quickly, greatly reducing its vulnerability to ground fire from hidden enemy positions near the base camp. It felt like the pilot waited until the last possible moment before he turned the engines on again and pulled out of the dive as we gracefully landed on the runway with some of our manhood and breakfast still intact.

Song Be was a much smaller military installation than the massive Bien Hoa base. It was blanketed with a fine layer of red dust, which seemed to have found its way into and on top of everything there. All of the dwellings were tents of varying sizes, with sandbags and tin to offer some protection. This was in direct contrast to the lush, tropical countryside about two hundred yards beyond its perimeter. I was to find out later that this geographical arrangement was typical for most of the firebases in Vietnam, regardless of their sizes.

An area had to be carved out of the jungle that would house the tents, artillery, bunkers, vehicles, and landing zones for various aircraft. This new area would be an enclave, surrounded and protected by a concertina (similar to barbed wire) system marked off by bunkers about every fifty yards or so. Then there was the outer perimeter, which was also cleared of trees and foliage, one to two hundred yards deep. Beyond it lay the tree line, typically comprised of thick jungle vegetation, ideal for the enemy to hide in. This outer perimeter or "free-fire zone" was heavily mined. The enemy had to cross it to reach the base camp. Anything that moved out there was fair game. This area was totally covered with layer after layer of concertina wire and claymore mines, which could be activated from the bunkers. There were even fifty-five gallon drums of Phu gas that also could be detonated from the bunker, incinerating any living thing that was unlucky enough to be in the general area.

But Song Be had one beautiful landmark that set it apart from many other base camps. Nearby, there was a solitary mountain, seemingly less than a mile beyond a section of the perimeter. At the top of it was a small firebase composed of a mortar platoon and communications station that had a panoramic view of the tropical landscape along with our dust-covered compound. But even with this breathtaking mountain amidst the lush, tropical jungle, it was becoming increasingly more apparent that we were now entering another outer perimeter—the realm of darkness.

Larry and I reported to our company headquarters, located near a mud hole, in a weather-beaten, dusty tent. This was the official rear area of D Company, 1st Battalion, 12th Cavalry of the First Air Cavalry Division. The red and white Gideon, reminiscent of the cavalry of the western frontier, hung over the flimsy wooden doorway. The rear staff was a company clerk and a 1st lieutenant, the executive officer. These two individuals were entrusted with keeping the highly mobile company supplied with food, ammunition, fresh troops (that would be us), and the most critical of all items—mail from home. We were issued our weapons, ammo, rucksacks, canteens, etc., and filled out some paperwork. The clerk pointed us in the general direction of the mess tent so we could get something to eat. It was about a hundred yards away, adjacent to the motor pool that serviced the trucks and jeeps for the base. After being "served" by the cook, we carried our tray of chow to the dining area (a few wooden picnic tables under a ragged and dusty tent) and sat down next to some other soldiers who, judging by their weathered and hardened appearance, had been there for quite some time.

They asked us what unit we were assigned to and immediately after we told them it was D Company, they responded, "Oh yeah, Dustoff Delta." We were informed that this unfortunate nickname was given to our unit because of the relatively high number of casualties suffered recently. "Dustoff" referred to the medevac helicopters called in to evacuate the wounded and "Delta" is the army radio term for the letter D, like "Alpha" is for A and "Bravo" is for the letter B. This news was most unsettling to say the least because the following day we were heading out to the LZ (landing zone) where our new company was gathered, making preparations for its next CA (combat assault). That night, we pulled bunker guard duty with two "short-timers" who were slated to return to "the world" (home) in a few weeks.

Like many soldiers who were nearing the end of their tour of duty, they were removed from direct combat operations in the "bush" (jungle/rice paddy) for several reasons. First, except for a few who enjoyed killing and wanted to continue the gruesome task, the overwhelming majority of "grunts" (infantrymen) would jump at the chance to get out and stay out of the bush. Consequently, as a reward for doing one's share of "humping" (carrying an eighty-pound pack and hunting for enemy troops in the bush for eight to eleven months), a rear job opportunity is presented, usually as a bunker guard, helicopter loader, or company clerk. Second, and probably the main reason to pull someone out as he approaches his departure date, is plain old safety. It stands to reason that the closer one gets to getting out alive and in one functional piece, the more nervous one becomes. At some point during the war, the army in its infinite wisdom came to the realization that a nervous soldier could be a danger to his unit. In a sense, one regresses to becoming as dangerous as a cherry the closer one comes to going home.

Anyway, these two short-timers passed us a "bowl" (a pipe filled with marijuana) as we sat on top of the bunker next to our machine guns, watching the marvelous Southeast Asian sunset. A few Cobra gunships were making their way home from a mission of raining death on some unsuspecting "gooks" (North Vietnamese soldiers or Viet Cong guerillas), while a medevac was hurriedly bringing some casualties in from another direction. I could feel the atmosphere of death begin to filter through my soul for the first time.

Over the course of the night, they gave us straight talk of what the war, and particularly the bush, was all about. We asked for the truth, and that was what we got. The operative word was *survival*. There was no talk of goals, objectives, victory, God and country, or anything else other than surviving the year in any manner one could. It was absolutely senseless that we were even still there anymore. Our nation was on the verge of civil revolt over it and we had already committed to pulling out in the near future. Yet, Americans continued killing an enemy who really was no enemy since he was willing to leave us alone. We were the ones who came after him on search-and-destroy missions that always ended with loss of life on both sides. We were hunting him and he was waiting to ambush us for seeking him out in his own land.

They informed us that there is no such thing as troop morale, since all anyone wanted to do was survive and go home. They told us that a fellow soldier recently executed one of the first sergeants in another company during a firefight with enemy troops. The first sergeant was repeatedly causing problems, so a group took up a collection and paid one of their own to "waste him" during a firefight, making it appear like it was an accident. Several officers had also been killed within the past month when a "frag" (grenade) was tossed into their bunker while they were sleeping. We were informed of the growing tension between blacks and whites, "heads" (pot smokers) and "juicers" (beer drinkers), draftees and "lifers" (career soldiers), etc. The worrisome thing about all this was that these people were all American soldiers in the same unit and it was getting worse by the day. Morale was decaying even while offensive combat operations were maintaining their gruesome work. As I pondered these disturbing events, mesmerized by the setting sun from atop our bunker, medevacs were bringing in more wounded and dead from outside the relative safety of our dust-ridden base. In my gut, I felt the eerie sensation that I was entering the outer layer of the rings of hell.

We met our "slick" (Huey transport helicopter) on the helipad the next morning. Larry and I, along with the mail and other supplies, were headed to the forward LZ where Delta Company was getting some rest after humping the bush for a few weeks. We had our full gear on and it was the first time I entered a helicopter with a loaded weapon. We instinctively sat at the edge, with our feet dangling out, as we quickly became airborne over our barren, heavily wired perimeter and headed toward the dense jungle foliage interspersed with clearings of elephant grass. As we looked into each other's eyes, we suddenly realized that this was for real. The door gunner seemed fairly relaxed as he repositioned his M60 machine gun and began reading a paperback as we flew about five hundred feet above the ground. All we could see below were endless miles of lush jungle, with an occasional meandering creek or small river. It seemed that entire armies could be hidden in this vast, blanketed wilderness and no one would be the wiser.

Before long, a clearing emerged in the distance ahead, and we realized that it was our destination. It was a rather small forward landing zone, typical for units of the Air Cavalry, as they stayed for relatively short periods of time before moving on to another area of operation (AO). Surveying the area as we were about to land, I could see that it was nothing more than about an acre or two of dirt surrounded by hastily built bunkers (more like dirt holes fortified with sandbags) and a few well-positioned artillery pieces. The impression was one of a series of rodent mounds in the middle of the jungle. A small dust storm was stirred up as we landed just outside the perimeter. The inhabitants covered their eyes and turned their backs on the source of the disturbance. We stepped off the Huey with our weapons and equipment as a group of guys without shirts and sporting deep tans, approached the aircraft and began to unload the supplies.

Not five minutes went by until we were introduced as the "FNGs" (f___king new guys), an endearing term relegated to the new arrivals to a unit. Larry and I were assigned to the third platoon, but to different squads. We parted for a while as we were introduced to the seven or eight men in our squad. It was at this point that I first met Sgt. Bill Wood, my squad leader. He was a fairly rugged soldier who had a calming presence and readily made me feel welcome. He was a born leader and I was fortunate to have been assigned to his squad.

A few minutes later I heard some words that deeply disturbed me at the time. One of my squad members warned me about not throwing any frags in thick jungle terrain because one of our men recently had to fall on one with his helmet to protect others and "we had to pick his guts off the vines and put them back in." He mentioned this in a matter-of-fact fashion with which I would soon become familiar. There was little time to grieve or discuss casualties, as the business of survival does not permit such luxuries. One just went on staying alive the best way one could.

I never really had an opportunity to follow up his statement with any questions since my main focus was to make preparations for my first combat aerial assault just a few days away. Yet, these words haunted me for so many years that I really questioned whether I misheard him or simply dreamed them up. In the words of the noted psychoanalyst Carl Jung, "Imagination imitates and competes with reality." Vietnam was a place where the boundaries between reality, fantasy, and dreams shifted back and forth. Undoubtedly, at least in this instance, these boundaries didn't become more defined over the years. Finally, in October 2007, I became determined to see if in fact there was any truth to these words, as the search became another step in my lifelong quest to integrate my experiences from the war. It was not long before my Internet search revealed a rather startling discovery in the person of John Baca:

Medal of Honor Citation

John P. Baca, Specialist Forth Class, U.S. Army, Company D, 1st Battalion, 12th Cavalry, 1st Cavalry Division, Phuoc Long Province, Republic of Vietnam, 10 February 1970.

For conspicuous gallantry and intrepidity in action at the risk of his life above and beyond the call of duty. Sp4 Baca, Company D, distinguished himself while serving on a recoilless rifle team during a night ambush mission. A platoon from his company was sent to investigate the detonation of an automatic ambush device forward to his unit's main position and soon came under intense enemy fire from concealed positions along the trail. Hearing the heavy firing from the platoon position and realizing that his recoilless team could assist the members of the besieged patrol, Sp 4 Baca led his team through a hail of enemy fire to a firing position within the patrol's defensive perimeter. As they prepared to engage the enemy, a fragmentation grenade was thrown into the midst of the patrol. Fully aware of the danger to his comrades, Sp 4 unhesitatingly, and with complete disregard for his own safety, covered the grenade with his steel helmet and fell on it as the grenade exploded, thereby absorbing the lethal fragments and concussions with his body. His gallant action and total disregard for his personal well being saved 8 men from serious injury or death. The extraordinary courage and selflessness displayed by Sp 4 Baca, at the risk of his life, are in the highest traditions of the military service and reflect great credit on him, his unit, and the U.S. Army.

Well, there it was in black-and-white print—confirmation that a lingering memory of a tragedy was indeed true. Just seven days prior to my arrival in the same company, a soldier risked his life to save others and, for his exceptional bravery, was awarded our nation's highest medal for valor, the Medal of Honor. But to my surprise and delight, the story doesn't end there. Miraculously, John Baca survived the severe wounds he received during that February 10, 1970, ambush. A humble man, he rarely speaks about it publicly. He prefers to share an incident that occurred about six weeks earlier, on Christmas Day, 1969.

Baca was walking ahead of his unit, acting as "point," when he surprised a young North Vietnamese soldier sitting alone on top of a bunker in the jungle. Baca saw that the soldier could not reach his rifle quickly, and, not wanting to shoot him, yelled in Vietnamese for him to surrender. Not only was he able to take his "Christmas gift" alive and unharmed, the young man, twenty years later, was among the Vietnamese that Baca worked with building a medical clinic in 1990. (He returned to Vietnam with a group of ten men from the Veterans' Vietnam Restoration Project. The group spent eight weeks working alongside Vietnamese building a health clinic in a village north of Hanoi.)

To be sure, this was a story for the ages. But the only thing I was told at the time was about how they picked his entrails off the jungle vines. It was never mentioned if he lived or died. As I was to discover later, no matter how severely wounded a soldier was, the last thing you recall is that you believe he was still alive when he was hastily placed on a medevac helicopter. If he didn't return at a later date, like some would from minor wounds, you hardly ever knew what happened to him. Since you had to get back to the serious business of survival, the wounded comrade soon became history and rarely discussed while one was still in Vietnam. It was during the unguarded moments in nightmares many years later that such memories clamored to be heard from again.

The following day my buddy Larry, the other FNG who arrived with me, and I were summoned by my squad leader, Bill Wood, to accompany him toward a dirt mound just outside the perimeter of our LZ. Another squad member, Jim Waulk, greeted us as Larry and I were provided with the opportunity to engage in some target practice in order to adjust the sights on our newly issued weapons. Bill and Jim seemed to be close friends. Jim usually walked point for our squad and they joined us as they calibrated their own M-16s.

Even though we were there to fight a war and people were killed on a regular basis, there was absolutely no way any one of us could predict what would happen in less than forty-eight hours from the time we were joking around target shooting at Coke cans. These casual moments are still frozen in time for me as I write these words, envisioning the scenario as it surrealistically unfolds in my mind. But the clock would not stand still. The hours were steadily and inexorably inching toward that appointed time when Bill and Jim would be killed as they stood next to each other on a jungle trail in Phuoc Long Province on February 20, 1970.

Larry and I would each have our part to play on that fateful day. I would be holding Bill Wood in my arms as he was bleeding to death on a jungle floor, absolutely powerless to save his life. Larry would be called from another squad to help carry Jim's decapitated body wrapped in a poncho for several days in the jungle until another helicopter arrived to retrieve him as well. Perhaps they accompanied each other on the flight home to their beloved state of Ohio, along with the other flag-draped aluminum caskets that were returning to loved ones. The shirt I was wearing would be soaked in Bill's blood and I would not be able to spare enough water to totally cleanse my hands from the dried red fluid as I prepared my evening meal. I will continue to play this reel in my memory as we innocently take our target practice on cans placed on a dirt mound, hoping beyond hope that I can forestall or even prevent what will happen the day after tomorrow.

But happen it did. These two guys who welcomed us into the unit would not have much longer to live, while Larry and I would make it home alive and in one piece, at least physically. We would serve our last six months stateside together as we completed our two-year stint in the army. But John Gmack and Richard Timmons would return home in the same manner as these two soldiers who were shooting tin cans outside the LZ with us on this day. They would be reunited with the scores of those who preceded them over the centuries—those who never returned to the arms of their loved ones. A part of us left with them, as a part of them remained with us, an eternal brotherhood that connects us with one another at the juncture between life and death and beyond.

Helicopters Everywhere

Vietnam has already gone down in history as the "helicopter war." In fact, the terms *helicopter* and *Vietnam* are, for all intents and purposes, inseparable. Even today, some thirty-seven years later, the unmistakable, mesmerizing sound of a National Guard Huey flying overhead from the Niagara Falls Air Base never fails to halt me in my tracks, instantly transporting me back to another time. I feel compelled to stand motionless and follow its fading image in the distance until I can no longer hear the sound of the rotor blades. Somehow its spell over me seems to grow with the passing years. Ours was a "love-hate" relationship that was cultivated over many hours flying at treetop level or hundreds of feet in the air. Endearingly nicknamed the "slick," I experienced the Huey either as my lifeline or potential coffin, depending upon our destination. It was certainly a most welcomed sight as we were waiting to be extracted from the middle of a jungle after several weeks of sweat, toil, and death. Conversely, I dreaded the sight of the cursed thing when we were preparing for a combat aerial assault into some other God-forsaken heart of darkness for no apparent purpose. But regardless of which direction we were headed after boarding the ubiquitous aircraft, I hated flying. Like many of my fellow grunts, I felt much safer on the ground in my own element, regardless of how hostile it may have been at any given time. I felt that I could fend for myself better maneuvering with my feet on the ground. Whether one called it swamp, jungle, mud, or dirt … it was my security. Perhaps if we had been issued something resembling a parachute, I would have been able to hold on to the illusion that I had a chance of landing safely on top of some tree if we were going down.

Our lives were spent going from a forward firebase to jungles and periodically to large base camps. The landscape of Vietnam was peppered with these enclaves of varying sizes, much like cavalry outposts on the American frontier. Every one of them had a helicopter pad since flying was usually the only way you arrived or left the "fort." We even coined the term "skying out" to describe this mode of travel that became our way of life. Perhaps that is why soldiers in First Air Cavalry were called "sky troopers." My fear of flying spiked dramatically whenever a helicopter was shot down or crashed because of mechanical failure. That is why we all placed such a premium on boarding or exiting as quickly as possible.

Pilots and door gunners became nervous whenever they touched down to pick us up or to drop us off. It was here that they felt most vulnerable to ground fire or booby traps. Conversely, I became more nervous as our altitude approached fifty feet, as jumping off at this height would not have a good ending. Even if I discarded my eighty-pound rucksack and weapon, my chances of survival would be slim unless I landed in water deep enough to absorb the impact. Frankly, I would have done anything to avoid being inside a helicopter if it was headed for a crash. The charred bodies of crash victims were always on my mind whenever we boarded for a mission or to be transported from one firebase to another.

These unfortunate souls were referred to as "crispy critters" by our recovery teams and the sobering phrase "fly or fry" was casually made by the pilots and door gunners. A fate worse than dying in this manner is surviving in the state of blackened, living tissue. I vividly recall several of us watching in horror as three such survivors were medically stabilized in a tent that was being used as a makeshift hospital. We were pulling guard duty at a nearby bunker, adjacent to the medevac helipad, when the poor souls were flown in. Every square inch of skin was charred like a large, burnt potato that was roasted over a campfire. It was impossible to determine the race of the individuals. In fact, we initially had difficulty determining at which end their heads were located. The IV bottle served as a visual marker, since it is usually positioned near the upper body where the arms are. My first reaction was that I hoped and prayed that none of them survived. I would wish to be dead rather than to go on existing like a piece of burnt meat that the flies would soon be circling above, as they do for all decaying matter.

But while I was still a cherry during my first few weeks in Vietnam, my experience with helicopters was limited to a pure adrenaline rush, void of the suddenness of death that could end my life in the blink of an eye. Helicopters were everywhere. Firebases were bustling with the activity of helicopters all day long. They were engaged in the ceaseless movement of taking off, landing, or flying overhead. At times it rivaled the entranceway to a honeybee colony. The most plentiful and versatile of the group was the Huey UH. It was used as a troop carrier for air assaults, as well as one of the primary modes of transportation between firebases. It could also be used as a gunship when modified with a minigun and rocket launchers. For the most part, it offered little or no protection for the crew, especially the door gunners who were totally exposed to the elements. The troops who rode in Hueys with their feet dangling from the sides, just above the skids, could almost be picked off with a medium-priced pellet or BB gun from your local Kmart as they approached for a landing.

For the wounded though, the helicopters bearing the bold red cross of the medevac were a godsend, an answer to a desperate prayer. Made up entirely of volunteers, the medevac teams would place their lives in jeopardy in order to extract our wounded, even while the enemy was still in the immediate area and the landing zone was far from secure. We even had one landing in the jungle in pitch darkness to extract someone who apparently had malaria, with a dangerously high fever. As we took turns caring for him, we were anxiously waiting for word from our company commander on what to do with him. He seemed to be getting worse and daylight was many hours away. I specifically recall that his fever had to reach 105 degrees in order for him to be considered serious enough to be evacuated to a hospital. We all had selfish reasons for hoping that our medic would be able to keep the fever below that magic number—no one wanted a medevac to land near our defensive perimeter in the middle of night with its headlight beaming to secure a landing sight.

But it was not to be. Fortunately for everyone, all went well that time and he was safely evacuated to a field hospital. I don't recall that he returned to our unit and it wasn't until recently, when I spoke with our former platoon sergeant, that I actually discovered what happened to him. It seems that, during his hospitalization, it was discovered he was born with only one kidney, news even to him. This wonderful piece of information made him ineligible for the army and he was medically discharged on the spot.

However, while I was enjoying the relative innocence of a cherry during those first few weeks, I felt pure excitement at the mere sound or sight of a helicopter. This adrenaline rush was epitomized in my first combat aerial assault. I was still enjoying the relative innocence of never having been in actual combat. For that reason, the experience was relegated to being one of a wild ride, much like the helicopter assault scene in the movie *Apocalypse Now*. The entire company of about one hundred soldiers was taking flight in at least a dozen Hueys lined up in a staggered battle formation. We were close enough to helicopters on either side to see the faces of our fellow soldiers and the flight helmets of the pilots and door gunners. With our feet dangling over the sides hundreds of feet above the ground, it occurred to me, in one glorious instant, that I was participating in a full-blown cavalry charge like those of bygone days. Flashing before me was the scene from *Charge of the Light Brigade* as well as a collage of other cavalry charges from various movies during my childhood, all of which I reenacted countless times with Marx playsets on our living room floor with my best childhood friend, George.

There was something magical about this first aerial assault, mainly because I thought of it as still part of a world of make believe where no one gets hurt or dies. It was also the only time that I felt any *espirit de corps* while in Vietnam. This is what I had always fantasized that war would be like—soldiers lined up and charging into battle. I felt indestructible. My heart was racing and adrenaline was pouring through my veins as we cut through the tropical sky, swiftly heading toward our destination to meet the enemy head on. It felt as if nothing and no one could stop this aerial machinery. With only about one hundred of us in twelve helicopters, I thought we had more than enough to conquer anything that lay ahead. In retrospect, if I were given a choice on how I would die in combat, it would have been then and there during that first, glorious assault. In fact, the scenario would involve our small band heading straight into the communist capitol of Hanoi, fully realizing that none of us would come out alive. But it sure would have been a glorious way to die … charging straight into the gates of hell as one unit, dying a warrior's death in a blazing moment—the cavalry charge of my childhood fantasies.

I knew we were approaching our landing zone when the Cobra gunships peeled away from our formation. These flying raptors were very sleek aircraft with only a pilot and gunner, seated in tandem, in a helicopter that thought it was a fighter plane. Accordingly, their airframe, weapons platform, and high performance made no apologies for their intended design—to rain death from above on whatever was below. They were true killing machines. It was at this specific moment in time that the reality of war hit me. As the Cobras dropped altitude, it was obvious that they were headed directly toward our intended landing zone to "soften it up" for our landing.

When we finally caught up to them, they were already circling the clearing where we were to land and spraying the area with their mini guns and rockets. We were informed in cherry school the week before that if a Cobra passed over a football field while firing its mini gun, a bullet would be placed in every eight square inches. In this manner, a rabbit, regardless of its location anywhere on the field, would be hit by at least one round—even if it was standing motionless, hoping to go undetected. Our Huey finally descended but hovered a few feet above the elephant grass, which was six to eight feet high. The size of the clearing seemed to be able to safely accommodate four helicopters at a time. The pilots and door gunners, who were always anxious to get airborne again, were even more pressured to dump us off as quickly as possible to make way for the next flight, while the Cobras continued their pounding of the outer perimeter of the LZ.

In my ignorance, I was waiting for the pilot to land before I exited the aircraft. But this was not to be, at least not today. The elephant grass was apparently too risky for a landing, so we would have to exit while hovering above it. Not knowing what I was going to land in was one thing, but being strapped with an eighty-pound rucksack, grenades, ammo, etc., made me ponder my options. I quickly realized that there were no options as the door gunner, nervously focusing on the wooded area where his machine gun was pointed, kept motioning for us to jump off his helicopter. So jump we did, but not before I could shave a few feet off my fall by positioning myself on the skid. The elephant grass cushioned my fall as I rolled on the ground. Similar scenarios were unfolding all around our landing zone as troopers disappeared into the tall grass. Our first wave quickly secured the area for the rest of the company. Cobras were still circling and dive bombing like German Stukas from World War II, as they continued to wreak havoc on the thick foliage just behind the tree line.

We all breathed a sigh of relief when we discovered that we had not made any contact with the enemy and suffered no casualties—at least none inflicted by the gooks. It soon became evident that two soldiers had either sprained or broken their ankles jumping off the helicopters. Under the circumstances, I'm surprised that more of us hadn't been injured. Anyway, one of the helicopters was recalled to evacuate these two very lucky souls back to the main base. At that moment, I wished I could have joined them. The glorious cavalry charge was over. The grueling fate of the infantryman now lay ahead. Somewhere ahead of us was the North Vietnamese bunker complex that we had come to attack and destroy. The enemy knew we were here and was waiting for us. As I would discover during this first mission and subsequent encounters, they were very patient. We quickly exchanged the air mobility of the cavalry for the fate of the grunt. Regardless of all the high-tech advances in warfare, we were now relegated to the fighting methods that existed during the American Revolutionary War nearly two hundred years earlier, except this time the roles were reversed. We were the "imperial invaders" who were trained in conventional warfare. The Viet Cong were the "minutemen," defending their homeland using the ambush techniques that our ancestors successfully used to defeat British redcoats.

To be sure, the Cobras, jets, B-52 bombers, and artillery all shared in bringing death to this elusive enemy from various distances, usually from many miles away. After they locked onto their targets, it was a matter of pushing a button or a lever. They rarely got to see the destruction they left behind. With the infantry it was an entirely different matter. We not only witnessed their handiwork, but also added to the carnage at close range. As our platoon approached the area near the bunker complex, we managed to surprise a few NVA soldiers and opened fire, hitting several of them. They quickly retreated toward their bunker complex, which was hidden some distance away.

Cobra gunships were recalled to pound the section of the hill where we believed the bunkers to be located. Since we were in very dense jungle, all I could see were lush trees and thick bushes. The foliage was so thick that I would actually have to step on top of a bunker to notice it. Between the heat and humidity conspiring with the eighty-pound load I was carrying, the strain of humping the bush became as much of an enemy as anything else in the jungle. I soon learned to position a green towel on my neck and shoulders to prevent the straps of the rucksack from further digging into my skin and muscle. Loose corners of the towel also became quite handy for wiping the sweat from my eyes and forehead, which tended to compromise my vision. All in all, being in the infantry in 1970 just plain SUCKED—much like it did in 1776, 1861, 1914, 1944, and 1950.

Although I would be participating in other cavalry charges, it would never again be the same. We knew that, following breakfast the next morning, we would be making preparations to assault the bunker complex we came to destroy. Ours was the point squad as we approached our date with destiny. Death would be ushered in from nowhere and just as quickly recede, only to return at a later date. Bill Wood and Jim Waulk breathed no more. I now knew firsthand what awaited me after the aerial charge once we had landed to begin our death hunt. I stepped over an invisible line. Everything was the same but somehow different—forevermore.

War is Drugs

In many respects, this has been one of the most difficult chapters for me to write. Initially, I planned to avoid any serious mention about drug use, mine or anyone else's, for a number of reasons. However, the more I tried to avoid or gloss over the topic, the more I felt that I was exercising that age-old defense mechanism of denial, one that I became all too familiar with after my return home. War was bad enough, but war and drug abuse was even worse. Yet it was that reality which many of us experienced during that surreal period of our lives. Drugs, especially the ubiquitous marijuana, gave the war a psychedelic dimension for those who indulged.

Many of my current friends and colleagues can't believe how freely I smoked marijuana, when for so many years I haven't smoked a single cigarette or drunk an alcoholic beverage. Sadly, I continue to witness the ravages of drug abuse in the lives of people on a daily basis in my clinical practice. Therefore, I find it necessary to inform the reader that I am ardently opposed to even the experimental or recreational use of any illicit drugs. But the time was 1970 and the place was Vietnam. The following description of drug use reflects the mind-set of a confused young soldier who was caught up in a war he did not believe in and defiantly resisted at every opportunity. Drug use was a two-sided coin of attempting to cope with the trauma of war and bond with brethren who collectively joined in defiance against it.

Somewhere up there with helicopters, the word *drugs* is frequently associated with the Vietnam War. While some degree of drug use by U.S. troops was there from the beginning, it wasn't until after the Tet Offensive in 1968 that it became widespread. Limited mostly to marijuana in the earlier years, it reached its zenith in the latter half of 1970 with the arrival of high-grade heroin. By this time an increasing number of American troops were draftees. This was especially true for those unfortunate enough to end up in the infantry, a specialty for which no sane individual would volunteer, especially at a time when the war was already a lost cause. For high school dropouts coming from a lower socioeconomic household like I did, the choices were limited. And being a draftee essentially offered no real choice. You were routed to an MOS (Military Occupational Specialty) where the need was the greatest. Since the vast majority of the casualties were from the infantry, that is where the largest number of vacancies existed.

Some of my more fortunate fellow draftees with college degrees or technical skills were offered other avenues like army intelligence, signal corps, military police, etc. Therefore, it was no surprise that the draftees in most specialties mirrored the rebellion and unrest of their fellow nineteen-year-olds at home. By 1969, nearly 70 percent of the Army Infantry consisted of draftees. When I arrived in Vietnam, the counterculture of the sixties was heavily represented within the ranks of the U.S. military. Nevertheless, we trudged on—sweating, hurting, killing, dying, and watching others die. Living in fear for our lives and trying to cope with the inner pain that was compounding with interest in our souls, drugs offered an instant, readily available, and inexpensive mode of blessed relief, however brief. For many of us, drugs also provided an avenue of defiance against the insanity of the war in which we were forced to participate.

Right from day one in cherry school, when we received our orientation to helicopter assault and jungle school training, I was introduced to high-grade marijuana. Supposedly, it was laced with opium, hence the name "OJ" for opium joint. Since we were on a large base bustling with rear echelon personnel, including military police, the only safe place to smoke the stuff was inside one of the bunkers that were strategically situated around the vast fortified perimeter of our compound. Most of these bunkers were unmanned during the daytime, making them an ideal place for the gathering of the likeminded whenever the opportunity presented itself. We quickly learned to be opportunistic. It was at these gatherings, as we passed the bowl around, that we commiserated about the unenviable situation we would be in for the following year. For all intents and purposes, this became *our* support group.

During those two short weeks, we returned to those same bunkers in the evening for guard duty and picked up where we left off during the day. I must say from the outset that not everyone smoked "dew" (an endearing term for marijuana). But if you were from New York or California, the chances were better than average that you did. From the start it seemed that most of the draftees were relegated into two basic groups, "heads" and "juicers." The first group, of which I became an instant member, consisted of those who got high the natural way—smoking dew. After all, as our draftee subculture readily noted, "man made brew, but God made dew." To a man, we were dead set against the war and defiantly compliant at best. The second group was comprised mostly of soldiers from the southern states and remote places like Nebraska and West Virginia. The juicers would get drunk whenever we returned to a forward firebase or rear area, which was well supplied with alcoholic beverages. Some of the heartier ones would even carry booze in their rucksacks to drink while in the bush. Although I enjoyed drinking beer before I arrived in Vietnam, and even during basic and infantry training, I suddenly developed a revulsion even to the smell of it.

Then there was a third group that we referred to as the "lifers" (many of them were also juicers). There were times when we considered them as much the enemy as the Viet Cong. They were composed of the regular military, those who made a career out of maintaining the operation of the army's "green machine," which we held personally responsible for prolonging the insanity and death that hovered over us on a daily basis. As we heads viewed things at the time, the lifers worked for the politicians and businessmen who profited from the war. Of course, there were a few exceptions, like Bill Wood. He was one of those individuals who didn't fit into any of the above categories. He was respected by his men as well as by his superiors for his integrity. We also felt a certain degree of camaraderie with lower-ranking officers and sergeants who wanted to avoid contact with the VC and NVA as much as we did. Most of them would also return to civilian life when their tours were over. But as a rule, the volatile nature of our times seldom allowed the luxury of gray areas in Vietnam. Friend or potential foe had to be immediately identified or suffer the consequences. It didn't take long before I perceived many of the lifers as enemies and felt a growing sense of hatred for them as our casualties mounted.

Nearly 100 percent of the drugs we used were obtained from the South Vietnamese people. This was at least one source of profit for which we didn't mind being the "victims." They quickly learned to identify who they could safely approach with their goods by relying on the same markers we used to recognize members of our own brotherhood. One of the premier telltale signs was the multicolored, beaded necklace or bracelet that was worn with an air of proud defiance as we mingled with lifers and juicers. We would flash the peace sign with our index and middle fingers to accent our defiance against the war and acknowledge our brother on the receiving end. It wasn't complicated.

Heads could only trust other heads. With few exceptions, the following reasoning applied—if you smoked dew, then you were not a lifer; you were against the war and you could be trusted. The lifers and juicers knew we smoked but could do nothing about it. After all, we were all armed to the teeth. An uneasy and tacit truce existed. Everyone knew exactly what the beaded group with their bandanas and cassette recorders were doing in the bunkers, as the unmistakable aroma, accompanied by the sweet sound of *Abbey Road* or *Led Zeppelin*, gently drifted through the air.

The regular use of marijuana was generally reserved for the rear area and forward firebases. One had to have access to a bunker where there was a relative degree of safety. The beloved bowl would be passed around for what seemed like an eternity. There was no holding back on how much one partook in this sacred ceremony. There were times that we smoked so much dew that I actually had to excuse myself and step outside to have a cigarette break. On a few occasions, we even blew the smoke through the barrel of our weapon—unloaded of course. It was the ultimate statement of defiance and bonding, all rolled into one

Every bunker was loaded with enough ammunition to repel an invading army. In addition to M16s and M60 machine guns, there were about a dozen clappers, each one hooked to a claymore mine, which were strategically placed outside the perimeter, along with the endless rows of concertina wire. Protected inside the confines of the sandbag and metal reinforced bunker, one soldier could hold off a human wave attack if necessary. But the thing I had a problem with were the crates of frags that were used as stools while we passed the bowl. Try as hard as I could, I was unable to suppress the thought that somehow one of these frags would spontaneously explode and set the rest of them off (as if one frag wouldn't have done the job well enough). Adding to this obsession was the phenomena of the marijuana seeds popping out of the bowl and landing near or on one the crates. We were all familiar with being burned whenever one of those seeds landed on an arm or leg, sometimes even burning through our jungle fatigues which went unnoticed until it had time to reach the skin. My answer to averting disaster was quite simple—remove the crates and place them outside the bunker. Irrational as it may seem, I would much rather have taken the chance that the crate would be hit by a 122 rocket (which would really set the frags off) than a tiny seed that self-extinguishes in less than twenty seconds. My buddies kidded me because I could always be found in the bunker with the frag crates placed just outside the entrance.

The May 1970 *Life Magazine* article that Mrs. Gmack sent me about John's unit with First Air Cavalry Division aptly describes the role of marijuana with some of the grunts.

> After the jungle, firebase defense is like garrison duty, and the men relish it. Alpha (Company) splits into two roughly equal groups for the evening parties: the "juicers" lay in supplies of cold beer, while the "smokers" roll their joints and pack the pipe bowls with strong Vietnamese marijuana. Estimates on marijuana users within Alpha vary from Captain Utermahlen's low of 7 percent up to the senior pothead in the company's enthusiastic 85 percent. "We pass the pipe around," says a squad leader, "and we ask what the hell are we doing here?"
> Among the grunts there is a general taboo against smoking grass in the field, although some do: "We had one guy who was on grass all the time, and he won the Silver Star. He had it down to an exact science. He'd feel the breeze blowing away from the lifers, and he'd say, 'Hey, the wind's right. Let's get nice.'"
> Utermahlen is resolutely opposed to marijuana. "It has no place in the field where you rely on quick thought and reflexes. I know the people who smoke it, but I can never catch them."

Marijuana smoking is so extensive that anything more that a token enforcement would antagonize a dangerously high percentage of the company. No commander as perceptive as Utermahlen cares to risk confrontation of that nature in Vietnam just now. So downwind from Firebase Betty at night, it sometimes smells as though a large haystack were burning. Utermahlen's views on military appearance are also relaxed. "What they wear or look like out in the field is very low on my list of priorities. It's one of the compromises I make. As long as a man does his job, I don't care if he wears peace beads or symbols or if he shaves."

Getting high was altogether different in the bush. It wasn't until my third or fourth month in Vietnam that I actually smoked grass (a.k.a. dew) while on a mission. For one thing, it was most inconvenient being burdened with carrying so much weight and ammunition. I had a miniature pipe that I pulled out and smoked when we broke for meals or if the jungle was so thick that the entire platoon was being held up while the point man hacked a trail with his machete. But I really didn't get very high from the two or three quick drags off the pipe. It was more of a mild buzz, similar to having a few sips of wine or beer. In a sense, it was more like the relaxed feeling I got from a cigarette. It steadied my nerves, but I was as hypervigilent as ever. I felt more a part of the jungle, like I belonged there. But this had its down side.

There was a big juicer in front of me, I believe from Kansas, whose disapproving look could kill. In fact, I wondered if he entertained the notion of shooting me "accidentally" if a firefight broke out. After all, it wouldn't be the first time something like that happened. By 1970, Americans killing Americans was becoming an all too familiar occurrence. Then I thought, "If I was thinking this about him, maybe he thinks I might do it to him … so then it would be a matter of self-protection." I just remember the hatred in his eyes and, no doubt, he remembers the same in mine. This was insanity, pure and simple. Neither one of us said a word. The other negative aspect about smoking in the bush was having to put my rucksack back on and carrying the beast in the grueling tropical heat, since everything I owned I carried on my back. Needless to say, that was the first and last time I risked smoking grass while on a combat mission.

Marijuana wasn't the only drug to make its entrance in the life of the GI. Pure opium could be found in any small hamlet at the home of a *papa-san,* a sort of village elder. It was here that I had my first and last experience with the "brown devil" that ravaged so many souls over the century. A friend accompanied me to my initiation at a little village that we walked to from our base camp about a mile away. Once inside the hut, we placed our weapons against the wall and lay down on a rough carpet. Papa-san slowly and methodically stirred the brown substance over the pipe until it melted. He then handed it to me and, with a beaming smile beneath his long, thin beard, he motioned for me to inhale the sweet delight.

I readily inhaled until my lungs were full to capacity. I held my breath for some time and then gently exhaled the stuff dreams are made of back into the atmosphere. Although my weapon was within reach, I was so intoxicated, in a most beautiful way of course, that my condition would have rendered any attempt to secure it an abysmal failure. My mental orientation and psychomotor reaction time were, for all intents and purposes, nonfunctional. Fortunately, the tiny hamlet remained GI friendly while we were there during the daytime. Our very, very slow walk back to the base felt like we were walking on an earthbound cloud, hovering just a few inches above the road. My opium smoking began and ended on that day, as it left me in a vulnerable and totally defenseless position, even in a relatively safe area.

The third drug that I dabbled in during my tour in Vietnam was "speed." I was introduced to my first amphetamine, endearingly referred to as a "LRRP pill" (Long Range Recon Patrol), by one of the most unusual guys I ever met. He was a staff sergeant and had been in the army for some years; technically, this made him a lifer. But this was not applicable to him (obviously there are exceptions to almost every rule). He was on his third tour and was a sniper. I was informed that he obtained the pills from a medic who dispensed them to the grunts to help them stay awake for overnight patrols and ambushes. He asked me to accompany him to one of the watchtowers at our base camp. Positioned about forty or fifty feet above the ground, it provided a panoramic view of the base as well as the road that paralleled our side of the perimeter in the direction of a small town. It was here that he turned me on to this most unusual drug.

He presented me with two pills, which I readily washed down with a swig of Coke. In all my drug sampling in Vietnam, I can't recall a single occasion when I asked what kind of an effect I could expect from ingesting the new product. Part of the intrigue was not having any clue what would happen to me. This sort of reasoning, if one could call it that, was intrinsic to the whole Vietnam experience of being caught up in an endless series of new frontiers, within and without. I was already under the effect of the dew as I waited for the effect of the pills. In the meantime, my buddy pulled out his M-14 with the attached scope of a sniper and pointed at the villagers who were riding an open mini bus toward town. I would have guessed the distance to be about three hundred yards, not very long by sniper standards. Before I knew what happened, a shot rang out and he started laughing. He handed me the binoculars to verify his target. The people in the mini bus scattered by the roadside after the shot blew out one of the rear tires, causing the vehicle to come to an abrupt halt. Thankfully, no one was hurt.

We were soon approached by an officer who questioned us about what had happened; the sergeant told him that he was adjusting his scope and needed some target practice, and he left us alone. This was a smart move on his part, considering with whom he was dealing and that he was positioned in a tower. When it was my turn, I fired a shot toward the rear tire of a motor scooter just before it was out of sight around a bend in the road. I was tentative about getting too close for fear of hitting the rider. It never occurred to me that he could be injured if the scooter overturned should the tire blow out. Anyway, I can't say for sure if I hit the tire. I do know that I was starting to feel an accelerated sense of hypervigilance, which was made worse by firing the weapon. I was beginning to feel on edge, while at the same time a sense of euphoria was emerging. I did the next logical thing, asking for a few more pills to enhance this seductive sensation that was permeating through my psyche.

Four more pills set me on a course of sensations that I hoped would never end. But end it did about eight hours later and, as the saying goes, "What goes up must come down." I was experiencing this first major "crash" (period of time when the effects of a drug begin to wear off) shortly after returning to my own bunker for guard duty. Smoking a few bowls with the guys helped ease coming down, but it also resulted in my mind drifting into fantasies that were getting more and more bizarre. The sky was less black and a hint of reddish orange was subtly rising. The entire night seemed to have slipped by and dawn was now before me. I was awake the entire night and everything was getting bright with the approaching daylight. Soon the merciless sun would enter the picture and make my life that much worse. Fortunately, our company had two more days before we returned to the bush, and I would be able to recover with a good night's sleep. I could understand how one of these LRRP pills could help one stay awake on guard duty or while positioned in an ambush mode. But ingesting them by the handful like I did would be to court disaster. Hypervigilance crossed the boundary and quickly transformed into paranoia. We already seemed to have an abundance of both.

My subsequent encounters with amphetamines were even more emotionally brutal than the LRRP pills. Unbeknownst to me at the time, this drug comes in various forms with different degrees of potency. I might have been able to smoke some dew in the bush, but I never entertained the notion of taking speed while on a mission. For one thing, I already knew that I couldn't limit myself to the recommended dosage of one pill. I had to get high and one pill wouldn't do it. And getting high on this stuff in the bush is nothing less than an accelerated death wish.

There were two other forms of speed that could be obtained from the Vietnamese people. The more plentiful of the two came in a bottle and resembled cough syrup in its sweetness, but with the texture of beef bouillon. This was the infamous Obesitol, believed to be a product from France. It was prescribed as an appetite suppressant, hence the root word "obese." However, one would be hard-pressed to see the need for such a product in a war-torn country where the average person was struggling just to obtain his daily nourishment. Of course there were exceptions, primarily in the form of overweight and corrupt South Vietnamese generals and politicians, the fat cats of the war effort who cared little for their own people or their American allies dying by the hundreds each week. Obesitol was readily available in bottles, which were clearly labeled. For maximum effect, the proper procedure was to guzzle it down quickly and then wash the sweet, nauseating taste from memory with large gulps of soda. In less than a half hour, the ride of a lifetime would be in the initial stages. It was a pure, visceral adrenaline rush—accented by hypervigilance, paranoia, and intense euphoria. Unfortunately, much like its first cousin the LRRP pills, it was a nasty high to come down from. The crash from this nectar was even more precipitous, followed by a gnawing depression and sense of despair, as if being in Vietnam wasn't bad enough. I revisited this cycle a few more times, until I got caught off guard and was ordered on a mission before I had a chance to recover while remaining on our forward firebase, as described in the following story.

The search-and-destroy missions of the American Division's 11th Light Infantry Brigade, where I spent the second half of my tour after the court-martial, were more conducive to abusing speed. Typically, we would operate in a platoon-sized unit and would get dropped off by helicopter in the bush in a location where enemy troops had been sighted. We were a quick reaction force that rarely stayed out more than three or four days at a time, followed by a return to our forward firebase, San Juan Hill, or rear area, Duc Pho, for a three- or four-day rest period. On this particular occasion, sometime in January 1971, a short month before I completed my tour in this forsaken place, we returned from a mission and were informed that we would have a full week's recovery period with only perimeter guard duty on the firebase. This presented an ideal opportunity for me and my buddies to really "let it all hang out" and (over) indulge ourselves in our drug(s) of choice pretty much around the clock for three or four days, followed by a much-needed rest from our "recovery period."

I readily obtained about a half dozen bottles of Obesitol, ingesting them at a rate of two bottles a day, and began my plunge into the land of euphoria and pure adrenaline which I planned to maintain for as long as possible before descending into the major despair that was sure to follow. Most of my buddies were employing what is now referred to as "polypharmacy" in their partying, but all of us would be smoking dew as we passed the bowl nonstop. This was serious drug abuse. I believe I was the only one who had been without sleep for seventy-two hours when the unconscionable was heard around the compound, "Pack up, we got orders to assemble at the pad in an hour to hit the bush … we're gonna go waste some dinks."

Even with the few remaining brain cells that were operational and fueling my growing paranoia, I realized that my body would not be able to carry the heavy rucksack on my back in the steaming hot jungle. I was already dehydrated and had not had much nourishment in three days. To say that my thinking was also less than optimal after three days without any sleep would be an understatement. Had I not already been court-martialed for disobeying a direct order, the decision would have been pretty straightforward. I now found myself on the brink of refusing another direct order, not because I didn't want to go (I never wanted to go) but because I was mentally and physically unable. However, if I explained the why of it all, I would most certainly be court-martialed again and discharged for "failure to adapt" to the insanity of war where we were killing for no reason and dying for the same.

For some crazy reason I decided to pack my gear and head out to the helicopter pad, already loading up with tired and weary soldiers, as the rotor blades were stirring up the ever familiar burnt red dust cloud. This time, I made the conscious choice not to pack any claymore mines for setting up automatic ambushes. Since this is carefully done with setting up a tripwire mechanism attached to a battery, I knew that I would not be in any shape mentally or physically to do such a delicate task. Besides, one has to remember where he placed the claymore the following morning when it's time to deactivate and retrieve it.

Freudian psychoanalytic theory postulates that our behavior is multi-determined and rooted in our unconscious; a single act has more than one motivational impetus propelling it to the surface from a concealed source. Likewise, my decision to go ahead on this mission was no exception. It was more than going against my better judgment—most things were in Nam. It was something far deeper, most likely rooted in childhood. After all those years of playing with toy soldiers and army games with my friends, the thought of failing as a soldier, regardless of the reason, was something that was unthinkable—even if it cost me my life. I felt I could probably muster enough adrenaline to engage in a firefight if we got hit in or near our landing zone in the jungle. But I definitely knew that I was in no shape to hump the bush with all the weight I had to carry except for a brief period. Sometimes we had to trudge through thick vegetation at a snail's pace, so that even a half-mile could take hours, before we set up our perimeter for the night and had a meal.

I was far too exhausted to be anxious about the flight. I made sure that I sat in the middle and not in my usual position by the side with my feet dangling out, for fear of passing out from exhaustion and falling out of the helicopter. I was already feeling somewhat lightheaded. I don't remember much about the ride. We landed in a large clearing and the pilots apparently felt safe enough to touch down. This was welcome by all, especially me, as I would have fallen like a lead balloon if I had to jump off with all the additional weight. It was good news, too, that there was no contact with the enemy and everyone was safe.

It was only mid-afternoon, and we were informed that we had to hump some distance to reach our objective and set up our NDP (night defensive perimeter). Fortunately we were on flat terrain and would be following a dry creek bed so that we wouldn't have to struggle with hills or thick jungle vegetation. Another bit of good news was that it was not our squad's turn to walk point on this particular day. This was especially welcome news for everyone but the point squad. Leading the way, they were the most vulnerable. It is much easier to walk into an ambush along a trail or accessible pathway, like a dry creek bed flanked by thick vegetation on both sides, than blazing a trail with a machete through vines and thick vegetation. In the latter scenario, the enemy is unable to anticipate where we will be making our appearance in order to wait for us. For us, this dry creek bed was an unusually open area to be traversing. Harsh as it may sound, I was beyond caring about what might happen to the poor guys in the point squad who got hit. We all took our turns and had to be numb to what happened to the unfortunate souls who got it that particular day. Tomorrow might be my turn to die.

Unfortunately for me, all the good news ended there. Regardless of all these ideal circumstances going for me, the fact remained that I still had to hump the creek bed in the blazing hot sun and humidity in a totally depleted condition. I could already feel and hear my heart pounding, seemingly wanting to exit from my chest to find a more suitable home. I had no time before we left the firebase to trade my M-14 in for a lighter M-16. Those few extra pounds that have to be constantly held up were going to make a difference, as was the heavier ammo that the larger weapon required. We were soon making our way single file along the serpentine course of the creek bed. Being in the open offered no relief from the direct rays of the afternoon sun. Half an hour into the mission, I fell back on the creek bank in a dazed condition and landed in a sitting position. I made the decision that I could no longer continue, regardless of the consequences. One by one, the rest of the platoon filed by, some giving encouragement or a brief glance, others apparently not noticing. Someone must have notified our medic, who arrived as the last of the grunts were going by. He poured some water on my head and told me to get going because they were not going to stop until we arrived at our destination. He encouraged me saying, "You can do it," and proceeded to follow the others. All of a sudden, I was looking at the back of the last guy, an M-60 machine gunner, as he made his way past me and headed toward a bend in the creek. As he made the turn, I realized that I was alone.

I now had a choice of staying here and facing the enemy, dying from heat exhaustion, or, if I was lucky enough to survive the next few days, being permanently separated from my unit without a radio. To say that I was "up the creek without a paddle" would have been a gross understatement. I also knew that my heart was literally close to bursting and fully believed that the next time I hit the ground, I would be dead from "natural causes." Basically, I found myself in the unenviable position of choosing how I was going to die. I believe most people do not want to die alone and I was no exception. I also figured that if my heart burst, it would be an instantaneous death and I would be spared the suffering of some of those who I witnessed dying a much slower death and in great pain and horror. I managed to get up, but my legs were now trembling. I knew I had to discard some items to lighten the load, but the problem was that none of us was carrying anything superfluous. The first items to go were the two M-60 ammo belts. I had no energy to toss them and no time to try hiding them, so I left them where they dropped. I believe that I also discarded my smoke grenades and a few canteens of water and most certainly my helmet.

I continued along the creek bed until I caught up with the rest, but remained with the tail end squad. My guys were somewhere in the middle. Before long, I could hear my heart thumping in my chest and sensed the end would soon be near. Luckily, the word was being passed down to take a break, and we all sat on the creek bank. I took the next step and removed my entire rucksack, determined to carry only my weapon, some ammo, and water. I didn't care about the rest of my gear, including the food rations, remaining water, etc. I wanted only to live a little longer. We rested about ten minutes, when word came down again that we would be setting up for the night about a hundred yards ahead. What a tremendous, live-saving relief! With my gear back on, I rejoined my squad.

As it turned out, they hadn't even realized what happened to me. They were almost as exhausted and were in pure survival mode themselves. We set up our NDP and I ate a can of C-Ration and drank some more water. The medic came to check on me around dusk and gave me a small capsule to help settle my nerves. I was assigned the last watch for guard duty which meant I could have an uninterrupted night's sleep. It is doubtful if I could have stayed awake for the required full hour for an earlier shift. I fell into a deep sleep and, although rested, I was still not fully recovered the next day. We got a late start and humped for a relatively short distance. We had a heavy rain that night, so I was able to replenish my water supply. After this harrowing experience with speed, my remaining time in Nam was strictly limited to smoking dew.

The third form of amphetamine available was in a small vial that one snapped the neckpiece off to access the magic elixir. It was also made by a French pharmaceutical company judging by the writing on the glass. This was pure methamphetamine, or "meth," which also came in a crystal form back home. It was by far the most potent of the three amphetamine cousins. It was the only drug that one could actually say was rather difficult to obtain in Vietnam. I was only able to purchase a vial on two occasions but always had it on my radar screen. I could readily appreciate how it could plunge someone into certain ruin by its intensely seducing effect. We were in a large rear area, Bien Hoa, when a buddy brought it over to me, along with a can of Pepsi. He covered the vial with a part of his shirt and snapped the top of the vial off and poured the contents into the can. It was a tiny container and I seriously questioned whether there was even enough for one of us, let alone to share. One has to remember the mind-set while in the rear area, especially in a large, relatively safe one like we were presently enjoying, was to "get stoned to the max."

We each consumed about half of the can and smoked a cigarette.

Since it was a large rear area, much like a military base back home, there were no readily available bunkers nearby where we could smoke some dew. We just walked around in the midst of the rear echelon personnel, who seemingly were engaged in their daily tasks. Before long I felt a peculiar sensation, like my scalp was tingling and set to blast off like a spacecraft, accompanied by the intense visceral reaction that I'd become all too familiar with while getting airborne on a Huey. It was a feeling of pure euphoria, unadulterated by the presence of any other substances in my system like dew. It felt like the Cadillac version of amphetamines, much more cerebral and lacking the rough edges of its weaker cousins, LRRP pills and Obesitol. This was pure speed. No way could one take this in the bush and live. This was strictly meant to be a rear area high.

The abuse of amphetamines did not go unnoticed by the army. One of the great ironies made its debut at our company headquarters tent in Duc Pho. We could hardly believe our eyes as we walked in one day to get our mail and noticed a drug awareness sign by the first sergeant's desk (if it's one thing we were not lacking, it was an awareness of drugs … they were everywhere!). Anyway, the fairly good-sized sign depicted a disheveled, unshaven young man with bulging eyes and a look of terror on his face—certainly not unlike many of us on various occasions. The caption above his greasy and uncombed head read in bold letters, "SPEED KILLS." Not M-16s, grenades, booby traps, bombs, Cobra helicopters, B-52s, ambushes, RPGs, etc. I have to believe that at least one, maybe two, soldiers may have died from amphetamines, most likely from an undetected heart defect or else they were in a similar situation like I was earlier in the bush. The army's "war on drugs," as it was often referred to, was dedicated to saving lives so these same soldiers could be flown back into the jungle to continue fighting a war that was already deemed a lost cause; in essence, so that they could, once again, have the opportunity to die for nothing.

As potentially dangerous a drug as the amphetamines were, their adverse impact on American troops was dwarfed in comparison to the scourge that was being unleashed on us in 1970. Seemingly out of nowhere and overnight, King Heroin entered the fray and was taking no prisoners. I first heard it referred to as "scag" or "smack" while still with the Air Cav. Sometimes it was even called "coke," most likely because it came in a fine, white powder form. Unabashedly, most of the heroin "copped" (purchased) by American soldiers steadily hovered around the 98 percent pure range. Compared to its anemic and adulterated distant cousin that was called by the same name on the streets of New York City, it was in a league all its own. Drug addicts in the U.S. were lucky to obtain heroin that was near the 10 percent pure mark.

Being nearly tenfold more powerful, it overwhelmed and chained its victims almost instantly. Even more than the stimulants, this is one drug that definitely could and should not be used on a combat mission. For one thing, it had the opposite effect of speed, especially in the early distribution phase before one's body became acclimated to its sedating presence. It seduced the individual into a semiconscious state of euphoria. It was also very different in one other major area—physical dependence, otherwise known as addiction. For example, following a speed run (three or more consecutive days of amphetamine abuse with no sleep and minimal nutritional intake), one crashes for a few days and generally feels replenished enough to go on a mission. This was not the case with heroin. After three or four days of this extremely potent narcotic in one's system, an inner beast rearing its twin ugly heads in the form of physical and mental craving is unleashed on the newly imprisoned soul.

I am very fortunate that, due to circumstances, I was spared the hell that some of my friends suffered from the merciless, innocent-looking white powder. First of all, I have always had a revulsion, fear if you will, to needles. To actually tie a tourniquet around my arm and have another soldier, or worse yet, myself, insert a hypodermic needle of questionable sterilization into my vein was unthinkable to me. It was difficult enough watching others do this while in our bunker, where dust and dirt were some of the more sanitary aspects of the setting. I fell asleep on more than one occasion after my shift of guard duty with a plastic bag of dew on my chest, only to be awakened by a rat the size of my miniature dachshund helping himself to the delicious contents. Ever the animal lover, I simply grabbed him with one hand, while securing the bag with the other, and tossed him out into the night to fend for himself. It seemed like even the rats wanted to get high to escape the misery that was their lot in Nam.

There was a report circulating among the troops that if you snorted heroin through your nose, it would be almost impossible to get addicted. And, if you sprinkled it in a cigarette or joint, there was absolutely no chance of getting hooked. Most of us believed this falsehood since it was generated from a very reliable source—other heads. In this regard, I was fortunate that my use of the substance was limited to only two occasions, as the threat of flying back into the bush was always hanging over my head. The prospect of going on another mission was the main reason that my overall heavy drug use was curtailed. I needed to have a reasonable amount of alertness, as lives were at stake. Moreover, my body had to be ready for the grueling punishment it would undergo while humping the bush.

This was not the case for those who didn't possess this particular mindset (e.g., door gunners, artillery personnel, and other grunts who now had permanent assignments on the firebase for having done their time in the bush). Not having to hump through the bush carrying heavy loads like an army mule with the prospect of a firefight always present afforded some of them the dubious luxury of becoming full-time heroin addicts. Once they became addicted, their main task was to continue shooting, smoking, or snorting the stuff to prevent the grueling withdrawal. They seemed normal (a term used very loosely in this context) to everyone else and were capable of doing their jobs. They would intermingle with us at night in a bunker, or else we would party with them in their hooch (any structure or dwelling with a roof over it, be it made from tin, wood, etc; some were more elegant than others). It was during this time that they reloaded their veins with the poison that was eroding their will. The invisible cords of addiction were slowly strangulating its victims in the manner of a reticulated python. I remember being with some door gunners and crew chiefs in their hooch while we were enjoying the music of their reel-to-reel tape recorder and hearing the prophetic lyrics to a song, "With tombstones in their eyes." If the adage, "The eyes are the window to the soul," has any merit, then these disturbing words accurately captured the reflection that was being mirrored in their gaze. Even more frightening was the fact that it was some of these same airmen who would be flying us on combat aerial assaults the following day.

It was heroin that finally exposed the rampant drug abuse in Vietnam when American troops were returning home to the mainstream of society as full-fledged addicts. Accustomed to high-grade heroin, they were unable to obtain anything of similar quality on the street to prevent the withdrawal symptoms from emerging shortly after they arrived back home. It was after I got married in 1975 and had completed a master's degree at the University of Buffalo that a small paperback book captured my attention while browsing through a local bookstore. A title like *Heroes and Heroin* was hard to pass up.

In between the numerous moves we made during the first five years of our marriage and studying for my doctorate in psychology, the book was lost. Luckily, I made the acquaintance of a local psychiatrist a few years ago during a presentation he was making about psychiatric medications. He confirmed that he in fact was the same Dr. Brian Joseph who was quoted several times in the book while serving in Vietnam and treating soldiers who were addicts. There were several photographs of him as well. He noted that he had an extra copy and would be delighted to send it to me. *Heroes and Heroin* was based on an award-winning ABC-TV documentary on drug addiction in the military. The back cover displayed the shocking statistics that "in the first four months of 1971, over 1,000 men from the Marines alone were discharged for drug-related offenses…" My tour of duty ended in late February 1971 and I can assure you that the Army, a much larger military branch, was far ahead of our Marine brethren in these numbers.

The Enemy

It certainly goes without saying that you cannot have a war without an enemy. If some person, group, or army attacks your house or homeland, then identifying the enemy is easy enough. After all, it would seem only fitting to defend one's territory, which is necessary for survival. Another truism is that you need to have opposing forces willing to fight each other in order to have a war, a rather obvious concept echoed in the well-known sixties chant, "What if they gave a war and nobody came?"

This second concept is more complicated in that it goes beyond the immediate reaction of primary survival that kicks in when defending against an enemy attack. In this latter instance, someone is "giving a war" along the lines of "giving a party" and hoping for a good turn-out. Although somewhat of an oversimplification, "giving a war" is something that is almost exclusively determined by politicians who are entrusted with serving the good of the people who elected them to office. They are in the unenviable position of deciding who our enemies are. Since we are involved in areas that extend far beyond our national boundaries, anyone who threatens these interests is a potential enemy. In essence, our national interests set the stage and become the "homeland" that needs to be defended.

But this is where things get complicated. Our elected officials have to convince the average person that his or her way of life is legitimately being threatened half a world away. In the case of Vietnam, the threat of communism had to be convincingly packaged and sold to the American public, thus setting the stage for sending troops to defend the cause of freedom against communist domination. Never having tasted defeat, we were convinced that this foreign enterprise would involve little more than a "police action" or a "mopping-up operation." Very few indeed had any notion about the motivation and resiliency of our new enemy. We simply ignored the lessons of history.

Vietnam was a nation that had been invaded numerous times and had suffered the agonies of war far more than the average American can imagine. Putting things in perspective in 2006, a Vietnamese government official described the ten-year-long war with the United States as a "mere blip" on their country's long history. Just prior to our involvement, the French were soundly defeated at a little known place called Dien Bien Phu in 1954. Tens of thousands of elite paratroopers and famed foreign legionnaires were convincingly defeated by a tenacious communist Vietnamese force led by General Giap, the same military leader we would be facing when we stepped ashore and throughout the entire war. But like many American soldiers who fought in this unpopular war, I was never really interested in the history of the nation where my last breath may have been taken. It was only recently that I developed an interest in how the French fared during their attempt to conquer the communist forces there from 1946 to 1954. A classic text by Bernard Fall entitled *Hell in a Very Small Place: The Siege of Dien Bien Phu* chronicled this final showdown, which was actually staged by the French in an effort to entice the communist Vietnamese to a conventional battle in which the French were certain they would be victorious.

Despite having the advantage of tanks and aircraft (the communists had neither), the French were surrounded and defeated in conventional warfare. The truly remarkable tenacity of this very same enemy was equaled by its resiliency and adaptability. Knowing that the United States was far superior to the French, both in numbers and technology, they quickly learned that conventional warfare would soon spell disaster for their overmatched forces. They reverted to guerilla tactics to inflict the damage and protract the war, as they quickly disappeared like ghosts into the thick jungle after ambushing us.

Not long after U.S ground forces were finally pulled out in 1975, communist forces easily transformed into a conventional army and swept through South Vietnam with tanks and artillery, shattering the armies of our former South Vietnamese allies in record time. Just as we infantrymen predicted, the communist tanks were rolling into the outskirts of Saigon, the former capitol, as the last helicopter was evacuating American personnel from the roof of our embassy building. Just four years later in 1979, the communist Chinese massed tens of thousands of troops along their mutual border. They were planning to teach the Vietnamese a "punitive lesson" about who is really in charge of Southeast Asia. I had little doubt about the outcome of this showdown. The Chinese army was soundly thrashed and beaten back with a series of well-executed counterattacks. It was mighty communist China that was taught the hard lesson. The Vietnamese were truly an enemy to respect and admire. Their suffering was on a grand scale and matched only by their forgiveness for our inflicting so much of it on them and their families.

For obvious reasons, I considered the Viet Cong guerilla (VC) and North Vietnamese Army soldier (NVA) my sworn enemies, especially when my life or the lives of my friends were directly threatened. This fact was one that was quite clear and generally understood by all of us. But identifying who was our enemy did not end with such an obvious statement. It seemed that enemies could be found at any given time in our immediate surroundings. For starters, almost every officer, with the exception of a few platoon leaders or company commanders, was considered by many of the grunts in our infantry unit a potential enemy. We made a distinction between officers who, like the rest of us, were there because they had to be and realized it was a senseless, losing proposition. Consequently, these sensible types refused to volunteer us for stupid and deadly missions at battalion-level briefings as best as they could. Much to their credit, they avoided contact with VC and NVA during search-and-destroy missions.

Unfortunately, there were those reckless, stupid, or glory-seeking characters who saw waning opportunities for a career-advancing promotion before the war ended. The army had a simple formula: more medals, individually or as a unit, translated into highly desirable bonus points for one's personnel file that would be instrumental during promotion time. After all, the war wouldn't last forever, and such opportunities for glory (invariably measured by enemy body count) were steadily slipping away for such blinded fools. They were our enemy because we knew they were motivated by their personal ambitions or failings and needlessly placed the rest of us at risk. By 1970, a number of these officers and noncommissioned officers were selectively being targeted by their own troops—ushering the term "fragging."

There was one glory-seeking sergeant major with the First Air Cavalry who insisted on leading our unit on a mission in order to impress an Australian advisor. He was foolhardy enough to lead a charge toward a sniper who had the unit temporarily pinned down. Fortunately, he was the only one who charged toward the enemy position. He paid for this foolish act with his life. My friend Larry had to help carry his massive, burdensome corpse for four days. He was placed outside our perimeter the third evening because the stench of his decomposing body in the hot, humid climate was getting unbearable. It is better that he died alone, for he had the potential to have many others killed alongside him. Another classic example of a lifer who alienated his own soldiers, mostly comprised of draftees, appeared in the October 23, 1970, article in *Life Magazine*, sent to me by John Gmack's mother when I finally confronted my year in Vietnam.

The sudden appearance of Neanderthal man would have hardly caused a greater stir than the arrival, in the middle of the mission, of a company's new first sergeant—a 44-year-old, six-foot-two, big-bellied, 257-pound giant with a bikinied girl tattooed over 12 inches of forearm. The draftees instantly read about his 25 years of Army service in his seamed face, and they avoided him like an alien being. Captain Utermahlen was uneasy, unwelcoming. It was a sad and unequal contest from the start: a high school dropout asked to administer and discipline a young company where 50 percent of the GIs have college time.

The first sergeant had served with the same battalion in 1965–66, until he was wounded, but the Army since then had altered beyond his comprehension. "Things have changed. Before, everyone was gung ho and wanted to mix it up with Charlie. Now it seems everyone's trying to avoid him." He paused to mop sweat from his brow with the tattooed girl. "I'm still out to kill gooks; that is what I get paid for. The only thing you can do is force men into contact, but with their attitude now, I don't think we can go on like this for long." Back at the firebase, he announced his dislike of the casual way soldiers responded to some of Utermahlen's less urgent orders. The litter of abandoned ammunition at the firebase also annoyed him. Loose talk about fragging incensed him. He finally reached an insupportable level of frustration. Twice when his patience gave out, he drew and leveled his pistol to enforce orders. The second time, the young soldier he had been arguing with about garbage called his bluff and ran off to get his M16 rifle. As the two readied for an incredible high-noon showdown in the middle of the firebase, other soldiers intervened. There was no shooting but, at Captain Utermahlen's request, the first sergeant was reassigned to the States.

Many of us even considered the majority of the ARVNs—our South Vietnamese allies—as sort of an enemy by default. I absolutely resented the fact that their infantry units would be relegated to the relative safety of defending the base camp and sleeping in the "luxury accommodations" offered within a bunker complex, while we flew into jungle terrain to embark on high risk search-and-destroy missions and spent days and nights soaked from monsoon rains. After all, it was their war to win or lose with the communists who were invading their homeland. This was a reversal of roles to the nth degree. We all sensed that it would be only a matter of time after our ground troops pulled out before the South Vietnamese military would collapse like a house of cards. Our infantry units had the best insight into the motivation and fighting capacity of both Vietnamese groups. The South Vietnamese Army's motivation to fight was even less than ours by 1970. Unfortunately, it was not so for our communist foes, the NVA and VC. Despite the hundreds of thousands that we killed over the course of the war, including the incessant bombing of their homeland, they were growing more determined by the day. Not a very good indicator of what was in store after we pulled out over the next few years, as history certainly proved this to be the case.

Then, of course, there was the civilian population to deal with on a regular basis. The vast majority was poor and desperate as they tried to eke out a living in the midst of war. I felt very conflicted about them. My feelings ran the entire gamut from pity and compassion to outright rage and loathing. My heart was stirred by their suffering and plight, with apparently no relief in the foreseeable future. But I was also enraged at times because it was their fault that I was sent here against my will in the first place. Making things worse was the realization that some of them were actually VC guerillas who were dedicated to killing us whenever they had the chance. At the very least, some of them provided details about our positions or movements that were utilized for rocket and mortar attacks. For such reasons, none of them could be trusted, as everyone was a potential enemy. Bear in mind that I spent the second half of my tour with the 11th Light Infantry Brigade (LIB), the unit that was responsible for the infamous My Lai massacre in 1968. Although our Charlie Company was not the same one that was earlier under the command of Lt. William Calley, this infamy and scourge continued to permeate all aspects of our relationship with each other and the Vietnamese people. Confusion and hatred had a most fertile breeding ground.

In carefully reasoned retrospect, it turns out our main enemy was none other than the faceless politicians and investors who were twelve thousand miles from the actual site of the killing fields. Fueled by the motive of greed in its purest form, they were busy enjoying the Christmas parties and numerous perks afforded by sycophant lobbyists representing the various corporate sponsors of hell on earth. War, after all, is big business. They made sure that we were well supplied so that we could continue the carnage. There is nothing like a protracted war to help refine their products and increase the profit margin. Such individuals will forever remain the enemy of Americans in uniform.

The Vietnamese People

The day I set foot in the Republic of South Vietnam to start my one-year tour of duty as an infantryman, the Vietnamese people had been a war-torn country since I was four years old and still living in Hungary. And there were five more years of death and destruction to go. First, it was the French attempt to restrain communism throughout the entire nation, and now it was America's turn to at least keep the southern half a semblance of a democracy. Like many of my comrades of 1969–70, I was interested only in staying alive and returning home in one piece. It was survival, pure and simple. Neither our politics nor the history of these people held any interest for me—that is, unless it somehow contributed to expediting my ticket home.

But it would have been impossible to be human and not be affected by their plight, especially while sojourning in their land and participating in its destruction. And a most beautiful land it was, despite vast areas strewn with bomb craters. For even the old craters that littered the tropical landscape would fill up with the monsoon rain and spring forth with new life. They also made excellent swimming holes for the Vietnamese children, as well as American troops. For the most part, war seemed to be accepted as a way of life for the Vietnamese people. Suffering was frequently present or just around the corner. I wasn't there very long before I realized that we had all the helicopters, fighter jets, bombers, tanks, starlight night scopes, armor, Cobra gunships, etc. The enemy, the Viet Cong and the North Vietnamese Army we were fighting, was seriously lacking in all these departments. By now we had killed hundreds of thousands of them, and we were the ones on the track to withdrawing our forces. Why, with all our technology, were we the ones losing the war?

Certainly they were well armed with automatic weapons and rocket-propelled grenades, but that was about it. Compared to the firepower we possessed, it was truly a case of David and Goliath. I remember as a young boy eagerly awaiting the next month's edition of a colorful encyclopedia that my father would purchase for me at the supermarket. One of the editions depicted a victorious David as he stood with one leg on the slain Goliath's chest, while he held the giant's decapitated head by a thick lock of hair. He was defiantly brandishing the Philistine's massive sword, which he used to behead the behemoth, for all the combatants on both sides of the battlefield to witness. But he had slain Goliath with only a sling. The giant's body was heavily clad in thick armor, and his brightly adorned helmet was lying nearby. The helmet had an area that left only the forehead exposed. Apparently, this made a perfect target for a shepherd boy who had been groomed for the task years before. Unknown to his giant foe was the fact that David had previously slain lions and bears that had threatened his sheep with the very same sling.

It was during one particular mission that the concept of the enemy's "sling" emerged for me. One of the methods we employed for locating the Viet Cong guerillas or North Vietnamese troops was by using communist soldiers who defected to our side. They would then be assigned to an air cavalry company that was scheduled for a search-and-destroy mission near their former unit's area of operation. They were called "Kit Carson" scouts, a term modeled after the famous frontier guide who tracked the Indians for the cavalry in the American West. We were fortunate to have one who not only was a former sergeant in the North Vietnamese Army, but also learned enough English to be conversational.

We had established our night defensive perimeter and were having our dinner when a few of us struck up an interesting conversation with him. We were curious what his job was while he was in the army of the North. We were awestruck by his answer. Basically, he would begin his journey in North Vietnam where he was assigned to carry a 122 rocket all the way to a launch pad, somewhere in South Vietnam, typically situated near a U.S. military installation. We all could identify with being on the receiving end of this weapon while we were in a base camp.

He would carry this massive projectile via mostly narrow jungle trails through Laos and Cambodia, finally swerving east into South Vietnam. This several-hundred-mile journey would sometimes take up to three months. He would then return the same way and repeat the process. He had been doing this for four years without a break. Moreover, the entire landscape was swarming with individuals just like him. They were like soldier ants, carrying their loads in single file, with a singular purpose. This hearty soul was truly an army of one. It was at that very moment that I realized exactly why they were winning the war. Judging by the expressions on the other troopers' faces, they had also come to the same conclusion.

Another soldier had come to this conclusion about two years earlier. He was not an infantryman, but a physician who was decorated for valor when he provided medical care to enemy soldiers. I first became aware of Gordon Livingston, MD, last year when I was thumbing through the *Clinical Psychiatry News* and read a review about his most recent book, *Too Soon Old, Too Late Smart: Thirty True Things You Need to Know Now*. It was a rather catchy title, so I read on and discovered that he was also a Vietnam veteran. However, what struck a chord with me was a mock prayer that he wrote on Easter Sunday, 1969, and handed out to high-ranking officers and journalists who were present while stationed in Vietnam. He called it "The Blackhorse Prayer," after the name of his unit, the 11th Armored Cavalry Regiment:

God, our Heavenly Father, hear our prayer. We acknowledge our shortcomings and ask thy help in being better soldiers for thee. Grant us, O Lord, those things we need to do thy work more effectively. Give us this day a gun that will fire ten thousand rounds a second, a napalm that will burn for a week. Help us to bring death and destruction wherever we go, for we do it in thy name and therefore it is meet and just. We thank thee for this war, fully mindful that, while it is not the best of all wars, it is better than no war at all. We remember that Christ said "I came not to send peace, but a sword," and we pledge ourselves in all our works to be like Him. Forget not the least of thy children as they hide from us in the jungles; bring them under our merciful hand that we may end their suffering. In all things, O God, assist us, for we do our noble work in the knowledge that only with thy help can we avoid the catastrophe of peace that threatens us ever. All of which we ask in the name of thy son, George Patton. Amen. [1]

Not only was Colonel George Patton III, son of the immortal General George Patton, present in the group, but so also was General Creighton Abrams, commander of U.S. forces in Vietnam. This mock prayer so incensed the command that Dr. Livingston was arrested and threatened with a court-martial. The fact that he was a graduate of West Point and John Hopkins Medical School was probably the main reason he was sent home only as "an embarrassment to the command." A court-martial of a decorated officer with such an exceptional educational pedigree would have further damaged the already floundering war effort. Gordon Livingston resigned his commission from the army and committed himself to the antiwar movement. He has been a practicing psychiatrist for the past four decades. He returned to Vietnam in 1995 with seventeen soldiers from his former unit. Also in their company was his son Michael, who he adopted from an orphanage while he was there twenty-six years earlier.

Dr. Livingston's book is an accumulation of insight and wisdom about human nature that could only have been discovered after many years of practicing psychotherapy. My main reason for purchasing it was to discover how he arrived at the conclusion that the war was not winnable. Much like our unit, the Black Horse Regiment had a difficult time trying to locate the elusive enemy. Reportedly, our superior technological prowess developed a device called the "people sniffer." This top-secret brainchild of an idea was hung from a low flying helicopter and was designed to register the ammonia contained in human urine. In this manner, we were able to hone in on Viet Cong troop concentrations. Once high enough levels of ammonia were detected, we would simply pinpoint the coordinates and destroy them with a massive artillery barrage. Major Livingston recalled being present at a regimental briefing in 1968 that was attended by a puzzled infantry captain. Apparently, his men were patrolling a certain area when they discovered buckets of urine hanging from the trees. He remembered the embarrassed expressions on the faces of Colonel Patton and his intelligence officer. We were targeting buckets of urine with $250 artillery rounds all across South Vietnam. He recalled that it was "the moment I knew we were going to lose the war."

He also witnessed firsthand the massive destruction we were raining on the very land that we were trying to keep liberated from communism. I'm not referring to North Vietnam, where we sent endless bomber streams that delivered payloads in excess of what was dropped on Nazi Germany during the entire course of World War II. This was South Vietnam, where the U.S. forces were stationed amidst the South Vietnamese people. I can distinctly remember patrolling expansive areas of triple canopy jungle (three separate layers of treetops at different heights) where there wasn't even a small monkey to be found.

On one occasion when we received sniper fire, the entire company of nearly one hundred men would pull back a mile and a massive air strike would be called in. Our company commander radioed headquarters and reported that we were engaged with a "sizeable enemy force." This was the only way to get our government to spend millions of dollars for a bombing raid. If he told them it was only one sniper, he would have been ordered to have us hunt him down ourselves. Past experience had taught us that this was too costly in human life—namely ours! Such a call would have also seriously jeopardized any career advancements the company commander may have been entertaining. As an added bonus, our commander could then estimate that the bombs resulted in fifty to one hundred "probable kills." Once you start on the path of untruth, you have to carry it to its logical conclusion. Perhaps this is where the infamous "fuzzy math" had its origin.

My basic point is that, by employing such tactics and a wealth of others, we were literally destroying vast areas of South Vietnam, the very land we were trying to save. Even worse were the untold numbers of collateral damage to the lives of the Vietnamese people along with their domestic livestock and native wildlife. Perhaps the greatest destruction was not even with the massive bombing but with the extensive use of defoliants like Agent Orange and other pesticides designed to eradicate the foliage in an effort to prevent the enemy from using it as a refuge. The Vietnamese people, both North and South, would suffer horrendously from the aftermath long after the last American soldier left Vietnamese soil. Many of these same American soldiers who patrolled the jungles that were sprayed would incur the harmful rippling effects for years to come.

Although Livingston's book was filled with a wealth of wisdom and honesty, it was his compassion that captivated me the most. For many of us, our sense of compassion is borne out of intense inner struggle. Dr. Livingston was no stranger to personal tragedy, as two of his sons met death at a young age. One of his sons suffered from depression and eventually committed suicide; another one died from leukemia at the age of six. Even as a practicing psychiatrist, he was powerless to prevent his son from taking his own life. His attempt to donate his own bone marrow for a transplant for his six-year-old son also failed. He buried two of his sons within a thirteen-month period. Here was a man who was personally and deeply knowledgeable about grief.

> Grief is a subject I have come to know well. Indeed it was the subject of my life for a long time. I wrote a book about it, trying to find my way around it. What I learned is that there is no way around it; you just have to go through it. In that journey I experienced hopelessness, contemplated suicide, and learned that I was not alone. Certain that there could be no comfort in words, I came to realize that words, my own and those of others, were all I had to frame my experience, first my despair and finally a fragile belief that my life still had meaning.
>
> Thirteen years later, my sons, though frozen in time, remain a living presence for me. I have, largely, forgiven myself for not being able to save them. I have reconciled myself to growing old without them. They will not, as I once confidently assumed, bury me. I have forsaken any belief in an orderly universe and a just God. But I have not relinquished my love for them nor my longing that, against all reason, I will see them again … I envy those who can retain their faith through such a loss and even imagine a purpose to it. I cannot. But still I hope for a reunion with the soul of my departed son, so what kind of Agnostic am I? [2]

As I read these words, I feel a certain degree of sadness that he did not believe that a loving God is available to provide him with immeasurable comfort in the midst of his profound losses. I certainly do not mean to imply that his pain would be totally absolved or that he would suddenly become privy to the exact reasons why such tragedies occurred. I'm referring to a supernatural type of "peace that passes understanding," which could only emanate from God himself. I have been a Christian for many years and I'm still baffled by the words, "For God so loved the world that He gave His only begotten son; that whosoever believeth in Him shall not perish but have everlasting life." It is only by faith, a priceless gift itself, that I can have any appreciation of the pain God Himself felt when He allowed His son Jesus Christ to hang and bleed on the cross so that we all may partake of eternal life. Therein lies the profound mystery of the ages; He endured death so that we may have life. It doesn't make sense, but then again, God's ways are not our ways. Yet, I also feel an honest searching and openness in Gordon's heart and pray he will discover God to be faithful to the words "and they will seek me and find me when they search for me with all their heart."

Many images cross my mind as I write these words concerning the Vietnamese people, but one stands out in a most unusual way. I was still with the First Air Cavalry because I distinctly remember that the incident occurred just outside our base camp in Song Be. I was one of about three soldiers who were "volunteered" to ride shotgun on a garbage truck. This meant that we had to ride with the garbage in the back. I would have gladly taken Dramamine for the nausea if it were available. The contents of the truck were mainly the waste products from the various field kitchens. I soon discovered that the only thing worse than army chow is used army chow. Anyway, we couldn't understand why armed guards were needed for such a sorry assignment, as no self-respecting enemy would see the value of getting anywhere near this wretched vehicle.

It soon occurred to us that since this was not a dump truck, the garbage had to be removed by manpower—meaning, by us. As we were approaching the dumpsite, we noticed a large group of Vietnamese people eagerly awaiting our arrival. Instinctively, we drew our weapons but quickly realized that they were unarmed. The younger ones swarmed our truck as it slowed down and jumped right into the middle of the garbage. We soon realized that they were the ones who would manually clear it off the truck. For their labor, they were rewarded with the privilege of keeping any of the refuse for themselves. There was a well-represented cross-section of people that included children, adults, and elderly. Most of them were interested in whatever edible scraps they could find digging through the cesspool-worthy debris. It wasn't long before I noticed that a number of the adults and elderly were missing at least one limb; they would work that much harder to procure whatever they could find to eat and proceeded to do just that as soon as they discovered something.

We just watched in silence and disbelief that this is what human beings were reduced to in order to survive. At some point, I remember glancing over the side of the truck and making eye contact with a Vietnamese girl who I guessed to be in her late teens, pretty much about our age. She had a beautiful face and long, flowing black hair. Her clothes were ragged, and she propped herself up with a crudely made crutch; one leg was amputated below the knee. The bandages around her stump were partially soaked through with blood, indicating that perhaps it was a recent injury.

Her piercing gaze totally disarmed me. Her dark brown eyes revealed a deep sorrow and pain, but without a shred of self-pity. Reflected in her "window to the soul" was an inner strength and determination that was forged by generations of suffering and survival. She never smiled; she just looked at me with the silence, gentleness, and patience that epitomized the Vietnamese people. I sincerely hoped that it wasn't any of our weapons that resulted in the loss of her leg, but then wondered if that really mattered to her. Chances are that with only one leg, she would remain an outcast, struggling more than most to survive. She would have made a beautiful bride.

July 19, 2005, marked the death of the U.S. commanding general who will forever be associated with the Vietnam War. General Westmoreland was a handsome, distinguished-looking man who certainly looked the part of a commander. My most vivid memory of him was when he made a brief appearance in the 1974 documentary film, *Hearts and Minds*. I found it to be a disturbing movie at the time, as I had been out of the army for only three years. It was the first and only movie I saw about Vietnam for many years. I recently saw it again and found it to be a remarkably insightful overview of the war. During one particular scene, the retired general was dressed in civilian attire as he was being interviewed on his country estate. Nevertheless, he retained the countenance of a military heavyweight and looked as poised and distinguished as ever. His brief comment about the war concerned the Vietnamese people, whom he sincerely believed did not value life in the manner we do in Western society. Immediately, the film shifted to a group of Vietnamese women weeping by the fresh graves of their loved ones who were killed. The twofold U.S. policy for victory in Vietnam was military might, coupled with winning the "hearts and minds" of the Vietnamese people. It was impossible to accomplish the latter if our commanding general was unable to appreciate their humanity. Sadly, General Westmoreland insisted until he died that victory could have been accomplished if he had had more soldiers.

The Unknown War

Some fifteen years ago, I remember being glued to the TV on Sunday afternoons at 6:00 p.m. to view a documentary, *The Unknown War,* on a public television station. The authentic film footage was in black and white and was masterfully narrated by the soft-spoken Academy Award-winning actor, Sir Laurence Olivier. This captivating documentary was about the Eastern Front and the massive battles during World War II between Germany and Russia. Like many Americans, I was familiar with the war on the Western Front as we fought against Germany alongside our allies, England and France. I was equally familiar with the war in the Pacific with its large-scale naval battles and beachhead landings that were followed by brutal combat, island by island, with the Japanese Empire. Such campaigns were retold countless times in movies like *The Longest Day, A Bridge Too Far, Sands of Iwo Jima, Midway, Battle of the Bulge,* and many others, replete with our favorite movie stars playing heroes who came to the rescue or died trying. It is understandable that since the United States was not directly involved in the fighting on the Eastern Front, there was a lack of any significant interest by Hollywood to portray the battles that were fought on Russian soil. The title, *The Unknown War,* was a fitting one indeed.

The first thing I noticed during this documentary was the expansive scope of the battlefields and the incredible number of soldiers, German and Russian, who were involved in this butchery on such a grand scale. Putting things in perspective, the United States had about 400,000 soldiers killed in action when both Pacific and Western Front numbers were combined. Our principal allies, England and France, lost 350,000 and 212,000 military personnel, respectively. By comparison, Germany alone lost 5,000,000 men during the course of this Unknown War; Russian soldiers killed by their German counterparts numbered a staggering 10,000,000.

In retrospect, I believe that this TV program provided a way to be connected to my father, although unbeknownst to me at the time. After all, he was drafted into the Hungarian army which was allied with Germany to fight the Russians. Since Hungary bordered Germany, she had a "choice" of being an ally or victim of her powerful, ruthless neighbor. Like thousands of other Hungarian young men, my father could do little else but join Germany to fight the Russians. As much as I hated the heat, humidity, and jungles of Vietnam, I much preferred it to the brutal Russian winters where temperatures dropped to fifty degrees below zero.

My mother told me that one of the few times my father talked about the war was when he mentioned a sense of gratitude for a German officer who kicked him while he was sleeping, propped up against a tank. Waking him up saved him from freezing to death when he dropped from sheer exhaustion and fell asleep after a battle. Much like his American counterparts—my friends' fathers, combat veterans of the same war—he largely kept silent about the horrors he witnessed and participated in. Yet, these inner demons would occasionally find expression in ways that frightened me as a young boy. I can recall a handful of times when, after he had drunk a quantity of beer, there would be screaming in the middle of the night that woke me up from a sound sleep. Unknown to me at the time, he was experiencing nightmares about the war.

The most frightening scene occurred when I was about six years old and we were still living in Budapest. I walked into my parents' bedroom and discovered the presence of our next-door neighbor, who had come to my mother's aid. They were both trying to hold my father back from jumping out the sixth-story window while he was screaming. Thankfully, he woke up and sat on the bed, seemingly as frightened and bewildered as we were. By contrast, he was a sociable, good-humored, and hard-working provider during the daytime. Then, when I was ten years old, he was diagnosed with pancreatic cancer. Nine months and two major surgeries later, I saw my father reduced from a hulking 200-plus-pound man to a 120-pound, emaciated creature.

He was still my father. He was still my hero. I would visit him in the hospital on a daily basis and we would play chess. I don't recall seeing him for the last month of his life. I was probably shielded from him because of his deteriorating condition. But still, I would have wanted to be with him until the end. I believe that's the way it should be. He was my father, and I was his son.

I honestly believe that the first thing people want to forget when a war ends is that it ever existed. I think this is especially true for those of us who participated in combat. It was certainly true for my father and me, as well as countless others over the course of history. As each year goes by, I become more convinced that the emotional scars of war live on in households all over our land, long after the soldiers return home. I believe that my father did the best he could but, nevertheless, there was a part of him that he shut off from others and me during his life. I feel that I lost a part of my father before I was even born. It is inconceivable to me that it could have been otherwise.

I can certainly attest to the fact that I was less of a husband, friend, brother, and son to my loved ones because of Vietnam. If we had had children, no doubt they also would have been shortchanged to some degree. I don't mean to imply that I was necessarily bad in these roles, although there were occasions when that would have been an accurate description. What I mean to say is that I was first and foremost emotionally shut off from a part of myself in order to survive psychologically. Shutting down emotionally during war is necessary for daily *survival*, but continuing with this coping style in civilian life is maladaptive.

It baffles me to this day that, when I was thirty-one years old, I functioned as the clinical director of a Vietnam veterans' organization that was established in response to the treatment of an emerging reality of a mental condition—posttraumatic stress disorder (PTSD). Both the administration and I enthusiastically concurred that, given my unique background and training, I would be the ideal candidate for such a position. Not only would I be directly treating combat veterans suffering from PTSD, but I would also be responsible for clinical supervision of about a dozen mental health professionals at five different sites located within four counties around Western New York. It started out as quite an adventure, with an adrenaline rush that my current job as a clinical psychologist was not providing.

The adventure lasted about two years and turned out to be quite a wild ride for all of us who dared to take the plunge. To begin with, none of us, especially me, appreciated the enormity of the task upon which we were embarking. We were venturing into uncharted territory. But it was a cause we all strongly believed in—to make right the damage that was caused by the Vietnam War in veterans' lives. The time was 1981, only six years since the war officially ended and ten years since my return home. It never occurred to me or anyone else that I might be suffering from PTSD. Like my father before me, I unwittingly espoused the code of silence. Essentially this meant that absolutely nothing that might be going wrong in my present life had anything to do with my participation in "man's inhumanity to man." Frankly, I believed that these were two entirely separate realms that had no connection to each other whatsoever. More to the point, I went on with my life as if Vietnam had never been an issue for me personally.

Even as I was witnessing this connection in my patients, I remained clueless that many of my personal problems had similar roots. It was as if I was above it all. I had a PhD in psychology, was making a good living and had been married for six years, unlike many of my patients who were struggling in areas of employment and relationships. I had turned a blind eye to my own problems, which happened to be less evident but destructive nonetheless. I guess I was better at denial, but I'm convinced that this unique job opportunity exposed and even exacerbated my inner conflicts related to the war, even though I was struggling overtime to suppress them. I also had the complicity of the United States government, most of the population, and certainly the military. The entire nation wanted to forget about this military fiasco which caused so much pain and national dissent, not to mention the dreaded concept that rarely rises above a whisper among Americans—losing a war.

But politics aside, the Vietnam veteran was no different from scores of veterans of other wars, whether they were Americans, Russians, Hungarians, British, Vietnamese, etc. Those of us who returned home had a lifetime of dealing with the horror that we experienced. While the returning veterans of World War II were exuberantly greeted as victors and liberators, they, too, had to eventually retreat to the code of silence. After all, the war was over. Real men got on with their lives. In fact, there has been a commonly accepted lie on a massive scale that military service will "make a man out of you." I would certainly go so far as to agree that, during peace time, a few years of military service has the potential to instill discipline, teamwork, and a sense of pride for completing the training in many individuals who voluntarily join. But the idea that somehow serving in the infantry or other combat-related occupation during a war would automatically make one a better person is an outright lie. Regardless of the cause, we are placed in the role of being a destroyer of other human beings. It is inevitable and inescapable that a part of us will be destroyed or severely damaged in the process. A lie of equal proportion is that, having participated in death and destruction, one can now return home and pick up where one left off in life and maybe be more mature emotionally for having gone through such an "enlightening" experience.

As I write these words, I can't help but reflect on the fact that war makes everyone a loser. Some have lost their lives or caused the loss of life. Some have lost limbs or returned with injuries that will cause a life of pain. Some, especially those returning from Iraq and Afghanistan, will be suffering from traumatic brain injuries, which in some fashion adversely affects one of the most cherished human qualities—memory. Then there will be the scores of others silently suffering from the invisible wounds of their severed humanity.

Fortunately for our current veterans, the experiences of the Vietnam War helped to establish the reality of PTSD. Even with the progress that has been made in this area, there are still major hurtles to overcome for present-day combat veterans to access appropriate services. The first hurtle is the military itself. There still remains this macho-type warrior ethos that "real" soldiers or men either should not be affected by combat trauma or, if they are, they should be able to get over it or deal with it themselves. This is especially true of an all-volunteer military, where careers and promotions may be jeopardized for the individual soldier. If this major hurtle is somehow overcome, there still remains the shortage of mental health resources both in the military and at the Veterans Administration facilities to meet the needs of the fraction of soldiers that is seeking help. Not a week has gone by within the past few years when major concerns regarding these issues have not been raised in various publications by organizations representing psychologists, psychiatrists, and psychiatric nurse practitioners. I fear that scores of traumatized veterans have already begun their descent into the abyss of inner turmoil fueled by shame and guilt.

The terrain, politics, and even the country that my father fought in were as different from my circumstances as night and day. His were in the realm of epic tank and infantry battles with scores of aircraft on both sides joining in the mutual destruction on a grand scale. Hundreds, sometimes thousands, of frozen corpses littered the snow-covered landscape. Mine was in dense jungle terrain where we were involved in search-and-destroy missions as we hunted an enemy who was waiting in his ambush mode to strike us first. With total air superiority, we never had to wonder which side the aircraft was on that was flying overhead and bombing or strafing an identified target. But such differences fade when one considers the real essence of war—death and destruction.

Regardless of the scale of a battle, the war for each individual is fought on the small patch of land he is standing on, along with whatever may be within his field of vision. The horrors that unfold there are the images that become internalized within his soul. This patch of land is void of causes, politics, and grand strategies. The hype and inspiration of army bands and rousing, *esprit de corps* infantry training exercises have been banished from memory while humping the bush to arrive at the ambush site. Nothing can prepare one for the lightning strike of violence from nowhere that claims the life of the buddy next to you. Even worse is helplessly watching his last gasps of air as he escapes into eternity. His body, like the others around him, both friend and foe, soon become as cold and lifeless as the canteen or rifle butt. Still others, both friend and foe, can be heard moaning or screaming from pain. The rest of us, the lucky ones, will walk away this time, only to replay this scene again on another trail. This time, the blood on our sweat-drenched fatigues belongs to the poor guy who was standing next to us just far enough away to make the difference between life and death

Gruesome as it may sound, we can readily measure the dead and wounded. But what about the rest of us who were able to walk away? How do you count or measure the molecular rearrangement of the soul? What happened on the inside this time? After the shock wears off, can we arrive at a point where we can pretend it never happened? Then again, did it really happen, or am I having a bad dream from which I will soon awaken, still scared but relieved that, after all, it was only a dream?

Perhaps, then, this is the unknown war. It is the inner landscape every combat veteran brings home. It is first of all unknown to him because the whole inhumanity of it defies understanding on his part. Moreover, the sheer overwhelming nature of the trauma makes it virtually impossible to gain headway with any meaningful integration, even if he attempts to. This is more complicated by the fact that he needs to maintain survival mode, since the war still goes on and there's no time to try to make sense of what happened. Then, if he survives and goes home, the last thing he wants to do is recall the pain inside. His family wants the untainted soldier back. They are unable to emotionally enter into the silent horror he carried with him on his return trip home that continues to reside within his soul. The best they can do is to try to be understanding, but they will never *really* understand. Only those who went through the gates of hell along the way, regardless of which war or side, *will ever know.* Much like the savagery that took place on a grand scale on the Eastern front in World War II, the inner demons of the returning American soldier from Southeast Asia who tries to readjust to civilian life remain the unknown war to those around him.

It seems that, over the years, I made a meaningful connection with my father and every other soldier who ever was in combat, regardless of the side they were on, what war they fought in, or the scale of the battle. More than anything else, it is the realization that the battle is a deeply personal encounter, much like a religious experience. It matters not whether the deadly violence involved something massive like the Russian front tank battle or a D-Day invasion, or whether it was a squad-size patrol waiting to be ambushed on a trail in Phuc Long Province in Vietnam, near the Cambodian border.

The Last Mission

It was sometime in late January of 1971 and I had now been in Vietnam for nearly one year. In less than thirty days I would be on the "Freedom Bird" that would take me back home to the world. We were flying back in our helicopters to our base on San Juan Hill and I was thoroughly convinced that I had just completed my last mission with the 11th Light Infantry Brigade of the American Division. Every man in our platoon was soaked through to the skin. We had been in the jungle for well over a week and it had been pouring rain every day. The constant heavy rain washed my "bug juice" (insect repellent) off after each subsequent application, and I was riddled with mosquito bites from head to toe. But I was still preoccupied with something that had happened a couple of days into the mission.

It was around dusk, the time we usually set up our automatic ambushes comprised of claymore mines with a trip wire device. We were in an area with several well-worn trails, ideal geography for such an ambush as the trip wire is strung across the trail, waiting for the unfortunate soul to set it off. It is instant death. But that was not the case on this particular night. No sooner did I lie down to get some sleep than my claymore went off with the familiar, stunning explosion. It was always sudden. Shortly afterward I heard some yelling in Vietnamese and then a moaning sound. Someone survived and was in severe pain, about fifty or seventy-five yards from my position. Numerous trees and thick jungle vegetation separated us.

It was dark and the rain was unrelenting. The moaning continued throughout the night. I was beginning to feel a sense of relief after a period of silence, hoping that his suffering was over and he was dead.

But it was not to be. His moaning continued but was growing fainter; he was still alive and suffering. It is hard to say how long this went on in actual time, but he was silent shortly before daylight and my turn at guard duty. I was awake the entire night. The darkness was filled with the haunting symphony of steady raindrop pattering, accented with the waning death throes of human suffering. I was wrapped in my poncho liner in order to gain a measure of protection from the rain. I was helpless to provide him with any first aid. And in all honesty, I would have put him out of his misery if the opportunity presented itself. But neither option was before me, so I just lay there, powerless to do anything but shiver from being soaked to the skin.

My buddy who set the claymores with me was just waking up, and I asked him if he heard the sounds of the "dying dink" throughout the night. His answer still bewilders me to this day. He said that the explosion woke him up, but he "pretended" in his mind that it was "just a water buffalo" and was able to return to sleep. We heated up coffee water with some C4, which I removed from a deactivated claymore. This explosive compound takes on the character of a miniature flamethrower, quickly boiling water even in the middle of a downpour. The measly heating tablet issued by the army was barely adequate even in the best conditions; its barely visible bluish flame took forever to heat even a simple tin cup.

We then prepared to investigate the ambush site and retrieve a second claymore, which was set up on the other end of the trail. But I was unable to bring myself to go with him this time. He returned a short time later and handed me the helmet of a North Vietnamese soldier, along with the army belt that he had removed from the dead man. Both of them had a red communist star. The belt also was stained with blood. He wanted me to have them as "souvenirs" since I was going home in less than a month.

So here I was heading back to base camp with my souvenirs, convinced that all I would be doing was pulling some guard duty for the next few weeks until it was time to begin processing out to return home. I can still remember holding the NVA belt with the dried blood that was soaked into the fabric. Although the bloodstain covered only a relatively small area, about two square inches or so, I was growing increasingly more uncomfortable having it in my possession. I was with four other soldiers later that evening, including my buddy who was able to block out the moans of the dying NVA soldier, seated in a bunker passing the bowl. I can't recall his name, but he was a pretty normal guy, not the killer type like some we were familiar with and avoided as much as possible; smoking dew and socializing with them was counterproductive, as it ruined a perfectly good high. I guess I had a hard time understanding how a nice enough guy could maintain his sleep through the night even if it was a water buffalo or some other animal suffering. I realized that some of the guys who grew up on farms had to deal with the harsh realities of raising livestock, which would eventually be butchered. I guess you just get used to it.

All I remember is that I finally decided to give both my souvenirs to another soldier. I didn't want to take anything home that I hadn't brought with me when I first arrived. I wanted to leave Vietnam in Vietnam. I didn't even want to take the memory of this place with me. Maybe it was my way of trying to block it out and pretend it was a "water buffalo." My relief, however, was short-lived. Our squad leader came in the bunker to announce that several of us, including me, would be accompanying another group for a different kind of mission in the morning (Although he well knew that we smoked dew in the rear area, he was at a loss to do anything about it. Like many others in various levels of leadership, it was something they just had to accept as part of the war).

He was a rather unusual individual who hardly looked the part of a leader. In fact, he jokingly told us that he flunked out of Noncommissioned Officer School because they told him he "couldn't lead sheep to green pasture." Funny how I never forgot those words. He was somewhat small in stature with straight blonde hair and hailed from Connecticut, but he was proficient at killing. In fact, he was promoted to sergeant and made squad leader because of his fairly high body count. I don't remember him having any aspirations for pursuing a military career after the war. He just seemed to thrive on the dangers involved in combat, and it would be fair to say that he developed a degree of bloodlust. We felt confident in his ability to read maps, call in coordinates for air strikes, and sniff out ambushes. These things he did well. We just sensed that every time he met with the platoon leader or company commander, he was all too eager to volunteer our squad for whatever assignment was being considered that particular day.

I turned in early that evening knowing that we would be heading out sometime after breakfast. Sure enough, he showed up ready as ever and picked our machine gunner and me to accompany him for our mission. But something seemed radically different today. As we approached the helicopter pad, I could see only one Huey and two guys waiting for us while the engine was being revved up. These two guys were wearing the tiger-striped fatigues of our Echo Company.

To my knowledge, there were two types of specialists in that unit: recons and snipers. The former operated in five-man units and were inserted into the jungle to gather information about enemy troop movements. They would relay this information to headquarters and then it was our turn to go after the enemy in platoon- or company-sized units. But now there were only two of them, and they each had an M-14 like mine but theirs had scopes on them. No doubt about it, they were of the latter kind—they were snipers.

It was only at this point that the machine gunner and I were informed of the mission. The snipers already knew their part. We were to be inserted into a designated area in the jungle, just outside a small village where the Viet Cong were reportedly terrorizing the inhabitants. The plan was to have the snipers position themselves in the tree and pick their Viet Cong targets. Our job was to be positioned around the tree to protect them in case the enemy attempted to outflank them or surprise them from the rear. Actually, this is exactly what everyone, except the machine gunner, snipers and me, was hoping for. The rest of the platoon would be on stand by, ready to be flown in to outmaneuver the enemy should it attack us, much like a chess match.

I didn't like being a pawn. Besides, if this scenario played out as planned, it had all the makings of a potential disaster as far as I was concerned. The Viet Cong could be caught in the crossfire between the five of us and the rest of platoon. With the enemy between us, we could be shooting at each other as well. It's not like this was without precedent. I can count almost as many soldiers in both units I served with who were killed by accidents and friendly fire as were killed by the enemy. Since I had about a month left in Vietnam, this totally unexpected mission was beginning to unfold in my mind like a nightmare within a nightmare. The only positive note to the whole thing was that we would be in a stationary position for the entire five days. This meant that we wouldn't be humping around the bush with our full gear on.

As we were preparing to board the helicopter, someone in the immediate area heard my request for some reading material and handed me two paperback books to take for my reading enjoyment—*The Territorial Imperative* by Robert Ardrey and *The House of Seven Gables* by Nathaniel Hawthorne. To be sure, these were not the books I would have selected if I were provided with a choice in the matter. What I remember most about these books, which were as different from each other as night and day, was that neither one was what might be referred to as an easy read. I had time enough only to read about half of the *Territorial Imperative*, finishing the rest during my stint at Fort Hood a few months later.

Ironically, the *Territorial Imperative* was written by an ethologist, meticulously describing how vigorously an animal will defend its territory against an intruder. Essentially, his scientific investigations supported the concept that trespassers will pay a heavy price for invading someone else's homeland. Most of the time, the defender will risk his life to protect the area, which is essential for his own survival. It didn't take long before I realized that we were the invaders who had been paying dearly for our intrusion for the past five years. Since I was beginning to find the material unsettling, certainly something I didn't need under the circumstances, I put it away and began reading the other one. All I can remember about the other book was that it concerned a young girl who came to live in a mysterious old mansion somewhere in New England. Judging by this alone, the book would seem hardly more interesting than watching paint dry. But while I can't recall the details of the story, I remember falling in love with Hawthorne's unique writing style. In fact, this book launched me into reading most of his short stories as well as a number of his books during my college years and beyond.

The five of us were inserted into a small clearing in the jungle. We humped for only a short distance as we navigated our way through thick brush. The village was just ahead on the far side of the next clearing, a distance of about two hundred yards. The snipers picked their trees and the three of us set up our positions to form a semicircle that would cover their rear and two flanks. We were all within earshot of each other. Because of the denseness of the jungle, the three of us on the ground had poor visibility, even though the weather was quite nice. It was at times like these that our sense of hearing instantly became a biological sonar system, qualitatively transforming our hypervigilance to yet another level. I was able to read for hours while nestled in my listening post in the thick jungle foliage, hypersensitive to any and all sounds.

One becomes accustomed to the normal sounds that are peculiar to a certain area, like a lizard that makes a laughing noise, vocalizations of small monkeys, and even fairly good-size tortoises that crawl along the jungle floor. These are sounds that I'd learned to ignore. But sudden movements made by wild pigs and ground-dwelling birds always got my attention. I was reunited with some old acquaintances during our first night. As usual, I spread my poncho on the jungle floor for bedding and used my poncho liner as a blanket. Just as I was about to fall asleep, I heard familiar noises directly under me making a tapping sound against the plastic poncho. I can still recall the first time I heard this unusual sound nearly a year before. At the time it made me nervous since I was lying on top of whatever was making the incessant tapping, but I was too exhausted to move my bedding in the pitch-blackness of the jungle. When I lifted up my poncho in the morning, I discovered that I had made my bed in the middle of a termite thruway. The little critters were not going to change their well-traveled trail marked by scent glands just because I decided to sleep in the middle of the pathway leading to their termite mound. Noisy as they were, they were quite harmless. But it's a good thing I had sense enough that first time not to stick my hand under my bedding to feel around for the cause of the mysterious disturbance. Along with the busy termites, I noticed several scorpions nearby as well. Apparently, they found hiding under my poncho for the night a suitable temporary shelter.

Although there were no trails near our position, we still set up some claymore mines in key areas for added security and as an early warning system. I was hoping against hope to avoid all contact with the enemy, even more so than in times past. For one thing, I was "too short," as my departure date from this wretched place was fast approaching. But the main reason was that I felt unsettled not having at least a platoon of twenty-five or thirty soldiers around in case we were hit with a large enemy force (or, better yet, a company of about a hundred men as with the First Cav). Having a small group of five men in a recon mission with one of the main objectives to go undetected is of some consolation. But our job was to *be detected* in order to bait the enemy and bring it out in the open. This was the epitome of insanity. Nixon had already announced that Americans would be pulling out within the next year, handing the ground operations over to the South Vietnamese military. Yet, here we were hunting for enemy soldiers and simultaneously baiting them (with us as the bait), all in an effort to make "contact" and elevate our body count. Small wonder *The Territorial Imperative* was making me so uneasy. There was no just cause, liberation, democracy or any similar talk since the day I had been drafted—it was about doing your tour and going home alive. We were the intruders and the enemy was defending his homeland. I wanted to survive this year of hell and go home, never to think about it again.

It wasn't until about the third day that one of the snipers got off a shot and claimed he had a kill. I believe there was at least one subsequent shot, possibly two, later in the day. We were now on full alert, waiting to be surrounded and overrun during the night. I never felt so scared in my life; in my desperation, I fixed bayonet on my weapon for the first time. None of us slept that night. We took turns sleeping during the following day, still expecting the enemy to attack. We continued radio contact with the company commander, who was anxiously expecting us to be hit. A few more days went by and nothing happened. We were finally extracted from almost the exact spot we were inserted and headed back to base camp. Finally, a fitting end to a very stupid experiment—an experiment with my life.

Coming Home

For those of us fortunate enough to have escaped serious injury or death, there were two ways to complete one's tour in Vietnam—DEROS or ETS. The former meant that, after the completion of one year in Vietnam, there were still five or six months left to spend somewhere in the U.S. That is, after coming home to the family and neighborhood for a thirty-day leave, I would be reassigned to an Army base to complete my two years of active duty before I was relegated to that most enviable status of Inactive Army Reserve, with all the rights and privileges of being promoted to a full time civilian. The ETS route meant that I would be discharged from the army right out of Vietnam and be done with the whole thing and never have to deal with another active army assignment again. However, there was one catch—I would have to extend my tour forty-five more days in Vietnam in order to shave off five or six months of stateside duty that would be remaining on my two-year hitch.

I would probably have chosen the ETS route if, like many others, I could have been assigned a rear job in a relatively safe area for the last few months of my tour. But my defiant attitude precluded such a luxury and I had to get out as soon as my time was up. I just wanted to go home in the most expeditious manner possible. But even a rebel like me, was finally assigned to a rear area for the last few weeks. This was not as a reward, but rather as a safety measure. Like other infantrymen before me, as the time of my departure for home drew closer, I was becoming more nervous and prone to making mistakes. It's best for all concerned to reassign short timers to an area where the likelihood of combat is minimal.

I was reassigned to a unit in Chu Lai as a security guard. This was a large Army and Air Force base which some years later became identified with the TV series *China Beach*. It was here that I was reunited with Steve, a crew chief and door gunner who I met during my confinement in the stockade following my court-martial. He was also reassigned to a rear area job for his last few weeks. His assignment was somewhat more glamorous, as he drove a two-and-a-half-ton truck loaded with produce to the various mess halls scattered around the huge base. This was certainly more desirable than my job of guarding two very elderly Vietnamese *papa-sans* while they systematically went from one latrine to another to burn the human excrement located in large drums (affectionately referred to as the "shit detail").

I met with Steve and some others each night in various bunkers to pass the bowl and share our excitement about returning to the world. It seemed like there were no limits to our plans and dreams once we returned home. There was certainly no consideration or discussion about any potential adjustment problems we might encounter. The problem was being there; the solution was to get out. In essence, we collectively believed that whatever happened would be left behind. We would be like clean slates once we returned home. After all, going home was all we ever thought about—day and night, night and day. It is what kept us sane and was our hope if we made it out alive. Going home was what it was all about. Nothing could be simpler. We would pick up our lives where they left off a year ago. This line of fantasy was reinforced as we boarded a commercial airliner on that most anticipated of days. We were exiting this netherworld in the same manner as we arrived, except for one major difference—our jet aircraft was now miraculously transformed into the *Freedom Bird*.

We arrived at Sea Tac airport and it was February 1971. We were immediately greeted by about a half dozen photographers as we stepped off the plane onto American soil. Their flashbulbs were going off vigorously, as they seemed to be desperately attempting to include every one of us in their photographs. But this perceived altruism was short-lived. Like many others, they were there to make a buck from the war. For ten dollars, I could purchase a photograph of me as I touched down on the homeland. The murderous rage I felt toward them frightened me. Fortunately, there was little time to react as we were whisked through the airport terminal.

We were loaded on to the all-too-familiar olive drab buses and headed toward Fort Lewis, Washington. I was already feeling like a stranger in the wet February snow. Things began to feel familiar when we were on base and directed toward our temporary quarters—the familiar two-story chicken coup barracks of Fort Gordon fame. It was around midnight and we were hungry. After we were seated in a fairly nice mess hall, we were greeted by a first sergeant. He welcomed us home and said something that has echoed throughout the decades in my mind. The words were to the effect that our country thanks us for doing our job, but don't expect any thanks from any civilians. We should enjoy the steak and eggs that were being prepared for us and leave Vietnam behind and continue our lives where we left off the best we could.

We all sat in silence. I believe we all agreed. I realized this was an upscale mess hall when we heard the piped-in music as we started to feast on our steak and eggs banquet. The very first song I heard was by Creedence Clearwater Revival, "Have You Ever Seen the Rain?" The song was immediately immortalized in my mind. As Steve and I headed back to our barracks, we instinctively wondered where the bunkers were located. It quickly dawned on us that there would be no more bunkers. That little piece of dirt-laden real estate, which had provided us with the only real measure of security, was gone forever. Yes, they were dusty, filthy, and loaded with explosives and weapons, but it was there that we met with our buddies to talk about our dreams of going home. We were now home and already wanting to return to a "safe area." I sensed that something was not right, but was at a loss to articulate anything beyond feeling disoriented.

We were there for only a few days for processing before we headed for home—the old neighborhood. I would have a thirty-day leave before going to my final five-month assignment at Fort Hood to rejoin the cavalry. However, this time around, it would not be the air cavalry, but an armored cavalry unit. From the moment that I left Fort Lewis, I wanted to do whatever I could to forget where I spent the past year and every trace of memory associated with it. Dressed in an army uniform and sporting a deep tan in February, I felt self-conscious. I thought that everyone had to know where I had just been. The looks some people sent my way left me feeling even more out of place. I felt like a freak. No one offered a single word, just glances and stares. I now found myself all alone in a crowded airliner.

I arrived for a layover in Chicago. This was one massive airport interlaced with mini malls throughout the connecting concourses. I headed straight for one of the small clothing stores and purchased some civilian attire. Shedding my uniform had a two-fold purpose: helping me to forget where I had been and helping me to blend in with the population. This change of identity took place in an airport men's room. To make the change complete and permanent, I threw my uniform into the garbage can. With no visible trace of my former activity, I prepared for the last leg of my journey home. I left home alone one year ago and was returning in the same manner. I made a phone call to my mother and spoke with her for the first time in over a year. It was great to hear her voice. She informed me that some friends, including my girlfriend's family, were hoping to greet me at the airport. For some unknown reason, I kindly asked her to call and ask them not to be at the airport when I arrived. I would contact them individually later on. The rest of the day was a blur. My mother was in the kitchen drying dishes as I entered our apartment. She was happy and excited to see me, as were my brother and sister. After a round of hugs and kisses, we hung around the kitchen talking and eating. I had rehearsed this moment countless times over the past year and was glad to be home, but I felt numb and disoriented. I just couldn't bring myself to be as happy as my family was about having me safely home. Intuitively, I sensed that something was wrong.

The following four weeks of leave were filled with reconnecting with my high school fraternity and friends from the neighborhood. They were all welcoming and I don't recall paying for a single drink at the several taverns that historically served for our gatherings and partying in times past. I frequently heard the words, "Your money is no good here" as another beer was passed my way. Although I spent a considerable time with my girlfriend, I cannot recall any of our conversations. I find this to be a tremendous irony, as her letters which I read and re-read dozens of times in the jungle, served as my hope and lifeline. She was now in college and we were drifting apart after a nearly five-year relationship. Although we would remain on friendly terms for a few more years, I sensed that my first love was over. Strangely, as much as I detested the army, I felt a measure of security knowing that I would be going to Fort Hood soon for the last five months of my two-year induction. I was already drinking too much, and couldn't seem to fall asleep in my old bed. I finally ended up sleeping on the floor in the living room. Although it was natural for me, my family thought it was odd, especially without the use of a pillow.

Two distinct events that took place during my thirty-day leave stand out, even today. The first one unfolded following a night of drinking with six of my former fraternity brothers. Like many times before, we headed for George's, a small restaurant that specialized in chilidogs (or red hots if you were from Buffalo). One of my friends soon got into an argument with a man in his mid-thirties. Like the rest of us, he also had had too much to drink but should have known better than to start a commotion with someone who had the backing of a small army. Before we knew it, he pulled out a small pistol from his jacket and pointed it at my friend. I was just returning from the men's room located in the back of the restaurant. He didn't notice me approaching him from behind. Instinctively, I grabbed his gun and disarmed him. My friends were appropriately impressed and wanted to take the man outside and beat him up. I intervened and insisted we let him go before the police got involved. They agreed and we tossed the pistol into the Niagara River, which was about a hundred yards away. We quickly dispersed and went our separate ways.

It wasn't until I got home and was sitting in our kitchen that I began to appreciate the full impact of what had just transpired. The house was quiet as everyone was fast asleep. It was in this terrible stillness that I began to ruminate over the possible ways this night could have ended—all of them with tragic consequences. I felt scared and began to tremble. Then and there, I resolved not to seek the company of this group of friends again. God was watching over me and protected me from a terrible tragedy that easily could have happened to my friends, the man I had disarmed, or me. I was no stranger to taking risks, even before I went to Vietnam, but none of them involved the potential of loss of life or serious injury. This particular incident that unfolded in the early morning hours had all the makings of a death wish. Even though I was far from the jungles of Vietnam, I somehow managed to find myself in a predicament where a burst of violence was thrust upon me. But this was different—and avoidable. In some frightening way, I had become a catalyst of the equation that brought it about. I sensed that and it scared me enough to avoid the company of this reckless crew for the remainder of my leave. Instead, I spent more time with my girlfriend and some of my more moderate friends.

As traumatic as this incident proved to be, another one with far more life-changing implications was about to unfold a week later. It would be one that ushered in a true existential crisis. It was a Monday evening, and I walked to the corner tavern for a few beers to watch Monday Night Football. I had not been there for nearly two years. Surprisingly, there was only a half dozen patrons inside, also at the bar for the football game. I immediately recognized two former high school football stars that were in the same fraternity as me before I was drafted. They gave a warm greeting and offered to buy me a beer and invited me to sit next to them at the bar. They asked a few questions about Vietnam and filled me in on how some of our former fraternity brothers had fared over the past few years.

Before long, Monday Night Football was on and we shifted our primary focus to the action on the TV, providing our own commentaries throughout the game. At some point during the night, I experienced a flashback, but it was not about Vietnam. Ironically, it was about these same two friends who I remembered sitting on the same barstools watching a football game and talking mostly, if not exclusively, about football. Much like they were doing a few years before when we were all nineteen years old, they were interjecting their own glory days on the gridiron, now about three years past. It was during this sort of disassociated state that I had a most unusual epiphany.

It dawned on me, as I mentally disengaged from the dialogue with my two friends and drifted off to some other internal location, that they remained essentially unchanged during the past two years. I felt as though I had been transported to another world where I experienced and did things I could never tell anyone else. In fact, while we were in Vietnam, we routinely referred to our home or the United States as "the world." Geographically, we reduced the Planet Earth to two distinct locations, "the Nam" and "the world." You were either in one or the other, with one very important difference—those in "the Nam" constantly talked and dreamed about "the world," but those in "the world" never really knew that "the Nam" even existed.

So here I was observing these two guys providing play-by-play commentary on a football game, apparently clueless to anything outside this tavern, neighborhood, and surrounding Western New York area. I also realized that even if they expressed anything more than a passing interest in what the war was really like, I would be at a loss to describe my experiences. The best place for these memories was the burial ground located somewhere in the realm of my unconscious. It wasn't my tour in Vietnam per se that was the defining moment of this particular scenario. What disturbed me most at the ripe age of twenty-one was that it was entirely possible to go through life (in this instance, measured by a two-year span of time) and be sitting on the same old barstool. But more than that, it was sitting on the same barstool and being comfortable in that position. It was as if time stood still for them, while something else happened to me that I could not explain. Yet, as bizarre as it might seem, I felt pity for them rather than for myself. They didn't know that they didn't know. Even with all the trauma and hardship of war, I felt that I was in a far better place than they were. For whatever adverse affects the war had on my psyche, and there certainly were enough to last a lifetime, it propelled me to wrestle with core existential issues like What is the meaning of life? What is my purpose on this planet? Why was my life spared when others died? I realized that while such questions could be asked while sitting on a barstool, the answers would not be found there. I never returned.

Nam Attitude

As much as I detested being stationed there following my leave, I now believe that my five months at Fort Hood were most helpful for my transition back into society. Although we were housed in different barracks, it was a godsend to be reunited with Larry Toczek and John Meisenbach, two of the original five from Advanced Infantry Training. We were still numbed by the deaths of our friends, John Gmack and Richard Timmons, and, in a sense, were still awaiting their return to rejoin our little band. We recounted scores of others we met in Vietnam who also were killed for this senseless war. Even though the war was scaling back by 1971, American troops were still being sent to die for nothing. Above all else, we were angry to the core. We felt used and not much more than numbers in the green machine of the U.S. Army. We felt alienated from our peers who were still riding the "make love, not war" wave from the sixties. What many of them failed to understand was that we would be the first in line to reject war. I even spent forty-five days in the stockade for refusing a direct order, only to be reassigned to another unit to fight with and risk my life on a daily basis for five more months. No one else could have possibly understood what we went through or how we felt. Still, it was good that we had this time with each other to help us settle down and get reoriented to the world.

Someone once described the terrain surrounding Fort Hood as "nothing but miles and miles, for miles and miles." This was an accurate description if ever there was one. It was a flat expanse of land peppered with shrubbery and small, undernourished foliage that the locals referred to as "trees." I was in a cavalry unit again but hardly the same aerial mobile force that I spent my first seven months with in Vietnam.

I was assigned to Alpha Troop, 3rd Squadron, 1st Cavalry (First Regiment of Dragoons), of the 1st Armored Division. This was an armored cavalry regiment, comprised mostly of speedy, powerful Sheridan tanks and armored personnel carriers. This outfit was unique, however, since it was composed of two different types of soldiers. Half of them had completed their infantry or armor training a few weeks earlier and were permanently assigned to this new unit. Since the ground troops in Vietnam were already being scaled back, they were more than relieved that they would not be going off to war. They were cherries and, fortunately for them, would forever remain so. The rest of us were combat veterans who were defiant, angry, disillusioned, and suffering from PTSD without realizing it. We just wanted to be left alone. We were in no mood to play soldier by going on meaningless military exercises in this desert terrain. This was definitely not a good mix of military personnel and, to the credit of our first sergeant, the rules concerning our group were relaxed over the ensuing months. The problems became strikingly obvious a few days after our arrival, as more Vietnam veterans were arriving from their initial home leaves to wait out the remaining months in the army. Immediately following our morning roll call, where the customary head count was taken, we were ordered to line up for a "police call." Each company area, including the lawn and sidewalk, was to be kept free of trash by the soldiers who lived in the barracks. While we were conditioned to doing this during our basic training, the situation now was altogether different. The thought of bending down and picking up cigarette butts and gum wrappers ran against every fiber of my being. Sure enough, once we lined up and began to sweep the area, only about half of the troopers could be found bending down to pick up anything. This did not go unnoticed by our first sergeant who wisely observed without saying a word. He seemed to realize that he would be dealing with two different groups of men. The new recruits would be in his charge for the foreseeable future, while the defiant ones were only waiting for completion of their two-year stint and would soon be civilians—probably not soon enough, from his standpoint.

I took a liking to several of the new recruits and couldn't believe that the army was now taking what seemed like young kids. Most of the veterans were only one or two years older than these newly minted soldiers, but we felt like old men in many ways. We were hardened, disillusioned, and violated deep within our soul. We had aged far beyond our years. It was generally an unfair and awkward arrangement for all concerned but we made the best of it. We were all housed in the same barracks. I finally landed in a modern, brick building. No more bunk beds lined up like dominos in a pre-World War II wooden firetrap, as there were only eight of us in each of these spacious rooms.

The parking area adjoining our barracks building was a most unusual sight. Many of the combat veterans drove their vehicles back from leave so they had use of them for weekend jaunts away from the base. There was a fair number of brand new sporty and sleek Camaros, Corvettes, Mustangs, and Chargers that had been purchased with savings accumulated during the combat tour. Even more visually pleasing, however, was the large number of Chevy, Ford, and Volkswagen vans lined up with their psychedelic paint schemes. It was just another way for the returning soldiers to get integrated back into the hippie culture many of them were rudely extracted from when they were drafted. Although some of these vehicles belonged to the new recruits who would be staying at Fort Hood for an extended time, most of them were the proud property of the veterans. They were the ones painted with the glaring peace signs and distinctive graffiti of "potheads."

During the week, we were assigned to a cavalry troop composed of armored personnel carriers and Sheridan tanks, with a few jeeps thrown into the mix. There was certainly enough space to ride around in the expansive surrounding area. In a few weeks we became acclimated to our new rides and received our first official assignment, participating in war games. The army was testing its new, miniature, remote-controlled helicopter armed with video surveillance equipment. Our assignment was pretty straightforward. We were to be involved in a game of hide and seek, as we were to somehow attempt to camouflage these massive vehicles in desert terrain dotted with sagebrush and an occasional withered tree. No surprise that the little unarmed flying demon found us an easy mark every time. Immediately after we were detected, Cobra gunships were called in to "finish us off." Those of us who had fought in the jungles of Vietnam were provided with a frightening reminder of how threatening these killers from the sky really were. They certainly lived up to their billing as "death from above." Now being on the receiving end of these unarmed aircraft gave me a deeper appreciation for what the NVA and VC must have felt like dealing with their fully armed wrath. Fortunately for us, it was just a silly war exercise. Then one day, we received a briefing that the war games were temporarily suspended until further notice. We were delighted not to have to go kicking up dust storms and come back looking like we had been sanding dry wall all day. It seemed that our little nemesis, the unmanned "spy in the sky," was grounded. Rumor had it that it was shot down by one of the veterans who was guarding some facility in the desert. Although none of those participating in war games had live ammunition, those assigned to guard duty were fully armed. We were informed that the soldier in question was relieving himself near some sagebrush as the drone was hovering above him, to the amusement of the crew who was viewing the activity on their monitors. Apparently, in his irritation, he opened fire on the little demon and shot it down. It's a shame that we never found out who was responsible for this act of defiant heroism. We would have decorated him in a manner worthy of his deed. Our days of creating and chasing dust storms were over.

While we played soldier during the weekdays, the weekends were pretty much our own. John Meisenbach had a car, which became our ticket to get off the base whenever the weekend rolled around. Smoking marijuana was still a regular occurrence and certainly not limited to weekends. We would be passing a joint while riding on tanks or armored personnel carriers during field maneuvers. Rommel's Afrikakorps never had it so good. Vietnam veterans proved remarkably adaptable in this regard. I found it amusing while I was traversing the desert terrain that the last unit I served with in Vietnam, the 11th Light Infantry Brigade, went by the nickname "Jungle Warriors." Anyway, Austin was one of the most beautiful cities that I have ever been in, even to the present date. The tree-lined streets (real trees ... and green, too!) and breathtaking fountains around the University of Texas were a beautiful sight, especially to jungle transplants that were now living the unfamiliar life of desert rats.

It was during this window of time that two contemporary movements, The Jesus Revolution and Vietnam Veterans Against the War, were quite active on campus. Neither one of them appealed to any of us at the time, as we were fed up with anything hinting of an organization, regardless of how radical it might have been.

One weekend we visited Corpus Christi, a considerable distance from our base. The pure white sand beaches were a visual treat. About a dozen vans with the all too familiar psychedelic paint schemes joined us from our base, and were parked around our bonfire in wagon train fashion. So here we were, about thirty Vietnam veterans seated around a bonfire, listening to the tunes of Woodstock and passing the all-too-familiar and most beloved bowl—the magical contents of which had provided us with a mental escape while we were in the land of death. No more bunkers, no more helicopter assaults, no more weapons, no more ambushes, no more letters from home and counting every precious day remaining on the calendar. We were still alive. We had survived after all. But we were now in another land as we entered a different type of unknown territory. Some of us even talked about returning to Vietnam, as it was at least a familiar entity. I was beginning to hear the siren call myself, and it was scary and confusing. After all, coming home was the hope that kept me going each day while I was there. Now I found myself feeling homesick for the very place that I wanted desperately to blot from memory. I was now beginning to understand why some of the guys returned for second, and in some cases, even third tours in that forsaken place.

There was one incident during my stay at Fort Hood that provided me with a connection to some other feelings besides anger and defiance. Since the first sergeant relaxed some of the rules of comportment, one of the veterans from our building showed up one day for roll call with a baby raccoon on his shoulder, gently nestled against his neck. He found the orphan while on maneuvers on a tank somewhere out in the scrub brush. He was allowed to keep it in the barracks and the creature instantly became our mascot. Everyone thoroughly enjoyed playing with the friendly little critter, especially when he would search through our shirt pockets with his prehensile paws in hopes of finding an edible treat. Then one day, I found another apparently orphaned animal, an orange, tiger-stripped kitten. I adopted her and named her Foxy and she lived under my bed in a cardboard box for the next few months. For at least an hour a day the little raccoon and Foxy would play and chase each other under and on top of our beds. We enjoyed watching them frolicking and getting into just about everything. They even took naps together when they were all tuckered out. Then one day, Foxy got out of the building and a car accidentally ran over and killed her while she was darting across the street. I retrieved her body, which was lying by the curb, and buried her nearby. I remember getting teary and choked up at losing this little kitten. She had brought not only me but also a whole group of soldiers much-needed laughter and relief. The little raccoon looked for her playmate in vain for several days before abandoning the search. I believe the soldier took the little creature home with him when his stint was finally up. Even today as I write these words, some three and a half decades later, I feel warm affection for the memories of those two of God's creatures that touched our hearts at such a difficult and confusing time in our lives. Grief for Foxy in some way provided me with a measure of reassurance at the time that I still had tender feelings, dormant as they were. I was beginning to realize that I was still human after all.

It was a typical day, about a month before my discharge, that a group of us shuffled over to the mess hall for breakfast. But something unusual was about to unfold on this particular morning. Six of us were seated around a table, all Vietnam veterans. We noticed that the newly trained infantrymen were seated at a nearby table as a group. This was odd, because we were accustomed to them mixing with us at our table. I walked over and asked why they were not sitting with us. There was a brief silence as they proceeded to eat their breakfast, making only minimal eye contact with me. Before long, one of them turned toward me and said "Top (nickname for the first sergeant) told us to stay away from you guys as much as possible because you have a Nam attitude." So there it was. The army was distancing itself from the very soldiers who bore the brunt of war in order to reestablish a sanitized and peacetime version of soldiering—playing war games where no one gets hurt and returning to your comfortable barracks at day's end, much like a banker, teacher, or factory worker. Yes, we were angry, smoked marijuana on a daily basis, and were defiant to the core. We all knew this and actually took a certain degree of pride in our anti-military mindset. What we didn't realize at the time is just how violently ravaged our psyches had become. We were the infantry, the ones from time immemorial who did the fighting at close range, whether by sword, bow and arrow, muskets, or automatic rifles. We were the ones who returned home and would be dealing with haunting imagery for the rest of our lives. But we hadn't started out this way a year ago, and had no idea what was in store for us half a world away. But here we were, with our psychic pain covered with layer upon layer of anger and defiance. We needed help but didn't realize it. The Army, for its part, wanted to get rid of us in the most expedient manner possible. I certainly couldn't blame the first sergeant for wanting to keep the new recruits away from us. After all, we were damaged goods and our attitude was infecting everything around us. But it is also the very stuff that was instrumental to our survival, given the unique military and political climate of our time. We had a "Nam attitude" all right, but for the best reason in the world—we had just come back from Vietnam and were angry about how our country and military used and abused us. We had nowhere to turn except to each other for any sort of validation. The end of my two-year stint in the U.S. Army was approaching, the day when I would return to being a full-time civilian. My plan was to leave Vietnam, and everything associated with it, buried alongside Foxy at Fort Hood. From now on, it would be like it never happened. But here I am, some thirty-seven years later, and it feels more real with each passing day.

New Life

I moved back home to live with my family for the first two years following my discharge from the army. Although I was still technically in the Army Reserve for four more years, I was never called up to active duty. I abstained from smoking any more marijuana, as it had the uncanny effect at Fort Hood of transporting me back to Vietnam, the very place I wanted to escape. Ceaseless activity and goal-oriented behaviors soon became my primary coping mechanisms. Having obtained a GED while in Vietnam, I immediately enrolled in night school and was accepted as a full-time student at the University of Buffalo. I also obtained a full-time job at a shelter for homeless, alcoholic men. The year 1971 was when psychiatric hospitals were releasing mental patients to live in the community. Since many of them were woefully unprepared, they soon ended up in our shelter when their medication wore off.

My life became an unending series of charitable activities, fueled mostly by inner restlessness. Determined to sustain this new "healthy" lifestyle, I even quit smoking cigarettes. I continued to struggle with initiating and maintaining sleep. Since I was unable to sleep in a bed at all, I ended up getting what restless sleep I could while lying on the living room floor. But the nightmares and sweats went on unabated. Frequently upon awakening, I would find myself on the other side of our living room, some twenty feet from my original sleep area. This scenario continued for six months or more, until one night when it came to an abrupt end. Somehow on that fateful night, I got tangled up with a bamboo bookcase that housed a complete set of Compton's Encyclopedia. My mother believed it was important for our education to have this well-known reference material at hand. The entire family woke up to a loud crashing noise, followed by a series of moans and groans. They found me under the pile of books, along with the fallen bookcase. How ironic that it was made of bamboo, an all-too-familiar plant that laced the jungle trails, as well as my troubled dreams. That settled the issue of where I slept from that day on. Since sleeping on the floor actually proved to be dangerous, I was now able and willing to tolerate the discomfort of a bed. That bamboo bookcase saw service for many more years in my mother's apartment. I inherited it after she died and now have it in my finished basement area. It is a rather flimsy structure as bookcases go and it amazes me to this day that it was sturdy enough to support a complete set of encyclopedias. It is now a very much-pampered piece of furniture with rarely more than a few choice knick-knacks to weigh it down. Nevertheless, I have a deep affection for this precious item, as it presents a tangible link to the soul that was so troubled many years ago. It also is a testimony to my mother's insistence, regardless of her humble beginnings, of the importance of a good education.

I kept myself busy, but not busy enough to ignore the nagging sensation that somehow I was missing something. There was this inner feeling that continued to surface especially when I was alone and the only one still awake at night in the house. Then, without warning, I made a bold promise to myself—later that night, when everyone was sleeping, I would sit on the couch and stay there until I found the "truth." A yearning was welling up in my soul that was determined to settle for nothing less. I was never so determined about anything in my life.

Quite frankly, I had absolutely no idea how I would go about this undertaking. I was going to sit on that couch until I found what I was looking for, as grandiose and unrealistic as it sounds. After everyone was asleep, I sat down on that couch, just like I promised myself I would. I recall staring out the window at a cool, starlit November night. It was very quiet and, ever so slowly and imperceptibly, I began to experience a deep, inner peace. I found myself yearning for God, more than I wanted anything else before in my life, and I was single-minded in my quest. Unbeknownst to me at the time, the words of the prophet Jeremiah, "You will seek me and find me when you seek me with all your heart," were being fulfilled within my soul.

At a certain point there was a soft, gentle glow in the room and I sensed the presence of another person. Simultaneously, I was feeling a deep, inner peace that was beyond my understanding. This was not the artificial sense of well being that I was all too familiar with as the by-product of marijuana. I found myself yearning for the God of my childhood, the one I "prayed" to whenever I was lifting off in a helicopter or fired upon on a jungle trail, and then conveniently forgot when the danger passed. No, this time there was no danger to my life, just a nagging hunger within my soul. I wanted God not to rescue me from the threat of death but to give me life. I was not depressed, suicidal, or suffering from any psychiatric condition. I was suffering from a soul sickness, a deep existential crisis that only my Creator could cure. As that blessed evening progressed, this person began to take on the form of Jesus Christ, although barely perceptible in my mind.

Although I was raised a Roman Catholic and served as an altar boy when the Masses were in Latin, no Scripture verses came to mind. What did occur, however, was a series of images involving a Roman soldier. In some strange way, I was being presented with a set of outdated attire and weaponry, which included a helmet, breastplate, sword, sandals, etc. I should have been repelled by anything hinting of military. But in my mind's eye, I now had absolute trust in Jesus Christ, who was now real and alive in my presence. I didn't understand what was transpiring. All I knew for sure was that I had developed an unquenchable thirst for truth, which was being satisfied at the Fountain of Life. That night, I gently transitioned into a deep, peaceful sleep.

During the ensuing weeks, I gradually realized what happened to me that most memorable of nights. I obtained a copy of *Good News for Modern Man*, a book of the New Testament written in plain English. From the very beginning, the words came alive as I read about the life of Jesus Christ. It was as if I was hearing it all for the first time. In a very real sense, it was all new to me, because now I knew that His Spirit was dwelling within my soul. I returned to that same couch on a nightly basis while everyone was sleeping to read and digest these words of life. I did not view the parables and life of Jesus as just interesting stories anymore, but rather the reality of the unseen world fleshed out to explain the meaning of life. It wasn't long before I came across the Apostle Paul's description of spiritual warfare that "we do not battle against flesh and blood, but against rulers, against the authorities, against the powers of this dark world and against the spiritual forces of evil in heavenly realms. Therefore put on the full armor of God, so that when the day of evil comes, you may be able to stand your ground, and after you have done everything, to stand. Stand firm then, with the belt of truth buckled around your waist, with the breastplate of righteousness in place, and with your feet fitted with the readiness that comes from the gospel of peace. In addition to all this, take up the shield of faith, with which you can extinguish all the flaming arrows of the evil one. Take the helmet of salvation and the sword of the Spirit, which is the word of God."

Paul was describing the full outfitting of a Roman soldier preparing for battle that I envisioned. I was in a new army now, the Army of Christ. My enemy would be more crafty and deadly than any that stalked the jungles of Vietnam. I realized that there was a real devil who had legions under his command. I also had a vague sense that the greatest enemy I would be facing on a daily basis was my very self, saturated with my fallen nature and all the sins, habits, and struggles that could prove to be my undoing. Finally, if that weren't enough, I would also be facing a world that continues to be hostile to the new life that was recently imparted to me. The Bible I was reading was quite explicit about this triple threat—the world, the flesh, and the devil. But it also held the promise that God would continue to dwell within me causing me to be "more than conquerors through Christ."

A few weeks later, I had an unusual dream. I was being enveloped in darkness that I was absolutely powerless to stop. I feared for the destruction of my very existence, something beyond death itself. Then, just before the darkness consumed me, a soft, gentle, penetrating ray of light emerged to rescue me. This light became anchored in my very being, and I felt a reassurance that it would never be blotted out by any darkness. Some thirty-seven years later, I can still sense the indelible mark that this light made within me. It was the Holy Spirit given as a "seal of ownership," just as the Scriptures foretold. I would be returning many times to this interior realm in the ensuing years, as the darkness in its various forms and disguises would again threaten my existence. Sadly, many of these occasions would be self-induced. These early weeks marked the beginning of my new life in Christ. Like

John Bunyan's *Pilgrim's Progress*, my journey ahead would be filled by countless challenges, some victories, and my share of defeats. Through it all, I had to learn and relearn that the grace of God would always be sufficient. Ever so slowly, I had to begin the painful process of being divested of the layers of illusions, perpetuated by fear, anger, and pride, that have been my lot since childhood.

Sgt William "Bill" Wood
in Vietnam (photo courtesy
Sam & Bonnie Rhodes)

Bill Wood's final resting
place in Alliance, Ohio.

**Author reunited with Bill Wood during
visit to Alliance in 2002.**

**Ray Cage at gravesite of James Waulk, Jr., Washington
Court House, Ohio, during 2002 visit with his family.**

Photo of Bill Wood presented by author to Mrs. Beulah
Wood. Bill (lower right) is preparing a meal with his
squad in the bush (photo courtesy Ray Cage)

The Sub Shop in Alliance - Sam & Bonnie Rhodes, proprietors.

Inside the Sub Shop (left to right) Donna Fazekas, Paul Fazekas (author), Larry Wood, Bonnie (Wood) Rhodes, & Sam Rhodes.

Infamous "smoking" photo the author sent to Mrs. Trudy Gmack. Taken at Fort Gordon, Georgia (Advanced Infantry Training) it includes three members of the original "Five of Us." Richard Timmons (top center) and John Gmack (bottom center) were both killed in Vietnam; John Meisenbach (far right) was reunited with Larry Toczek and author at Fort Hood, Texas after completing combat tour.

John Gmack "humping the bush." (Photo courtesy of Mrs. Trudy Gmack)

Larry Toczek (left) and author (right) cleaning their weapons on a forward firebase.

Aerial view of a forward firebase.

Larry Toczek (left) and author (right) geared up to
board a Huey "slick" for a combat air assault.

**Author (center) "skying out" Air Cav style aboard a
Huey.**

A grunt's view from above during a combat air assault.

Huey "slick" helicopters flying in formation during combat
air assault, loaded with infantry. Photo taken from inside,
near door gunner's position.

Ray Cage (left),
machine gunner
and aspiring combat
photographer, and
Larry Toczek (right)
on a forward firebase.

Huey loading up grunts after
completing mission in Cambodia.

Making preparations to enjoy some of the four star
accommodations in the bush (jungle critters available in
various shapes & sizes at no extra charge).

Larry Toczek burning leeches off author's leg with a
cigarette.

A sign of the times. Seated between door gunner (left) and a
machine gunner (right), a soldier presents the "black power"
salute as their Huey extracts them from the bush.

**Another sign of the times– A C47 Chinook helicopter
door gunner proudly displays his 1970 "nose art"
depicting the "Zig-Zag" man.**

**Author (top center) with some of the boys
"relaxing" in a jungle clearing.**

Some of the boys enjoying the perks that come with
bunker guard duty on a forward firebase.

Three of the Kit Carson Scouts employed by the First Air
Cavalry to track down the Viet Cong and North Vietnamese
Army; they were the equal of any Apache or Crow scout used
by the US Cavalry a hundred years earlier.

Air Cavalry troopers taking a dinner break in the bush. Most of the time was certainly not spent in the "air" and most of the mobility for the "cavalry" part was putting one foot in front of the other. Carrying the eighty-pound rucksack, along with ammo and weapons, left one feeling like an army mule.

AH-1G Cobra gunship lifting off the helipad as it heads out for a mission. Cobras functioned as Stuka dive-bombers/fighter planes when they were assigned to protect our units on the ground. I am eternally grateful that they were on our side.

**Larry Toczek struggling with his rucksack
in the thick jungle foliage.**

**Larry Toczek "struggling" with a parrot in the foliage
of a Southern California bird sanctuary.**

Ray Cage (right) and author (left) with a fellow
grunt on a rear firebase in 1970.

Ray Cage (left) and author (right) at a mutual friend's house
in Buffalo, N.Y. (2002) flashing peace sign after all these
years.

Little Dylan being held in the loving arms of his father, Sgt. David McKeever (KIA in Iraq) (Photo courtesy of David McKeever Sr. – father, grandfather & Vietnam Veteran).

Eight-year-old David McKeever dressed in his first uniform proudly presenting the Cub Scout salute.

PART III

Reflections: The Human Cost of War

Semper Fi

When I went on eBay to order my own copy of the *Life Magazine* issue depicting John's unit, I noticed that there was a number of issues dealing with the ongoing war in Vietnam. I tried to focus on obtaining the ones that featured the war on the front cover. As always, *Life* presented a story of interest by combining dramatic photographs with concisely written articles. Not surprisingly, it was usually the photographs that left the more enduring images. It didn't take long for me to come across one such issue. I was immediately drawn to the May 22, 1970 cover, entitled "Our Forgotten Wounded." This issue possessed a glaringly unique front cover in that it showed two separate pieces on the war—one dealing with the U.S. invasion of Cambodia and the other with how we were treating our seriously wounded at hospitals throughout the United States.

Since I had been in Cambodia with my unit during that same time period, it was a bonus to have made such a discovery. Interestingly, the cover was horizontally divided in half and portrayed two separate photographs—the upper half was in color, while the lower picture was in black and white. The colored photo depicted a group of American soldiers with their shirts off, conversing and seemingly reassuring one another after an engagement with the enemy. Several of them had bandages covering what appeared to be minor wounds. The caption read: "U.S. troops on the Cambodian border." In stark contrast, the scene with the black-and-white photograph below was as forlorn as it was unconscionable, as it completed the caption with the words "And in a stateside VA hospital." It was reminiscent of a scene from Dante's *Inferno* in which the words "Abandon all hope, ye who enter here" are inscribed above the gate as one enters the first level of hell. The large, dimly lit hospital dorm with a high ceiling was overcrowded with beds in various positions, likened to the order of flattened dominos. One could make out a few pairs of bare feet as sheet-draped bodies of the seriously wounded servicemen were lined up in a seemingly lifeless formation of the forgotten. In the foreground was a shirtless, tragic figure slumped over in a wheelchair, with despair as his only companion. My first thought was, *If that were me, then I'd wish I were dead.*

As much as that picture grieved me, I was hardly prepared to deal with the even more depressing, black-and-white photograph that awaited me as I turned to the next page, entitled *"From Vietnam to a VA hospital: Assignment to neglect."* There he sat, naked and alone, strapped in a wheelchair in the shower room, helplessly waiting for someone to dry him off. His name was former Lance Corporal Marke Dumpert, who was "invalidated" from the Marine Corps after being wounded and was now a quadriplegic.

Sadness filtered through my soul. How could we just leave him there, so helpless and alone, like yesterday's trash? Here was the pride of the United States Marine Corps. This man survived one of the most grueling engagements of the war—the Battle of Khe Sanh—before he suffered a near-fatal wound from mortar attack while riding in a jeep on a firebase. Nearby—"In an enema room of the Bronx VA Hospital, disabled spinal injury patients wait up to four hours to be attended by a single aide." Deplorable conditions were also noted at the Wadsworth VA Hospital in Los Angeles, where a photograph showed "a doctor giving a spinal tap braces his patient against a breadbox." Physicians here considered the conditions "medieval" and "filthy." Another photo displayed a handwritten cardboard sign placed above a bed with the words "LEAKY ROOF! Move bed No. 6 when it RAINS! Thank you."

Most of the men referred to in this shameful exposé were paraplegic or quadriplegic. They had given their all when duty called and now desperately needed their country to come to their aid. One must remember that even under the best of circumstances, the vast majority of these wounded would have an uphill battle the rest of their lives. Many would continue to depend on others to care for them and be susceptible to additional medical and psychiatric complications. It was nothing short of immoral to treat them in such a neglectful manner.

Our troops in Vietnam, and now in Iraq and Afghanistan, had a phenomenal survival rate when they were wounded. They received the best medical and nursing care in the field hospitals. That issue has never been in question. It is what happened when they return home and require sustained, long-term care that problems of neglect emerge. As always, it comes down to our federal budget and lack of foresight.

According to the *Life Magazine* article, even the "showcase" VA hospital was noted as understaffed, with a single registered nurse being responsible for the care of as many as eighty veterans. Yet, for some unknown reason, Donald E. Johnson, the Veterans Administration director in 1970, publicly stated that the nation's wounded and suffering warriors received "care second to none." Apparently, Mr. Johnson never ventured through the wards of his own hospital system, the largest in the world, to witness the echoes of despair. A subsequent inquiry by the Senate placed the blame "directly on a series of cutbacks in the VA medical budget." Unfortunately, the rationale for such a travesty could be reduced to two problems: abysmally poor foresight and planning or simply a lack of caring about those who sacrificed their lives for their country. It's probably a combination of both, as lack of concern will ultimately result in haphazard planning. These two ingredients served only to feed one another in a downward spiral of moral decay.

Fast-forwarding from 1970 to 2005, and there is another budgetary crisis concerning the care for our disabled veterans. The cover of the July/August 2005 issue of the *Disabled American Veterans* (*DAV*) magazine presents a caricature of our current federal budget. Seated around a huge pie are pigs and fat cats in suits, gorging themselves on the federal budget pie, with names on the individual slices like "special interest," "pork-barrel spending," and "other special favors." Nearby, a disabled veteran, his leg amputated below the knee, stands with one hand supporting his crutch, while the other hand is holding a plate with a sliver of pie stuck with the sign, "Veterans Health Care." It continues to both baffle and anger me that we would revisit such a scene in our nation's history. Our combat wounded should receive the highest quality of care humanly possible after they have been evacuated from the battlefield, often at great risk to their comrades. There are also those civilian healthcare professionals who work tirelessly and in understaffed conditions to provide the care for veterans when they return home.

I found it hard to believe that the blatant neglect of the Vietnam veterans that was the subject of the *Life Magazine* exposé would be repeated with the wounded men and women of the new millennium. That is, until I read in the *DAV* magazine the shocking news that halfway through fiscal year 2005 the "Veterans Affairs medical facilities across the country have already run out of money and face huge deficits, an emergency situation if there ever was one." The article further notes that VA facilities are "cutting staff and limiting services even as the number of veterans seeking health care is on the rise." The following words of Randy Pleva, Sr., current president of Paralyzed Veterans of America (PVA), hearken back to the *Life Magazine* article of thirty-five years ago.

> PVA is disappointed, and I'm highly upset, by the Senate's failure to provide health care funding to sick and disabled veterans, as well as the new veterans returning from overseas. I can't believe that the Senate would do something like this. Taking care of veterans is an ongoing cost of our national defense and our fight against terrorism. Veterans are being constantly assured by the VA and those in Congress that the VA has the money it needs to meet its responsibilities, but every day we see reports that veterans are being turned away, other veterans are facing unconscionable delays, and entire health care networks are running deficits as a result of attempting to provide health care. Unfortunately, the Senate's vote against veterans sends a clear message to the men and women serving in the military and those contemplating service—we will send you off to fight our wars and defend America, but we don't want to care for you properly when you come home.

I also fear a more insidious and systematic process whereby emotionally troubled veterans will be gradually marginalized over the course of time, even if the proper care is available. Many of the combat veterans will be struggling with posttraumatic stress disorders, much like we did when we returned from Vietnam. Fortunately, we are now much more aware of the disorder and can screen more readily for it. However, it is one thing for a draftee who is already a civilian to seek out treatment and quite another for a professional soldier whose very career depends on performance and promotions in rank. Many of these individuals will, sadly, suffer in silence. This is one of the drawbacks of an all-volunteer military. Underscoring this point, I can recall a feature article in *Newsweek* this past year about the lineage in today's military families. The article noted the growing chasm between the warrior mind-set of our military from the main fabric of society. This makes it especially difficult for a combat veteran to seek help for psychological trauma, as his/her superiors can perceive it as a chink in the warrior's armor.

There have already been a number of inspiring stories in the media about severely wounded men and women and their courageous struggles to regain their lives. Miraculously, some amputees have returned to active duty with artificial limbs. They are to be greatly commended and are an inspiration to Americans everywhere, military or civilian. But the wounded for whom I have the most concern are the ones who sustained some type of head injury in combat.

Already, Traumatic Brain Injury (TBI) has received the dubious distinction of being referred to as the "signature wound" of the current war in Iraq and Afghanistan. Such injuries are more prevalent in combat where the majority of causalities are caused by explosions. My sensitivity and concern for these veterans come from many years of conducting neuropsychological evaluations of patients recovering from head injuries, usually from motor vehicle accidents. It is amazing how an injury that resulted in even a minor alteration in brain function adversely affected an individual's life. In fact, there is an entire subspecialty of neuropsychology within the psychological profession dealing with such disorders. Almost invariably, the one area that is affected is our memory.

A fully healthy individual takes no notice when such cognitive processes as attention, concentration, immediate memory, short-term memory, and long-term memory are operating in relative harmony. However, most traumatic head injuries will affect the memory or other cognitive processes in some fashion. Depending on the site and scope of the injury, it will ultimately impair any of a number of memory processes like learning new information, recalling previously learned material, visual spatial perception, reasoning, language, and others, thereby significantly reducing overall intellectual functioning. Related and emotional aspects of personality, like social judgment, impulse control, and motivation, are usually affected as well. Essentially, the person's core identity and ability to have mature, meaningful relationships is altered, in many cases permanently. Since many of these service men and women have spouses and children, the emotional and financial cost is exponentially that much greater. These individuals and their families will require long-term rehabilitation and care.

If a country sends its young men and women off to war, then at the very least it should be faithful in two things. First, an honest account must be provided about why the individual is being taken from his or her loved ones for an extended period of time, perhaps not to return alive, or to return forever changed. Second, veterans and their families should be awarded the best possible care that our nation can provide for their sacrifice when they return home.

According to folklore, there has always been a certain level of competition between the Army and Marine Corps, especially where members of their respective infantry units were concerned. Some of these competitive strivings have undoubtedly resulted in barroom altercations on more than one occasion. However, the caption under the last photograph in *Life Magazine* about the *Forgotten Wounded* would appear to put all such things in proper perspective.

> At the Bronx VA Hospital Marine veteran Frank Stoppiello, wounded in the Ashau Valley in Vietnam, gives a cigarette to quadriplegic Andrew Kmetz, an Army Veteran, as they wait for treatment. Because of overcrowding, they must share a corner with trashcans.

Semper Fi, my brothers, but God help America!

Invisible Wounds

From time immemorial, the end product of war has always been destruction. The price paid for liberation of a people or defense of a homeland has always been high in terms of the cost in human lives. I was raised by parents who were well acquainted with the horrors of war. My father was twenty-five years old when he was conscripted into the Hungarian Army during World War II to help the Germans stem the tide of the Russian onslaught that was heading west by 1944, straight for his homeland. He was in an infantry unit, which was assigned to a German Panzer Division. He would go on to fight the Russians in the Hungarian uprising of 1956 as a "Freedom Fighter" when they would once again be invading his beloved homeland. I have no memory of him saying anything about his role in either of these major events in his life.

My mother, on the other hand, was quite open about her experiences during the war. I can vividly recall her stocking our pantry with what seemed to be an abundance of canned goods when I was six years old. We could barely open the door to gain entrance. When I approached her about it, she became somewhat emotional and informed me that one should always be ready for an emergency—like a WAR! Since the supermarket where we regularly shopped was within walking distance, her answer was somewhat puzzling to me. For one thing, we were in America, not Europe; for another, we were not engaged in any war. But 1957 was also a time when some Americans were building fallout shelters in case of nuclear attack from Russia. By and large though, while my mother was operating in a hypervigilant state, most of our neighbors were calmly going about shopping for only a week's worth of groceries at a time.

I had no idea of the impact the war had on her mind-set. She was born in Tata, a small village in Hungary. In the closing months of the war, the village changed hands six times between the opposing armies, until the Russians finally prevailed. Her beloved uncle by marriage was Morris Fleischmann, a Jew who was being held with others in 1944 while awaiting deportation to a concentration camp. Knowing that he was hungry, my mother risked taking him some food while he was imprisoned in a holding compound surrounded by barbed wire and patrolled by the SS guards with their frightening dogs. She was immediately arrested and taken to the Gestapo, who planned to execute her the following morning. She pleaded with them that she was a Hungarian citizen who worked for a low-level government official in a nearby town. She was locked in a dark, cold basement and spent the entire night huddled near the door at the top of the stairs. The crack at the bottom of the door provided the only light, along with an equally miniscule amount of heat for comfort. Unashamedly, she told us that she thought about venturing down the stairs to relieve herself, but decided to do her business right where she sat. When morning finally arrived, the illumination through the small basement windows revealed the horror of corpses, which were stacked like cordwood, directly below the stairway where she spent the night. She was forever grateful that she hadn't ventured below. Her story checked out and the Gestapo released her that morning. Tragically, her Uncle Morris, who managed to survive the war in a concentration camp, died from malnutrition a few weeks after he was liberated by American troops. She never forgot the horror of that night and many others that she experienced when she was only seventeen years old.

Over the years, I began to realize that my father was not unusual in maintaining silence about his participation in the war. A number of my friends from childhood, and later on as an adult, had fathers who were just as silent about their war experiences in Europe or the Pacific theater. Although there were a few exceptions, this code of silence seemed to be the norm. I can recall several of the members of my high school fraternity who returned from Vietnam around 1968 and how the word was that somehow they had "changed." We welcomed them back by shaking their hands and passing them a beer. But beyond that, no one knew what to say to them. Occasionally some idiot would ask, "How many people did you kill?" followed by an uneasy period of silence.

One thing was for sure—they had in fact changed. They came around a few times trying to pick up where they left off with our group. But before long, they just stopped coming altogether. Aside from a few safe inquiries, my basic plan was to treat them as if they never left, as if they were "normal." At the time, I believed that this was the right thing to do, even though I sensed that they had changed in some dark, intangible way. They were present with us physically, as they socialized and even laughed along with the rest, but they appeared to be somewhere else whenever we made eye contact. Something happened to them while they were in Vietnam and they were now changed in a way that I did not understand. In all honesty, I lacked the desire and most certainly the capacity to understand. I was just happy that they were back in one piece and now we could continue having fun like the old days. But before long, it was my turn to be the guy they were welcoming back in a similar fashion. My friends were genuinely happy to have me back, but in a way that was consistent with my never having left the neighborhood. The circle was now complete.

The best way for me to forget about Vietnam was work and education, two prosocial activities that allowed me to direct my energies in a productive manner and direction. I plunged myself into my studies at the University of Buffalo while maintaining a full-time job working the third shift at the Terrace House, a shelter for homeless, alcoholic men in downtown Buffalo. Since I was already experiencing difficulty sleeping anyway, this seemed to be a very workable arrangement. I managed to obtain bachelor's and master's degrees in under three and a half years, while working full time at nights. In retrospect however, some of these activities were propelled by a compulsive drive fueled by inner restlessness.

It was during this time around 1974 that I had a chance meeting with one of my former fraternity brothers in a local coffee shop. He served with the U.S. Marine Corps as an infantryman the same year I was in Vietnam. We had met a few times with some former high school fraternity brothers when we first came home, but we never talked about our tours. We both tried to fit in and pick up where we had left off with our friends. Things were no different this time around.

We talked about the other guys and where we were presently working. As we parted, we exchanged platitudes about getting together at some later date. Two days later, I heard his name mentioned on the evening news. He was missing and presumed drowned in the Niagara River. Reportedly, he was drinking while scuba diving near Strawberry Island in the middle of the river. His body was recovered the following day. I was angry that he would be so foolish. As the years went by, I found myself engaged in behaviors that others judged to be just as reckless. By the grace of God, I lived through them.

Whenever we discuss the casualties of war, we invariably focus on those who died or were wounded. These are the statistics that are tallied after each battle or engagement. It is right that immediate attention be given to these numbers, for they provide feedback about the hazards that the troops are presently facing. In treating the wounded, our main objective is to assess and treat physical damage. After all, the medical and nursing personnel are specifically trained to identify damage to the tissue. It is something that can be seen, cut, sutured, and bandaged. Hopefully, with proper treatment, many of the injuries heal over time. But one cannot grow new arms or legs or have vision restored when there is permanent damage to the optic nerve. This is also true for certain spinal injuries that result in paraplegia, quadriplegia, or some other form of paralysis. Stories of the severely wounded who forge ahead with their lives despite numerous obstacles are inspirations for all of us. They are a godsend for fellow veterans who themselves are struggling with combat-related injuries.

Actor Kevin Bacon played the role of a father who lost a leg during the Spanish Civil War in the film *My Life as a Dog*. There was a scene where he was walking through the woods with his eight-year-old son who proudly said, "But Dad, you got a medal for losing your leg." His father responded with a gentle smile, "Son, I'd rather have the leg." But the boy's real hero was the next-door neighbor who happened to be a star athlete. He worshipped this young man who was kind to him and taught him how to play baseball. When World War II broke out, his friend enlisted in the army and was shipped to the European theater. One day the young boy received a package from him containing a German soldier's helmet, something he proudly displayed and which brought him a great deal of popularity with his peers. But he became disillusioned when his idol returned from the war in a less than heroic fashion and isolated himself by abusing alcohol. He finally had a chance confrontation with the war veteran and asked him if it was the fear of dying that bothered him so much during the war, to which his friend quietly answered, "It wasn't the fear of dying; it was the killing."

At the very heart of the matter, we are training and asking our troops to kill another human being. Much of the training deals with dehumanizing the enemy to a level where killing him becomes a natural act, like disposing of a cockroach or rodent. The enemy has no feelings; his only purpose is to kill you. A local combat veteran who served two tours in Vietnam as an army infantryman quoted his platoon sergeant as saying, "Our business is killing, and business is very good."

Hardly a month goes by when the professional newspapers or journals that I subscribe to don't mention something about posttraumatic stress disorder (PTSD) in reference to the troops deployed to Afghanistan or Iraq. Historically, war has always taken a sizeable toll on the soldiers who participated in combat—killing or seeing others killed. But it wasn't until 1985 that the American Psychiatric Association actually developed the diagnosis to help explain the mental impact of war on Vietnam veterans. Unfortunately, this was ten years after the war officially ended and a full twenty years after the war first began. But at least there was now a diagnosis that listed some of the signs and symptoms the veterans were experiencing many years after they returned home. The diagnosis was now officially in the Diagnostic and Statistical Manual of Mental Disorders (DSM).

This DSM is useful for diagnosing patients and assigning them a particular code. This is for their clinical record as well as well as for billing an insurance company for reimbursement. It also provides a generally accepted form of communication within the mental health community. However, it is based upon the "medical model," which focuses on specific signs and symptoms in order for a diagnosis to be made. In the case of PTSD, the diagnostic process begins with the person having been "exposed to a traumatic event or events that involved actual or threatened death or serious injury, or a threat to the physical integrity of self or others," and "the person's response involved intense fear, helplessness, or horror." Once it has been established that this in fact did occur, it is followed by an inquiry by the clinician to determine if there are any ongoing repercussions from the trauma in the person's life. Some of these include intrusive recollections, distressing dreams, flashbacks, avoiding activities that are related to the trauma, problems with emotional intimacy, sleep difficulties, irritability or angry outbursts, hypervigilance, etc. Finally, it has to be determined whether "the disturbance causes clinically significant distress or impairment in social, occupational, or other important areas of functioning."

How this "disturbance" plays out in an individual's life is based upon an interplay of factors unique to the person and his or her present life circumstances. For instance, I can recall almost failing my doctoral program in psychology in 1977 for a reason that utterly baffled me at the time. Even now, as I view a copy of my graduate transcripts, the grade D (unheard of in graduate school) stands in stark contrast to the mostly As marked with an occasional B listed in the document—courses such as advanced research and statistics, clinical psychology, factor analysis, and physiological psychology. Courses that are noted for a high level of difficulty were some of the ones that received the highest grade. Apparently, my intellectual functioning was reasonably intact. The one that was graded a D was a course called the Psychology of Aging and Death, and it was being taught by a new faculty member. Since this person was also on my dissertation committee, it was highly recommended that I take the course.

Initially, I had no problem with the title and figured it was going to be less intellectually demanding than other courses I had taken since it was also open to upper level undergraduates. The class ended up being composed of an equal number of graduate and undergraduate students. I can still recall one of the humorous and incisive comments one of the graduate students made about eulogies in general. He sarcastically noted that the deceased is invariably portrayed with a glowing tribute, regardless if the person was a scoundrel while he was alive. In addition to class attendance, the bulk of the course grade was based on two unusual projects. As a group we were required to attend a funeral home and observe the practice of mortuary science. I could not muster up the wherewithal to view a corpse again, so I did not go. We also had to write a personalized account of how we would like our own funeral service to be conducted.

The day the paper was due, I hurriedly managed to submit a handwritten half page of how I would want to be buried in a navy blue pin-striped suit. Although I never owned such a suit—I just remembered how nice one looked in the store window during a trip to Toronto in 1969 when I was giving serious consideration to joining the ranks of draft dodgers residing there. I had no explanation for my behavior and the professor had little choice but to give me a D, which is a failing grade in graduate school. I was emotionally frozen and avoided dealing with the topic of death as much as possible. The baffling part was that I couldn't even begin to identify the cause of my behavior. I didn't want to do the assignments, but I was at a loss to explain why. I believe the professor felt slighted, wrongly believing that it was sheer defiance on my part. This unexplained aberration placed a wedge between us that remained for the duration of my studies at the university.

The DSM describes the full spectrum of mental disorders that are experienced by the American public, ranging from schizophrenia, depression, personality disorders, and dementia, to various sexual dysfunctions, and ailments that are induced by licit and illicit drugs. In all, there are hundreds of diagnosable conditions for children and adults, to which each succeeding revision expands the growing list over the years. A copy of the manual is readily available at Barnes & Noble or may be purchased on the Internet. Its major strength is that it is descriptive in nature, allowing treatment targeting of specific symptoms for mental health practitioners. Unfortunately, this does not come without a price. According to Dr. Stanley Greenspan, "Concern among clinicians that the DSM approach, which is based on symptoms and surface phenomena rather than on a fuller range of feelings, beliefs, and thoughts, falls short as a foundation for clinicians and research work, and has fueled the trend in mental health care toward short-term, medication-based treatment." In an effort to complement the DSM, the Psychodynamic Diagnostic Manual (PDM) was recently published and had significant input from the various mental health professions. Dr. Greenspan notes that the purpose of the PDM is "to add breadth and depth to a diagnostic system (DSM) that has moved too far toward a reductionist view of human nature and experience." He further notes that the PDM "goes beyond the classification of disorder to such dimensions of human experience as the … capacity for relationships; quality of internal experience; and affective experience, expression, and communication

… a sense of 'unique signature' of each individual's experience of symptoms." His hope is that it will help clinicians "know the whole person" they are dealing with in a more systematic manner. [3]

Along with others in the mental health profession, I have been frustrated with the one-dimensional nature of the DSM diagnostic classification. It wasn't until I read a book by A.W. Tozer entitled *The Pursuit of God* that I was confronted with the timeless account of the inner struggle of one human being in a deeper way. He was describing the anguish experienced by Abraham the night before he was to sacrifice his son, Isaac, as instructed by God. Abraham's drama echoed the torment of someone who is about to commit an act that went against the very grain of his being—to kill another human. Although the fact that it was his own son that made his dilemma all the more painful, his mental agony is one for the ages. Tozer incisively described the core of this human drama as "made of *living spiritual tissue*; it is composed of the sentient, quivering stuff of which our whole being consists, and to touch it is to touch us where we feel pain. To tear it away is to injure us, to hurt us and make us bleed." [4]

The term "living spiritual tissue" is something that helps to describe the real wounds suffered by those who have experienced the horror of combat. It is this wounded invisible "tissue" that is the violation of the soul that is borne by the soldier. For example, Staff Sergeant Jesus Arriaga, who was on the cover of a news publication of the American Psychiatric Association, was interviewed about responding to the suicide bombing that killed three female Marines in June 2005. The article stated, "The horror of what he saw haunts him." It is such descriptors as "horror" and "haunts" that begin to describe the lacerations that are inflicted within the interior realm. Nine months afterwards, an Army veteran of the Iraq War describes himself as "feeling dead inside." These and many other Iraq and Afghan veterans who suffer these invisible wounds are professional soldiers who were better trained than many of the units that served in Vietnam. Yet, they are still "cursed" with being decent human beings, called to carry out or witness things that have the potential to defile their very soul—then doomed to carry this burden for the rest of their lives.

Visions of Daffodils

Midway through the TV program *Biography* that I was viewing several years ago came a quote from F. Scott Fitzgerald, "Show me a hero, and I'll show you a tragedy." Haunting words to be sure, especially when the program was about the most decorated American combat veteran of World War II, Audie Murphy. Along with the Medal of Honor, he received every decoration for valor, some more than once, that could be awarded by his country. For the first few years after his discharge from the army he had difficulty finding a job and ended up sleeping in a gymnasium, living off the disability pension he received for his war injuries. A few sympathetic men felt it was unacceptable and a national disgrace to have a Medal of Honor recipient living under these conditions and were instrumental in helping to launch his movie career.

His autobiography *To Hell and Back* became a bestseller, and his acting career was modestly successful. Then in 1955 he starred in a movie by the same title which was essentially about his conspicuous combat career in the European theater. It became the highest-grossing motion picture for Universal-International Studio until the movie *Jaws* was released in 1975. Unfortunately, his family and friends, as well as Audie himself, came to the realization that he never really came "back."

Although he came from very humble beginnings as the son of poor Texas sharecroppers, he had a remarkable career. He was successful not only as an actor, but also as a movie director, racehorse owner and breeder, poet, and songwriter. But for all of his external accomplishments, he continued to suffer from depression and insomnia—hallmark symptoms of PTSD. He became addicted to a prescription sleep medication for seven years, finally locking himself in a hotel room for a five-day agonizing and life-threatening detoxification. As his acting career began to fade, he became addicted to gambling to "feel alive," as he was quoted saying. Most of his free time he spent lying in bed in the converted garage that was attached to his family home with a .45 automatic weapon next to his bed. He was welcome to join the family at any time but rarely did so. For nearly twenty years, his busy movie career helped to stave off some of the ghosts of war. Now, with more time on his hands, they were managing to make their presence known in full force. He continued to be sporadically involved in movies and had just completed producing and starring in his last motion picture, *A Time for Dying*, when he called a close friend who was a director. Audie informed him that the movie was finished and that he was sitting by the phone with his loaded gun and was now ready to "blow my brains out." His friend severely admonished him by challenging him to do it and consider what impact it would have on all the kids in the country who idolized him. Apparently this struck a nerve and Audie began cursing at his friend and hung up the phone—a life-saving case of anger suddenly turned outward. His friend's ploy had worked, as Audie decided against suicide. Tragically, he died a short time later as a passenger in the crash of a private airplane.

Audie Murphy hardly looked the part of the great warrior. However, the hundreds of German soldiers who he was credited with killing, wounding, or capturing would probably beg to differ. He was rather diminutive in stature and had an innocent, boyish face that was mild even by Vienna Boys Choir standards. So much for appearances, much like the contrast that existed between his successful career and the battle with demons that had haunted him since he returned from the war. It is doubtful if there will ever be another military hero the magnitude of Audie Murphy. As young boys playing "war" in our backyards and around the Museum of Science, we emulated this remarkable man and were oblivious to his inner pain and near suicide. I often fantasized how intoxicating it would be to bask in such glory. This train of thought from childhood followed me on my flight to Vietnam, until the reality of war and death swiftly blotted it from memory. There is no way I could have anticipated the horror and the impact it would have on my being.

Ultimately, the specific effect combat trauma will have on an individual may well be as unique as a fingerprint. The DSM lists some of the common denominators, but they are general descriptors void of personal signatures. It is becoming clearer to the mental health community that PTSD has multiple determinants, no surprise to anyone with a basic understanding of Freudian psychoanalytic theory. The manner in which the specifics of combat trauma play out in an individual are determined by the interplay of a number of variables, including genetics, temperament, environment, extent of exposure to combat, and social support over the course of time. The Vietnam War introduced a new variable—the country's negative perception and reaction to the fighting soldier and the returning veteran. The conflict over the war itself on the home front, coupled with the public's mistreatment of the returning troops, helped to fuel the veteran's avoidance of dealing with the emotional aftermath it had on him. Dr. Robert Jay Lifton, a pioneering psychiatrist who was treating Vietnam veterans while the war was still in progress, authored a classic text on the subject entitled *Home from the War: Learning from Vietnam Veterans.* Psychologists and psychiatrists gleaned much of their material from thousands of hours in rap groups with combat veterans that they facilitated. One of the most startling revelations made by some of the veterans, was that somehow it would bring dishonor to their comrades who died in battle if a nation decided to withdraw its soldiers prior to securing "total victory." Lifton readily noted that politicians, "armchair warriors," and misguided combat veterans, in an effort to "honor" those who were killed in combat, have appealed to this sort of warrior ethos with remarkable effectiveness.

The book described a severe case of PTSD with the tragic story of Medal of Honor recipient Army Sergeant Dwight W. Johnson who rescued a buddy from a burning tank moments before it exploded, killing his other friends who were stuck inside. Acting on the rage that was unleashed within, he hunted down and killed up to twenty North Vietnamese soldiers in close quarters. He received psychiatric care for "depression caused by post-Vietnam adjustment problem." He continued to suffer from "persistent bad dreams" and survival guilt because his friends died. His treating psychiatrist related that he was tormented for "winning a high honor for the one time in his life when he lost complete control of himself." He was plagued by the fear of losing control in a similar manner while he was a civilian back in Detroit. A grocery store manager, who alleged that Johnson drew a gun on him in an armed robbery attempt, shot and killed him in 1971. According to his obituary in the New York Times, May 29, 1971, his mother stated, "Sometimes I wonder if Skip (Sergeant Johnson) tired of this life and needed someone else to pull the trigger."

Another tragic ending concerned Major Edward Alan Brudno, a fighter pilot who was shot down over North Vietnam in 1965. He was held captive as a prisoner of war for seven and a half years. He was allowed to write to his wife during this extended period of confinement. Two of his "dream sheets," a detailed description of his plans when he was reunited with his family, were published in the book *Dear America: Letters Home from Vietnam.* He wrote these letters only a week before his return home. Major Brudno committed suicide four months after his release. It was the day before his thirty-third birthday.

Not surprisingly, some have questioned the whole concept of PTSD as a legitimate diagnostic entity. Already a classic, *Stolen Valor: How the Vietnam Generation Was Robbed of its Heroes and its History* has made a significant contribution to dispelling many of the myths and misconceptions of the Vietnam veterans that have proliferated over the years. Moreover, the authors, B. G. Burkett and Glenda Whitley, have rightly exposed the scores of phonies that tarred the image of those who served in the war. They described the slipshod method employed by the Veterans Administration at the time in awarding PTSD disability claims to veterans who were never engaged in combat. But I believe that the authors may have gone too far in the opposite direction as they greatly minimized the disorder, if not altogether questioning its legitimacy. In presenting a lopsided view of the entire concept, they may have placed unnecessary barriers in the paths of individuals who continue to suffer silently from the trauma that war has left on their psyches. Since the book was published in 1998, it would be interesting to know how these authors would explain the high rates of PTSD and suicide of our returning troops from Iraq and Afghanistan. Although Burkett is a Vietnam veteran who honorably served as an ordinance supply officer, he admittedly did not experience the horrors of combat nor is he a mental health professional. Consequently, he is not in a position to discuss the impact of combat trauma from either a personal or professional perspective. Adding insult to injury, the authors even attempted to discredit any antiwar activism by highly decorated war heroes, as well as the Vietnam Veterans against the War movement, which was composed of a large number of combat-decorated veterans.

A more recent work, *Flashback: Posttraumatic Stress Disorder, Suicide, and the Lessons of War* (2006) by Penny Coleman, is an incisively written book by a photographer who was married to a Vietnam veteran suffering from PTSD who eventually committed suicide. In addition to sharing her own personal struggles over the years, she includes poignant narratives of other women who are finding themselves in similar situations as their family members are returning from tours in Iraq and Afghanistan. She strongly believes that the military is either denying or minimizing PTSD and its long-term impact on returning troops.

I certainly do not believe that everyone who was involved in combat has a death wish that will ultimately end up in his or her demise. However, it is my contention that for most of us war is an unnatural act and, if we participate in actual combat where killing is involved, it will fundamentally alter our souls. The specific manner in which this is done will depend on a number of individual characteristics that were previously mentioned. For example, I sincerely doubt that anyone reading this book is acquainted with someone who captured poisonous snakes with his bare hands as a way of engaging in thrill-seeking behaviors. But that is exactly what I did four years after returning from Vietnam.

I had just married and moved to Hattiesburg, Mississippi, in 1975 at the age of twenty-five to start my PhD in psychology at the University of Southern Mississippi. Donna and I moved there during the month of August. I was immediately mesmerized by the heat, humidity, and semi-tropical foliage. Living near a swamp only enticed me further into venturing into this high-risk activity. I had always enjoyed searching for snakes as a boy in the Buffalo area near where we lived. However, these specimens were limited to harmless garter snakes. Occasionally, I would come upon a smooth-scaled green snake or ring-tailed decay snake. A special treat would be the rare find of a milk snake, which was actually a subspecies of king snake, the only constrictor type in our region.

However, some of the rules had been changed. To begin with, the last time I was snake hunting (somewhat of a misnomer, since I released them unharmed), I was twelve years old. Moreover, I knew that the area in Mississippi where we were now residing was the natural habitat for all three species of pit vipers that are native to the United States—rattlesnakes, water moccasins, and copperheads. I could feel the adrenaline rush as I was preparing for my first venture into the swamp. I told my wife that I was just going for a stroll as I began to carefully walk the narrow trail that led me toward my destination. Before long, I was in the stalking mode with a stick that had a V shaped end to secure the head of the snake.

My first capture was a large water moccasin that I discovered sunning himself in a small glade, a short distance from a muddy pool. I remember observing him in wonder and in the beauty of his wild, natural element. He was a truly magnificent creature! I had come there to capture him but I was the one captivated by his deadly beauty. All I know is that I wanted to feel him, and the adrenaline was rushing through my veins. I was now operating on instinct as I carefully laid the stick aside and ever so slowly approached his coiled body basking in the sunlight. For some inexplicable reason, I felt compelled to capture him with my bare hands. He was surprised and angry as I made the one-handed grab around the back of his head, essentially neutralizing his poisonous fangs. After a brief period of admiring his raw, dangerous beauty, I released him unharmed. Since I wasn't always able to approach the snakes unnoticed, it became even more thrilling to determine the extent of their strike range and then go in for the capture after they tired of striking at me and their reaction time began to slow down. Most of the time the snake just wanted to escape, but I was fairly successful at blocking his path. My wife was the only one who eventually became privy to my high-risk behavior. I promised numerous times to stop but always returned for more. It wasn't just the poisonous snakes that were alluring, but the jungle-like feel of the terrain and the potential danger that awaited my arrival. These intense visceral payoffs called me back for repeated doses of adrenaline rush for the next eighteen months.

Finally, and mercifully, I was bitten on the thumb by a copperhead within fifty feet of the house that we were renting at the time. Ironically, it was also the only time that I was handling a poisonous snake with the "assistance" of my neighbor. I immediately attended to my injury but was not prepared for the excruciating pain that rapidly followed. My entire left arm swelled to double its original girth. The pain felt as if someone had intravenously injected lava into my veins. Fortunately, a neighbor was able to drive me to Forrest County Hospital in nearby Hattiesburg. I was hospitalized for four days, mainly because I had an allergic reaction to the antivenin. I also needed plastic surgery and a skin graft to repair the tissue damage to my thumb. My snake-chasing days came to an abrupt halt. I was informed that next time I would be better off taking my chances dealing with the venom, as the next allergic reaction to the antidote could be fatal. Another hard lesson learned by a very thickheaded man. Although this happened in 1977, my pride takes a well-deserved beating every time someone confronts me in a pharmacy or medical procedure inquiring if I am allergic to any medicine. I get the strangest looks when my written or verbal response is yes—antivenin. It's no mystery that there is only one way to make such a discovery.

Based upon my clinical and personal experience, I truly believe that there are many combat veterans who experience PTSD in some way, shape, or form. I have met some veterans who were so disabled that they were unable to maintain a semblance of normalcy in their lives. However, in one major area, I concur with Burkett and Whitley, authors of the book *Stolen Valor*. They did a commendable and much-needed exposé of the fakers who capitalized on the Hollywood image of the Vietnam veteran and duped the psychiatrists and psychologists in the Veterans Administration Healthcare system. It's an unfortunate blight on the mental health professions that they failed to corroborate their claims with their personnel files. Their military records were anything but consistent with the stories of their combat exploits. While there were many combat veterans who wanted desperately to forget about Vietnam and blend in with society, there were those who lied or exaggerated their war experience and grew deep roots within the veterans' medical system. Some of these individuals were never in Vietnam or were assigned to units or areas that were not directly participating in combat roles. Some went so far as to claim that their assignments were so top secret that no records were kept of their missions "behind enemy lines."

Most combat veterans generally avoid discussion of their painful memories of war. For its part, society has inadvertently encouraged this "let sleeping dogs lie" philosophy. Therefore, it is no surprise that interviews with those who participated in Normandy and Iwo Jima sixty years ago frequently end up with the old veteran getting choked up as he describes the man next to him who was killed. Long-buried emotions are seizing an opportunity for expression and integration. I remember meeting with an old friend about twenty years ago. He was a combat medic who was in Vietnam the same year that I was. We talked about old times over dinner, but neither of us made any reference to our tours in Vietnam. Instinctively, we avoided broaching the subject, much like our World War II brethren. It wasn't until we were in the parking lot, under the streetlight where our cars were parked, and ready to part company, that I mentioned the subject. I vividly recall the tail end of my words, "Doesn't it seem like it was all a dream?" My friend pensively looked at me and responded, "No, that was real. All this seems like a dream," and we parted until our next meeting fifteen years later.

Obviously, I never forgot our brief exchange, as the words managed to surface periodically over the years. It's as if the entire Vietnam experience was so intense and surrealistic that it somehow became the inner reference point by which ensuing experiences were filtered. Phenomena with such a foundationally unsettling capacity remind me of another of Freud's discoveries—primary versus secondary forms of thought. Primary process thinking is considered primitive, not regulated by such dimensions as time and space. This type of thought "is preverbal, expressing itself in images and symbols ... it is also prelogical, having no concept of time, mortality, limitation, or the impossibility that opposites can coexist.... It survives in the language of dreams, jokes, and hallucinations." It is the stuff of which dreams are made, "the royal road to the unconscious." For example, when we initially wake up from a particularly vivid or disturbing dream, it feels very real, sometimes even more so because of its intensity, compared to our familiar daily stream of consciousness. However, since it "doesn't make sense," we can readily dismiss it and "go on with our lives."

In direct contrast, secondary process thinking is what provides our individual lives and civilization with direction and stability. It is the structural foundation of all that guides our communication and inter-action with the external world of other people and the rest of the environment that we live in. Language, speech, rational thought, memory, planning, judgment, and impulse control are some of the main areas mediated by secondary process thinking. This unusual conversation with my Vietnam veteran buddy felt as if we were teetering somewhere between these two realms of the mind—primary and secondary process thought. This mental zone is often referred to as "derealization" within the field of psychiatry, "an alteration in the perception of experience of the external world so that it seems strange or unreal." Somehow we were able to compartmentalize this primitive and disturbing imagery of war and go about our daily lives. In a very real sense, however, we were denying a part of ourselves; we wanted to live as if all this never happened—like it was a bad dream and grist for the mechanism of forgetting and denial. Such intensely violent imagery was too much for us to bear, especially in the isolation that we, along with many others, had grown accustomed to after we returned home.

I noticed that I was becoming irritable and difficult to live with while writing these past few chapters, particularly this one. It was not just limited to inner restlessness; my wife graciously confirmed that I was "very much on edge." As I happened to share this dilemma with my friend Bill Stott, he readily quoted a verse from the poem *Daffodils* by Wordsworth that he recalled from his youth.

> For oft, when on my couch I lie
> In vacant or in pensive mood,
> They flash upon that inward eye
> Which is the bliss of solitude;
> And my heart with pleasure fills,
> And dances with the daffodils.

My friend quoted this piece, with particular focus on the words "They flash upon the inward eye," referring to the "inward eye" as the seat of imagery. He noted that the poet, during his repose and un-guarded moments, was enjoying the pleasant images of this flower that were soothing his soul. But the inward eye of those exposed to the horrors of war view images that have a totally different impact on their inner being. When a certain Medal of Honor recipient of the Vietnam War was interviewed about how it feels to be a hero, he nervously answered, "I tell people that I am no hero, why here I am as a grown man, and I'm still afraid of the dark … maybe because I know what could be out there."

Eleanor Grace

It was August 2004 and I was approaching the campus at D'Youville College, located near the Peace Bridge that connects the United States with our Canadian neighbors. The experience brought back memories as I drove by this grand structure on my way to the college. I recalled frequently crossing that bridge during the summer of '69 when I was tempted to remain in Canada and join the growing ranks of draft dodgers.

Since it was summer, there were relatively few students walking about the college campus. I parked my car and continued on to an interview with some faculty members in the Nursing Department. I was at the point in my life when I seriously considered applying for a full-time teaching position. I was a nurse practitioner, as well as a clinical psychologist, and I felt fortunate to have had such an opportunity. I casually walked up the stairs inside the Health Sciences Building and turned the corner to catch the elevator to the fifth floor en route to my meeting. I had just pressed the elevator button when my eyes became fixed on a memorial plaque located on the wall to my immediate left, with the following inscription:

In Memory of
Eleanor Grace Alexander, RN

Capt. U.S. Army
Killed Nov 30, 1967
In Line of Duty
Qui Nhon, Vietnam

"Our boys are dying over there, and they need nurses to care for them. I want to go."

I ended up accepting an assistant professorship for one year at the college before I returned to my first love—clinical practice. It was a memorable year as I met some fine people and tried my hand at academia. As a frequent passenger on the elevator, I couldn't help but glance at the name on the plaque, regardless of how large the crowd was that was waiting with me or how much of a hurry I was in. I often wondered if anyone else noticed the plaque. One day I posed the question to a class of freshman and sophomores enrolled in an entry-level nursing class. To my surprise and disappointment, no one had ever heard of her. Rest assured, they became acquainted with her and her sacrifice on that very day. Like most schools in our high-tech society, students practice their multimedia lifestyles as they walk through the campus, connected to their cell phones. One of the unfortunate by-products of all our technology seems to be a dimming awareness of the richness of our immediate environment.

It wasn't long before I inquired about Eleanor Grace from one of my neighbors on the fifth floor wing of the nursing department. Professor Judith Stanley was in the adjacent office and she informed me that a special memorial service was held each year on November 30, the day Eleanor Grace was killed. The faculty felt that it was important for the school to recall and honor the sacrifice she made to her country and particularly to wounded soldiers. Nursing students are especially encouraged to attend. A representative from the Student Nurses Association places a wreath beneath the bronze plaque next to the elevator. Each year, a scholarship in her name is awarded to a nursing student who exemplifies service to others.

Captain Alexander was a 1961 graduate of the D'Youville Department of Nursing. She was in the U.S. Army Nurse Corps and insisted on going to Vietnam so she could help the wounded. She was stationed with the 85th Evacuation Hospital but volunteered for temporary assignment in Pleiku to help with the heavy casualities suffered from the battle of Dak To. She was one of twenty-six Americans onboard a Caribou aircraft that was diverted to Nha Trang. Their airplane crashed into a mountainside about five miles south of Qui Nhon and there were no survivors. She died while serving others and was posthumously awarded a Bronze Star for Meritorious Service. She was twenty-seven years old when she died. I was deeply touched by a letter that was entered on her Vietnam Veteran Memorial Web page. A childhood friend, Brian Mulcare, wrote it.

The Game of WAR!

Dear Eleanor:

I've missed you these past four decades. What I remember most was our time together on "THE STOOP" in front of my family's house. The Korean War was going on in '52; I was 5 years old, you were 12. I preferred to consider you my friend rather than Baby-Sitter. We were watching my older brothers and their pals play a game called "WAR." We were not permitted to play this GAME, I was too young and you were a *GIRL*—Even though you could easily keep up with the boys of your age. It was a simple, tag-like game using a Spalding ball and a manhole cover. We were never "IT!"! The players were in an age bracket that missed the "DRAFT"—although my brother Dennis did enlist in the Marine Corps, he got out before THE NAM heated up. Irony is in full force here, for the observers of the game of WAR were actual participants in the real thing. We spoke last in the spring of '67 and wrote while you were in-country. I had just returned to Camp Lejeune, N.C. and my Mom died in Oct. '67. You sent me a condolence card from NAM. A month later you were gone also. It was a double loss for me, you were much a part of my family. Semper Fidelis, Eleanor. I miss you.

Love, Brian (Mulcare)
Cpl. USMC, 3rd Force Recon. '69

Learning about Eleanor Grace made me aware of a group that I had not previously given much consideration—women who served and died in Vietnam. Over six thousand women served in the military and in numerous civilian roles in Vietnam during the course of the war. The vast majority were nurses. In total, sixty-eight were killed—fifty-nine civilians and nine military. All nine of the women in the military who died were nurses—eight American and one Australian. I began to feel a tremendous sense of gratitude for all the nurses and physicians who served. Undoubtedly, they witnessed some horrific scenes of our dead and dying soldiers who were transported to field hospitals. As combat veterans, they had to carry these scenes and faces with them as they returned home. Perhaps more than many others, they had a more intimate exposure to the horrors of war.

KIA in Iraq

It had been several years since I had been confronted with the ghosts of Vietnam. The war in Iraq had been going on for over a year and the steadily mounting casualties were troubling me. About six or seven soldiers and marines had been killed this past year from the Buffalo area. The local media covered their stories with the usual family interviews and military funerals, as they were honored for their ultimate sacrifice. By this time, several things were going through my mind concerning the war. Having had intimate contact with families who lost loved ones in Vietnam over thirty years ago, I wondered how present survivors were dealing with their losses and I continued to pray for them. I was also concerned about the returning troops, especially those involved in direct combat roles of killing or witnessing the death of others firsthand. While there were differences between Vietnam and the current war in Iraq and Afghanistan, the trauma and fear of death had remained the same— it changes a person on the inside —it becomes a mark indelibly etched on one's soul. It was at this point that I began to reflect on how God might make me useful to these broken people.

I was sitting in front of the TV in early April 2004, engaged in my usual channel surfing. I stopped on one of the local news stations and heard the tail end of a story that shocked me into disbelief. The news report briefly showed a photo of a soldier with his wife and infant son, while announcing that he had just been killed in action in Iraq. It is while I found myself drawn to the screen that the newscaster announced, "Sgt. David McKeever was scheduled to complete his tour in two weeks." I was in emotional shock. I had known this soldier since he was ten years old. I had spoken with his older sister a few months ago, inquiring about him and his father, a friend of mine who was also a Vietnam veteran. It has been a few years since we had any contact with one another. She told me that David was married to a girl from Nebraska and had a baby boy, that he was in the Army and had been stationed in Iraq, and that he would be coming home soon.

I turned the TV off and sat on the couch in a silent, trance-like state. My little dachshund, Funny Face, sensing something was wrong, began to lick my hand in her effort to comfort me. I was numb. My mind drifted back to a particular afternoon about fifteen years ago that I spent with him and his younger brother, Tommy. I was teaching them how to quietly and carefully approach a small pond, so as not to disturb the wildlife—quite a challenge for nine- and ten-year-old boys. In this manner, we could all observe and enjoy the turtles, fish, and other woodland inhabitants that came to the water's edge.

The *Buffalo News* had the following write-up:

> David McKeever, a Vietnam veteran who was wounded in that war three decades ago, told a friend he was finally just starting to feel confident about his son who was sent to fight in Iraq last year. The 61-year-old veteran had good reason for saying goodbye to the jitters. His son, Army Sgt. David M. McKeever, was scheduled to leave Iraq on April 21. "I thought, I survived Vietnam and my son survived Iraq." The calmness was shattered Tuesday when he received word that his 25-year-old son was killed by a rocket-propelled grenade while on patrol with seven other soldiers in Baghdad on Monday night.
>
> McKeever, killed on April 5, was 15 days away from leaving Iraq and returning to his wife, Niki, a native of Kearney, Neb., and son Dylan. He joined the Army immediately after graduating from South Park High School in 1997. He was a member of the Army's 1st Armored Division and also served in Bosnia. McKeever is also survived by his parents, David, a Vietnam veteran, and Carol; a younger brother Thomas; and four sisters, Heather, Pam, Colleen and Carolyn.

He was very close to his younger brother Thomas (Tommy), and the newspaper quoted some of his thoughts and feelings.

Thomas McKeever, 24, of Buffalo, said in his eulogy that David was "a loving father, a devoted husband and a dedicated soldier. He served our country with honor and dignity and made us all feel proud of him." He recalled that his brother loved dogs and owned a golden retriever named Jazmyn. "When he'd go to the drive-through at McDonald's, he would order the dog a cheeseburger."

During the ensuing months after his son's military funeral, David and I had a number of lengthy telephone conversations. He would invariably get choked up whenever we talked about his son. We finally agreed to set aside an afternoon together and meet at the Small Boat Harbor in Lake Erie. We would take a boat ride in my sixteen-foot aluminum fishing boat. It was a beautiful, sunny afternoon, and a light breeze was blowing across the lake.

Since it was early afternoon, we had the lake and harbor area to ourselves. It's amazing how therapeutic a boat ride can be. In no time at all, one is magically transformed by the gentle, undulating motion of the waves. Over the years, I have taken a number of people in my boat, mostly to do some small-mouth bass fishing. Without exception, our conversations seem to take on an entirely different quality compared to the ones we have on shore. It was no different with David. Before long, we began to talk about our combat experiences in Vietnam—something we had never done before. Funny how you can know someone for so long and never share some of the most life-changing events you carry with you. Such was the case between my family and friends and me for many lonely years.

It was the first time I heard how he got wounded in 1966, while serving with the 4th Armored Cavalry Regiment of the First Infantry Division. He was driving his armored personnel carrier down a road and noticed a slight depression across the middle. He alerted his lieutenant, who was riding with him, that it looked suspicious and strongly urged him to order the column around it. Unfortunately, the officer insisted that he proceed straight ahead. The next thing David remembered was waking up in a rice paddy with a medic holding his head up so he wouldn't drown in the shallow water. Suddenly, he began to laugh out loud, telling me that he was afraid because his first thought as he regained consciousness was, "I'm really in trouble now for getting drunk and driving this thing into a ditch." He relied on the medic to explain what had happened. Then, in a very somber tone, he told me that he was the only survivor—the rest of the crew, including the lieutenant, was killed instantly.

It's still a mystery to him how he ended up in the rice paddy, a considerable distance from his vehicle. During his initial stay at the base hospital, he noticed a group of soldiers milling around the wreckage of an armored vehicle. He managed to go outside and join them and overheard an officer say, "It's hard to believe that there was one soldier who actually lived through this." He heard several of the men mention that they would really like to meet this guy, and David chimed in with them. "He's right here with us," said the officer, and everyone turned to look at the man standing directly behind him. David, who was standing behind everyone else, couldn't help but look to see if the man in question might be behind him, when the officer spoke up, "I don't know what you're looking for Mckeever, you're the man I'm talking about!" That was the first time he heard that his whole crew perished in the explosion. Moreover, he couldn't even recognize what remained of his own armored personnel carrier.

We spent about three hours on the boat. It was the first time we had gotten to really know each other. Afterwards, he invited me over to his car to look at some pictures of David, spanning the course of his abbreviated life. There were childhood scenes of opening presents on Christmas and Birthdays with the family, swimming in the backyard pool, and as a soldier with his wife, Niki, son, Dylan, and dog, Jazmyn. One of the striking features about the photos was that he and his brother, Tommy, seemed inseparable. I slowly took in each picture, carefully listening to David's tender commentary about his son, as he fought the tears, often unsuccessfully. But one picture seemed to stand out from all the rest for me. It was one of David at 8, wearing a uniform and a tender smile, proudly displaying the Cub Scout salute with his right hand.

As these delicate moments with David unfolded in his car, I recalled an art exhibit by Vietnam veterans that I had attended about twenty years earlier. A gifted artist and Vietnam veteran, Thomas Bashford, was displaying some unique pen and ink drawings. I bought several of them and they are still hanging on our living room wall. Interestingly, they have absolutely nothing to do with Vietnam, typical of most of his artwork. But there was one masterpiece that he had on display that particular day which captivated me with its haunting lure. This one *was about* the war, in a soul-piercing way. Actually, they were eight separate drawings portrayed in developmental sequence, tracing the rites of passage of an American boy. The first drawing depicted proud parents holding their infant son, followed by baby's first steps into his parents' waiting arms, his first haircut at the barber shop, going up to bat at a baseball game, his first junior high dance, driving his jalopy, in his Army uniform, and finally, a flag-draped coffin. These were the memories—pictures in the mind—left for surviving loved ones to ponder for a lifetime.

There is a very cruel irony to this father and son who were both awarded the Purple Heart; David Sr. was the only survivor of his crew in 1966 while his son, David, was the only one who died in his Humvee some thirty-seven years later.

Sometime after our boat ride I received a small package from David. The contents included a copy of the very same picture of his son in his Cub Scout uniform. How did he know, in the middle of his own grief, that this one was my favorite?

Sgt. David McKeever

It wasn't long before I received a phone call from David inviting me to attend a fundraiser for his son's widow, Niki, who was flying in from Nebraska. It was to be held in South Buffalo, at the American Legion Post # 64 on South Park Avenue. It was fitting since this is the neighborhood where David grew up and attended high school. I wanted to meet Niki and offer whatever words of comfort might be appropriate. David and the rest of the family had maintained regular contact with her and little Dylan, his grandson. In some ways, my expectations were different from when I met Bill Wood's widow thirty-two years after his death. She had been remarried to a wonderful, loving man with whom she had a daughter in college. Niki had been recently widowed and had a surviving son from her fallen husband. The loss was all too recent, just four months ago, and she would be in a different stage of the grieving process.

Buffalo is a wonderfully diverse city with a rich representation of people from various racial, ethnic, and cultural backgrounds. It is truly the city of good neighbors. As such, it is noted for having a great variety of ethnic cuisine and activities. If there is one thing that I learned over the years about an Irish event, it's that it is anything but subdued. The American Legion Post # 64 is located in the very heart of a neighborhood with a healthy concentration of Irish-American citizens, and the fundraising event for Sgt. David McKeever was no exception.

As soon as I approached the doorway entrance, I could hear a rock band playing in the background. Although there were many people milling about on the main floor, my attention was immediately directed toward a temporary memorial composed of pictures and medals, including a Purple Heart, in David's honor. I recognized some of the childhood photos that his father shared after our boat ride. They depicted his very full, yet short, life. Within a few minutes, I recognized David Sr. talking to someone in the crowd. Standing about six feet two and weighing upward of 260 pounds, he was hard to miss. We made eye contact and he immediately came over to greet me. We readily hugged each other and began to cry. It was the first time I had cried since learning of his son's death. I couldn't guess how many tears he had shed over the previous year. He then escorted me closer to the memorial and told me how much his son was admired and respected by his men. Before long, I made my way over to David's brother, Tommy, and then to his mother and sisters to express my condolences.

In typical Buffalo fashion, local merchants donated all of the food and beverages in an outpouring of support for David's surviving family. There was an abundance of pizza, chicken wings, and sub sandwiches, along with a full complement of beer and soft drinks. The neighborhood remembered its native son.

Not long after, I began scanning the crowd looking for Niki. Never having met her, I had only memories of photographs to guide me. I spotted someone standing with another young woman near a corner and immediately recognized her. She was a beautiful young lady with a round face, bright blue eyes, and long, curly blonde hair. I approached her and introduced myself as a friend of the family and expressed my sorrow for her deep loss. She was visibly exhausted from traveling and emotionally drained from talking to so many new people. Fortunately, her childhood friend accompanied her from Nebraska. I admired Niki's gentle spirit and natural demeanor. It was readily apparent that she had loved her husband deeply and that they were well suited for each other. They were planning for his return to civilian life as a firefighter after his second enlistment was up. Like the rest of David's family, she was anticipating his return from Iraq in a few weeks and was planning to meet him in Germany. Having made all the necessary arrangements, she was backing out of the driveway in Nebraska for the airport to catch her flight when another car pulled up behind her, and two men in army uniforms got out to inform her of the tragic news. Her blue eyes reflected the pain in her young soul.

About six months later, I received a phone call from David informing me that Post # 64 was having a dedication ceremony to rename the post in honor of his son's sacrifice for his country. I interrupted him when he began to ask me if I wanted to attend, letting him know that I wouldn't miss it for anything in the world! He told me that Niki would be there and would have three-year-old Dylan with her as well. Reportedly, this was the first American Legion Post in New York State to make a name change in honor of someone killed in the line of duty. I decided to ask my friend Bill Stott to accompany me to this event and he readily agreed. In fact, he arranged to have his congregation at St. Luke's Anglican Church present Niki with a sizeable donation for her and Dylan. We arrived at the ceremony, which was being held in the same place where his fundraiser was held a year earlier. It was a much more solemn occasion, but just as full of people who cared about Sgt. McKeever and his family. We sat down at a table set up in a large room resembling an auditorium with a stage at the other end. This is where the band had been playing at the fundraiser during the benefit the previous year. Bill informed me that what was currently the Post had been a neighborhood movie theater some years before. He fondly recalled many Saturday afternoons when he came to watch movies with his friends. South Buffalo also happened to be his old neighborhood.

The entire McKeever family was seated on the stage behind a long table. The podium was in the center and the speakers took their turns to honor their fallen hero. Speakers included his former high school principal and Assemblyman Mark Schroeder, and the former mayor of Buffalo, Jimmy Griffith. The audience included Legionnaires, friends and family, as well as the local Boy Scout troop. Niki and her mother were seated in the front row. Family members and dignitaries took turns expressing their sorrow and gratitude for David's sacrifice. Although many emotional and tender things were said, it was Niki's opening words that I will never forget—"David was my life."

Something unusual and refreshing began to unfold during this solemn ceremony. Three-year-old Dylan began to frolic on the stage with his female cousin, totally unaware of the seriousness of the occasion, as fellow Americans were honoring his deceased father, killed in battle. I couldn't help but wonder what was going through his young mind, as he was delighted to be playing on the stage like a typical toddler, near his family. Occasionally, his Uncle Tommy would intervene and redirect them, but for the most part he was content to let them play. After the ceremony, we gathered in the front room for refreshments. It was at that point that the greatly enlarged photograph of Sgt. David McKeever in his Army uniform was officially unveiled. From that day on, the American Legion Post on 1770 South Park Avenue will bear his name. I suspect that Dylan will return someday for a longer gaze at his father's photo to reflect on what took place there on that special day.

My Dearest Dylan

Dear Dylan:

It is March 30, 2006, and I'm spending a few days at the St. Columban Retreat Center in Derby, New York, on the shore of Lake Erie. I make it a point to come here a few times a year for a much-needed spiritual tune-up. It's a beautiful and peaceful place. I meditate, take walks, and enjoy afternoon naps. The quiet atmosphere is a most welcome respite from the hectic pace that exists outside these idyllic fifteen acres. Aside from exchanging a few pleasantries with the kitchen crew during meal times, I spend the rest of the time in solitude. Being away from the daily routines and stresses offers me an opportunity to connect with my deepest self. Placed on the small table in my room is a pamphlet with a brief quote from one of my favorite authors, Thomas Merton: "Solitude is to be preserved not as a luxury, but as a necessity."

I have been going on these retreats now for over fifteen years. Unlike a vacation with my wife, my focus is very much an inward one. I eventually rediscover that ultimately my only possession is my personal relationship with God. I have many things in my life to be grateful for, but they are all temporary, even my beloved wife. A widower dealing with the death of his wife reminded me of this as I was browsing through the bookstore in the basement and noticed a book that he wrote dealing with the loss of his beloved. Anyway, these retreats seemed to be serving as sort of markers on my life's journey.

In fact, it is primarily during these times of extended solitude that I'm reminded that my life *is* a journey. All too often I view myself as a physical being with a spiritual dimension. It is here that I realize that I have it in reverse; I am a spiritual being in a temporary earthly body.

It's here that I am able to take stock of the things that really matter. I reflect on the events in my life that God used to shape the person I am today. I am reminded not only of the events in my life since my last retreat, but also that God is revealing things that occurred much further back in my childhood. Within the safety of His presence, I am able to honestly examine the weaknesses that continue to plague me and diminish my relationship with Him and other people. I find myself shaking my head at the litany of resentment, pride, defiance, fear, insecurity, stubbornness, and plain old *knuckle-headedness* (I'm not sure if that is a word, but it fits!) to which I routinely succumb. I feel safe in doing this only because I have a heavenly Father who loves me far more than I can love myself. His mercy and loving-kindness bathe my spirit from within. He reveals very specifically how His love has sustained me over the years, regardless of my behavior. There were times that this love took the form of a painful correction so that I might learn an important lesson. At the time, I would have gladly renounced this chastisement if it were possible; but I am grateful that He didn't allow me to squirm out of it. I was again reassured that "all things work for the good to those who love God and are called according to His purpose." Over the years I had to read and reread this Scripture verse to realize that it doesn't mean all things are good or feel good, but simply that they will "work for the good."

It is a bright, sunny day, and the temperature must be in the mid fifties. Spring is making its presence felt more each passing day.

It is now May 13 and it has been six weeks since I began to write this letter to you. Once again, I'm back at the St. Columban retreat center. It seems that for some reason I had to wait until I returned to this special place before I could continue writing this letter to you. I guess there is something to be said for a "time and a place …" I spoke with your grandfather last month. It was the second anniversary of your father's death in Iraq, and he gets choked up whenever we talk about him. He mentioned that your uncle Tommy will be involved in some sort of tribute this Memorial Day when your father will be honored in Buffalo. For most Americans, it is a day off from work or school. Some will even reflect to varying degrees on the solemnity of the occasion. Others will remember their buddies who were killed. Families will visit the graves of their loved ones who died in a war. But for you, Dylan, it will always be a reminder that your father was killed in the service of his country. Your grandfather told me that one of the last things your father told him was that he was "afraid" to return to Iraq. He then told him that he, too, was afraid when he was in Vietnam. Maybe that's the best definition of courage, going on ahead despite being afraid. Your father is my hero. I will remember to pray for you and your mother this Memorial Day. Spring is nearly in full bloom now; everything is bustling with new life.

Peace and blessings,

Paul Fazekas

P. S. I don't know what impression was made on your young mind that day when the American Legion Post was renamed in honor of your father. I just know that from where I was sitting, I will always remember you as the spirited little boy who was playing with his cousin on the stage.

Good Enough Mothering

A long-time hobby of mine involves building, detailing, and painting World War II plastic model aircraft. Like most modelers, I purchase far more model kits than I have time to construct, a conservative ratio of about ten to one. The more experienced I become, the higher the standards are that I must live up to before the present project is deemed satisfactory. It also it takes increasingly more time and energy to complete each successive airplane. I find this sort of logic bewildering. However, I'm still a far cry from a certain dentist I read about in a modeling magazine who spends an average of forty hours just on the landing gear on single engine fighters. Even more impressive was the fact the he actually made a first-aid kit with a tiny red cross for the crew's compartment in his B-17 bomber. When someone questioned the rationale behind it, since it was not visible in the completed aircraft, he responded, "But I know it's in there." No doubt that's how he feels about the thousands of cavities he has filled over the years, as they remain hidden from public view. I don't know if one has to be somewhat obsessive-compulsive for this hobby or if it becomes an eventual by-product of being engrossed in countless hours spent fitting, sanding, and mulling over details. For me, it has always been somewhat of a love-hate relationship to be sure.

As interesting as the various propeller-driven aircraft are to me, I am even more fascinated by the personalities of the pilots who flew them. One such remarkable story caught my attention when channel surfing landed me on the History Channel. It was the story of two former enemies, Charlie Brown, who piloted an American B-17 bomber, and Franz Stigler, a German ace fighter pilot, who was flying in a Me

109 fighter.

It was December 20, 1943, and Lt. Charlie Brown was flying his first bombing mission over Germany. Although German fighters mauled his unit, he managed to keep his badly damaged airplane flying while heading for home to England. His tail gunner was killed and three other crewmembers were seriously wounded, while he himself sustained a shoulder injury. All of a sudden, a German fighter appeared flying alongside his right wing and waving at him. The fighter then pulled in front of him and motioned for him to land his bomber on German soil. Brown refused, and eventually the fighter pilot saluted him, rolled over, and flew out of sight. In 1986 the American airman began to search in earnest for the chivalrous German fighter pilot who mercifully allowed him and his crew to live despite their defiance against landing the plane.

They finally met in 1990 and have been close friends ever since. Franz Stigler was already a fighter ace when he flew alongside Brown's badly damaged B-17. He was moved emotionally when he noticed "the half-dead men" inside the American aircraft; "shooting them would be like shooting at a parachute." A number of other factors made this act of gallantry even more remarkable. Franz ended the war with twenty-eight aerial victories over American and British fighters and also shot down five four-engine bombers. He had earlier that day shot down two B-17s and one more would have made him eligible for the Knight's Cross, the supreme symbol of German aerial combat. More importantly, allowing an enemy aircraft to escape was a court-martial offense, punishable by death in front of a firing squad. Neither reward nor fear of retribution was enough to make this fighter pilot shoot down a helpless, yet still defiant, aircraft. Impressive as was the high-performance fighter under his control, the internal mechanism of the man far surpassed the Denier Benz engine of his nimble aircraft.

Not mentioned in the documentary was the fact that the Americans were not bombing a neutral territory, they were bombing Stigler's homeland. This was the place his wife and parents lived, where he attended school as a young boy, and the land of all his childhood memories. It is a well-known historical fact that tens of thousands of German civilians were killed as a result of the bombing raids by the allies throughout the war. This young fighter pilot certainly had a motive for revenge. Yet, when it came to the crucial moment, he chose to display the quality of mercy. There must have been something involved in the inner workings of his soul when he witnessed the faces of the wounded enemy who were returning from destroying his homeland. Even though he realized that his decision would probably result in them returning at a later date to continue the destruction, he still could not bring himself to shoot them down.

As I was reflecting on this most unusual event, I remembered a term used by psychoanalyst David Winnicott, called "good enough mothering." He was referring to the crucial role of an infant's and young child's caretakers in providing an emotionally responsive and trusting environment during those formative years of development. It is during this completely dependent and vulnerable period that a child internalizes a sense of self that lays the foundation of his or her core identity. Most importantly, the child intrinsically senses that his life is valued and priceless and the foundation for empathy is forged deep within the psyche. Undoubtedly, Franz Stigler was moved with compassion, the foundation for which was laid down by the very people who were on the receiving end of the bombing raids.

Good enough mothering certainly does not mean "perfect mothering" and it is not a guarantee that the child will internalize the love of the caretakers so that he may be able to value others in like manner. It refers to the childrearing process whereby a basic bond or attachment with the caretakers (usually the mother) is balanced with the child's growing need to become an autonomous individual with his own core identity, complemented by empathy for others and responsible decision making. It takes reasonably healthy parents to navigate through this developmental undertaking with their child. Echoing the words of Jesus, it allows a person to "love your neighbor as you love yourself." The question "Who is one's neighbor?" posed to Jesus was answered with the story of the Good Samaritan.

The story is about a man from Samaria who was traveling from Jerusalem to Jericho and noticed a man lying on the side of the road half-dead after being robbed and beaten. Several others had seen him earlier but chose to keep going without stopping to offer aid. The Samaritan, however, stopped to offer assistance and even paid for the victim's care with a local innkeeper. From this passage, it would seem that one's neighbor is anyone who comes into his field of vision or immediate physical proximity. Any such individual, then, is deserving of our acknowledgement, respect, and compassion, qualities that we would certainly want afforded to ourselves. But herein lies the rub—we can offer to others only that which we have been provided by those who cared for us. We cannot give what we don't have. If we have not been loved, then we will not be able to love others.

In conducting a child psychiatric examination, in addition to peer relations, one of the key areas I inquire about concerns a child's relationship with pets or other animals. Not surprisingly, research has repeatedly confirmed that there is a correlation between premeditated violent behaviors as adults who have a history of childhood cruelty toward animals. This confirms what we already knew to be the case. After all, our relationships with our pets are based upon emotional bonds, as these living creatures are entrusted to our care. A child who is incapable of appreciating the pain and suffering inflicted on an animal would have difficulty empathizing with a fellow human being. Even more tragic is one who actually derives pleasure from such acts.

We all come not only from different geographical locations and cultural backgrounds, but also with our own unique childhood histories. Regardless, it is my personal opinion that being in a war and actually participating in combat somehow alters one's inner being. Factors like personal predispositions, extent of combat, survivor guilt, witnessing death, or taking a life all would be expected to alter an individual's soul. In whatever way these variables make their unique contributions, the end product is a changed person. Unfortunately, many have to endure this change silently and alone for years, unable to understand why they have set out on a self-destructive course. Some are remarkably resilient, while others may be seared beyond their internal connection to humanity.

I vividly remember two individuals who possessed such diametrically opposite intrapsychic structures. I can remember the face of the first soldier, only because it reflected a hauntingly evil expression with his piercing dark brown eyes—a glaring vista into the "heart of darkness." We were actually from different companies and ended up pulling guard duty together in one of the bunkers on a forward firebase. We were supposed to alternate sleeping and guarding every two hours throughout the night. We were on a heightened alert because the enemy had recently been probing our position with mortars and small arms fire. He wore a leather necklace made of human fingers that he severed from the enemy troops he killed. Even more disturbing was the way he laughed as he described how he went about this gruesome task. Although I had been in Vietnam for about nine months and witnessed "man's inhumanity to man" many times over, I think it was at that moment that I received my introduction to a qualitatively different form of evil. It seemed that this unfortunate soul had somehow lost his connection with humanity. His wearing an American uniform did little to allay the unsettled feelings that I experienced throughout the night. I could not sleep when it was my turn and I had one hand on my weapon during the entire time. I felt like the enemy was *already inside* our perimeter.

The other incident is hazier in my memory. I was on a search-and-destroy mission with the 11th Light Infantry Brigade. One of our squad members accidentally shot and killed a Vietnamese woman. She had appeared out of nowhere and was unarmed. We returned to base later that day and tried to comfort him, but to no avail. The battalion commander came by later to talk to all of us about how such a tragedy unfortunately can happen during war. I remember that the soldier started crying. He wept inconsolably throughout the night and was taken to a hospital the next morning. We never heard from him again.

Sometimes I wonder what kind of life these two young men had when they returned home. Something essential for living was severed the last time I had seen them. I know that many others carried a lot of baggage when they returned to their loved ones. We all had changed.

Remember Me

It was a Sunday morning, much like many others I have known. My wife and I were scurrying out the door so we wouldn't be late for church—again. We complement each other in many areas, save one—we both habitually run late … for almost everything. This is one area where neither one of us has taken responsibility to make any meaningful improvements in over thirty years. We're still quite content to blame each other for allowing the minutes to somehow drift by, leaving the pair of us scampering to make up for lost time. It just happened to be the Sunday when the new associate pastor would be preaching his first sermon. At the time, we were attending a midsize evangelical church located about ten miles south of Buffalo.

The new minister was introduced after the worship music. Since it was the first Sunday of the month, the congregation would have the opportunity to participate in Holy Communion following the message from the pulpit. He began his sermon with the words of Jesus at the Last Supper instructing His disciples to "do this in remembrance of Me" as they broke bread and drank wine. His sermon focused on the meaning of communion for Christians. He then introduced the story about a Vietnam War medic, which immediately placed me on heightened alert status to the words that followed.

It was the year 1970, the same year I was in Vietnam, when a newly arrived medic, Brian Rooney, was performing a triage on a helipad. After he finished treating some wounded soldiers, he approached the body of what he mistakenly believed to be a dead man. He didn't like the idea of an American soldier dying far from his home without his name being known, so he leaned over the man's body to reach for the dog tags and got the surprise of his life. The soldier opened his eyes, grabbed Rooney's shirt as he pulled him close and said, "Remember me …" before dying. This incident haunted Brian Rooney for many years afterward. As a teacher and himself a disabled veteran in Los Angeles, he had occasion in 1993 to try and locate some veterans' memorials in his area. He soon discovered that there was no comprehensive archive of war memorials anywhere to be found. He was not only concerned about memorials dedicated to veterans killed during the Vietnam War, but also with memorials of all wars in which Americans sacrificed their lives for our freedom. His passion for war memorials was echoed during a hearing in April 27, 2004, to the U.S. Senate Committee on Energy and Natural Resources.

> That soldier that died in my arms in Vietnam created a deep scar in my heart, but in the course of time I have come to realize that he is much more than a single, nameless GI that died on a battlefield far from home. Through this work and legislation, that brave young American becomes every American that ever died for freedom, whether it was Concord or Gettysburg, Korea or North Africa, on the shores of Omaha beach or the streets of Baghdad…. In a sense every dying American soldier from the Revolutionary War to this present War on Terrorism is reaching up now to you, grasping your shirt, and pleading, "Remember me…." [5]

Brian discovered a disturbing trend of veterans' memorials across the country that were vandalized, neglected, or simply abolished each year. He further stated that "the thought of throwing out a veterans' memorial was unacceptable," so he created a non-profit organization, Remembering Veterans Who Earned Their Stripes (RVETS). The main purpose of this group was to create a national registry of veterans' memorials. Additionally, they continue to monitor these memorials annually and take steps to restore or save any that may be in jeopardy. Taking it one step further, Mr. Rooney plans to print the personal story of every American named on these memorials across our country. In this way, he hopes that present and future generations will become familiar with the individual lives that paid the ultimate sacrifice to preserve our freedom. He wants all of us to remember the price they paid.

U.S. Cavalry

My decades-long journey to confront the ghosts of Vietnam took a rather unexpected and circuitous route. It was sometime around the mid 1990s, nearly half a dozen years prior to dealing with the death of Bill Wood, that I began to have a renewed interest in the life and military campaigns of General George Armstrong Custer. I was particularly fascinated with his shocking defeat at the Little Big Horn River on June 25, 1876. Ironically, this major military disaster occurred during the same year that our nation was making preparations for the upcoming centennial celebration at the New York World's Fair. Because news traveled at a slower pace back then, most of the country found out about the Seventh Cavalry's defeat during the Fourth of July festivities. Some news writers at the time noted that it came as even more of a shock to the nation than the assassination of President Lincoln eleven years earlier.

To describe Custer as a controversial figure would be a major understatement. Obtaining the rank of major general at the age of twenty-two, he was without question the greatest cavalry commander of the Union army during the Civil War. In fact, it was largely due to his development of unconventional cavalry tactics that the North was able to finally match wits with the vaunted cavalry of the Confederacy. He personally led the charges of his brigade at Gettysburg that were instrumental in defeating General Lee's forces, and became an instant national hero. The nation was in disbelief that its greatest cavalry commander, along with every last man under his immediate command, was wiped out by a "band of savages" on a sunny Sunday afternoon. I can still remember the film *They Died with Their Boots On*, with Errol

Flynn as the dismounted General Custer making his last stand against the onslaught of thousands of Sioux and Cheyenne warriors. It was the quintessential scene of death and glory merged on the silver screen.

It was only within the past fifteen years that renewed interest in the "Custer Massacre" has emerged, largely due to recent archaeological findings at the battle site and a number of books on the subject. There was even a fairly accurate made-for-TV movie entitled *Son of the Morning Star,* based on the book by the same name. The movie nicely develops the rationale behind Custer dividing his over six hundred cavalrymen in three separate units as they approached the Indian village. He was obsessed with attacking them from different angles in an effort to surround them and prevent their possible escape. The real mystery about the battle over the past 125 years has revolved around the actual battle itself.

Since no white man lived to tell the tale of what happened, the Indians provided the only eyewitness accounts. For the most part, their versions were largely ignored and deemed unreliable. Moreover, many of their warriors feared for their own safety, as an attitude of retaliation prevailed for a number of years after the battle. When pressed, they would either keep silent or relate versions that placed the soldiers in a more favorable light. The only thing that was known for certain was that Custer and over two hundred men were killed in the engagement. Since the rest of his battered regiment was pinned down three miles away, all they could relate was that they heard the fighting and saw dust clouds gathering in Custer's direction from the warriors' ponies. A brief attempt to send a relief column was swiftly repulsed by the Indians. Surprisingly, the surviving companies of the 7th Cavalry Regiment were just as shocked to learn of Custer's fate a few days later when General Terry's unit relieved them. Up until that moment, they believed that Custer routed the Indians and was chasing them as they tried to make their escape. This was a logical conclusion since both Custer's men and the entire Indian village seemed to have disappeared. The relief column soon discovered the naked and mutilated corpses of over two hundred soldiers strewn around the hills, having baked in the hot sun for several days.

The nation was so angered by the incident that it was referred to as the "Custer Massacre" for years. The fact that the 7th Cavalry had sought out and initiated the attack on the Indian village was totally ignored. The battle that was immortalized as "Custer's Last Stand" had all the ingredients that make for legend. The search for factual information takes a back seat until people are ready to hear the "truth." Until recently, many of us believed the Hollywood version of the last stand: Custer and his brave men were driven to a hill by thousands of savage Indians and forced to dismount and fight to the last man as they repeatedly repulsed human wave attacks until they finally ran out of bullets; unable to properly defend themselves, they were massacred.

Several scholarly investigations have been conducted over the past fifteen years relative to this infamous battle. Having read everything I could find on the topic, my two favorites were by John S. Gray, MD, a retired physiology professor. The first one was entitled *Centennial Campaign: The Sioux War of 1876*, which places the Battle of the Little Bighorn within the broad context of cultural differences, political scandal, military blunders and detailed description of the battle, and culminates with the army's relentless pursuit of the foe that defeated its soldiers. His second book on the subject, *Custer's Last Campaign: Mitch Boyer and the Little Bighorn Reconstructed*, challenges the legendary beliefs about the battle that have been handed down over generations. He closely examines Indian accounts of the fight and reconciles seemingly contradictory versions made by them and soldiers who were only a few miles away on that fateful day.

I was particularly impressed by what Dr. Gray referred to as the "time motion analysis" he employed to rule in or rule out the reported accounts by Indians who were the only eyewitnesses to the battle, along with the soldiers' versions who were in the general vicinity. As his analysis began to take shape by "connecting the dots," the criteria for systematic examination of ensuing reports became more stringent. The present version of the battle, which is backed by the meticulous research of Dr. Gray and others, is quite different from the one that has been portrayed over the years. General Custer wasn't just simply outnumbered by a "horde of savages" and "overwhelmed by vastly superior forces" in a series of major onslaughts. Rather, he was tactically outmaneuvered and his men for the most part were outfought by a determined foe.

The "last stand" also was not a matter of two hundred dismounted cavalrymen in a defensive circle with Custer in the center while thousands of Indians simply overwhelmed them. We now know that the two hundred men under his immediate command were further divided into smaller units about a mile apart from each other while Custer was preoccupied with searching for a crossing point in the Little Big Horn River so that he could continue his attack on the Indian village. He was well aware by this time that Major Reno's attack from the other end of the massive village had been repelled. In fact, Reno with over 150 men was already fighting to keep his own command from being annihilated.

True to his nature, General Custer was in an offensive mode until the very last moments of the fight. Tragically, he witnessed the systematic destruction of his companies while they were positioned in holding formations, separated from each other on nearby hills. Custer and about eighty of his remaining troopers made their famous "last stand" on a hill, surrounded by ravines and other hills, with no cover other than their dead horses and the bodies of fallen soldiers. Meanwhile, the Indians were not so foolish as to rush them, thereby sustaining heavy causalities. They were content to snipe at them from concealed positions with bows and arrows and rifles from the surrounding low-level brush. Custer's men were systematically eliminated by an intelligent and clever foe that utilized the topography to its full advantage. Not until there were only a handful of troopers left, Custer reportedly among them, did the Indians launch a full-scale attack.

Indian accounts consistently reported that Custer was a true warrior, who kept fighting until he was killed. Many soldiers lay wounded around the battlefield when the fighting was over. They were beaten to death with clubs, stripped of their uniforms, and dismembered by warriors as well as squaws and old women, to prevent them from seeking revenge in the afterlife. This was a customary religious practice among the Plains tribes. General Custer himself was left intact except for pierced eardrums, so that he would be able to listen to the Indians' needs and the promises that he had made them when he entered the next life. So ended the battle for the five companies of the 7th cavalry and their famed general of horse soldiers. Unlike the grand *Charge of the Light Brigade* scene portrayed by Hollywood, the end was inglorious, at best.

An equally fascinating aspect of the George Armstrong Custer story were the personality profiles of the officers and overall constellation of the cavalry troopers who marched with him that day to Valhalla. His personal entourage included several relatives who died with him. His younger brother, Captain Tom Custer, who commanded E company, was found next to him on top of the hill. Tom was a hero of the Civil War and is the only soldier ever to have been awarded the Medal of Honor—twice. Lieutenant James Calhoun was his brother-in-law and commanded C Company. His nephew, Artie Custer, was a civilian reporter assigned to cover the campaign. Captain Miles Keogh, a close friend, was an Irish immigrant who was in charge of I company and a fierce and seasoned trooper. By contrast, Major Marcus Reno, his second in command, and Captain Frederick Benteen, who was in charge of the pack train, were his bitter rivals. Both men were also highly decorated Civil War veterans, but were pinned down on a hill three miles away with about three hundred men and over fifty wounded following an initial failed attempt to rout the Indians from another direction.

Custer's ever-faithful wife, Libbie, who lived to a ripe old age, relentlessly maintained that these two men failed her husband and were responsible for his defeat that fateful day. Amazingly, this controversy continues among history buffs to this day. The 7th Cavalry Regiment, numbering over six hundred men, was hardly the finely honed fighting machine portrayed in movies and books. While the regiment had its share of seasoned fighters, they were in the minority. There was an assortment of recent immigrants from Ireland and Italy, with some of the latter barely able to speak English. In fact, some historians believe that the courier, Sgt. Rosario, who Custer sent for reinforcements in order to coordinate his attack, was misunderstood due to his broken English as he attempted to describe new developments in the ensuing battle. Also, many of the men who went on the campaign were raw recruits.

Finally, the 7th Cavalry, which had been commanded by Custer since its inception in 1866 and long touted as "Indian fighters," had only one victory over the Plains tribes in ten years of chasing them. In 1868, Custer and his regiment surrounded a sleeping Cheyenne village near the Washita River by their winter camp. Chief Black Kettle was flying an American flag from his tepee to signal his truce with the United States government. While Custer's band was playing "Gary

Owen," the soldiers charged on horseback from four sides in the pre-dawn hours, totally surprising the villagers. Over 150 Indians were killed, while many more were captured and marched back with the troopers. Their teepees, possessions, and livestock were destroyed.

It was lucky for Custer that he pulled his regiment out as swiftly as he did, as several thousand warriors from other tribes and camps in the surrounding area were swiftly moving toward the sound of the gunfire. During the fight, one of Custer's majors and twenty troopers went in pursuit of some Indians and were ambushed; there were no survivors. Custer's bitter rivals, Reno and Benteen, blamed him for not rescuing the group. Years later, the tables were turned, as a number of troopers now blamed Reno and Benteen for not coming to Custer's assistance. From what I have studied, they would have met the same fate if they had been foolish enough to leave their defensive perimeter to face a numerically and tactically superior enemy in the open. In summary, on that day of June 25, 1876, everything that could go wrong did go wrong for the regiment.

I find it amazing that, of all the wars and major battles that the United States has been engaged in over the past several hundred years, the two that are the most remembered had relatively few causalities. One only has to recall various movies and a large number of paintings of the battles. Combined, the Alamo and the Little Big Horn had about five hundred killed in action. These numbers are dwarfed by comparison to Gettysburg, Antietam, Normandy, Iwo Jima, and countless other major battles where thousands of Americans died, often in only a matter of a few hours. Other than their historical significance, what makes these battles memorable is that in each case the entire command was annihilated.

In the case of the Alamo, the handful of civilian survivors' and the Mexican Army's versions of the battle were relatively consistent and acceptable enough to be marked down as "truth." Although there is some speculation as to how Davy Crockett actually died, the order of battle remains uncontested. However, the shroud of mystery surrounding the fate of Custer's regiment has only partially been unveiled with the recent archeological findings. Most of this evidence is based upon digging up cartridge shells and using their locations to speculate on the sequence of troop movements and tactical cohesion. Nevertheless, it does provide a more objective account that can be thrown into the hopper of educated guesswork.

It takes a long time for us to change a perception about something once an image is implanted in our mind. This is certainly the case for the Battle of the Little Big Horn. Immediately after the incident, reporters were inflaming the public by depicting it as a massacre, an appropriate enough word to be sure, since Custer and every trooper in his five companies was killed. Additionally, many paintings about the battle have been done over the years. Interestingly, the quality and particulars of the works on canvas reflected the current perception and historical presentation of the event. For example, one of the first paintings depicted Indians who actually had red-colored skin, wearing only a skimpy cloth and adorned like peacocks at the peak of mating season, with their brightly colored feathers pointing toward the sunny Montana sky. At first glance it makes one think of Montezuma's Aztec warriors, but in place of Fernando Cortez we have General Custer in the center of his doomed troopers, wielding a saber at the onslaught of these "red" men. The warriors depicted in this piece were not Plains Indians, and neither Custer nor any of his cavalrymen took their swords with them on the campaign.

Another painting, while more accurate in coloration of the warriors, nevertheless has the vast majority wearing full headdresses, each one dressed like a war chief. At least Custer is without the sword or flowing yellow hair that he routinely had cut short while on summer campaigns. The most recent painting depicted Custer and only about a dozen troopers in the final stage of the battle. Although they were badly mauled and completely surrounded, their Indian tormenters were still cautiously waiting before rushing in to finish them off. It appears that each successive painting over the years portrayed a more accurate representation of the "last stand," making each rendition a few degrees less glorious.

To General Custer's credit, he admired the Indians and wrote a book, *My Life on the Plains*, which reflected his intimate knowledge of American Indian culture. While many politicians in Washington were in favor of totally exterminating the tribes, he championed the cause to place them on reservations and gradually integrate them into the white man's culture. A realist, he knew that the days of the Sioux and

Cheyenne freely roaming the plains were over and that the only hope of keeping them alive was the reservation. In fact, he testified in Washington against President Grant's brother for his corruption toward the reservation Indians. The president's brother was diverting supplies of food and clothing intended for the reservations and misusing it for his own profit. Custer may have been brash, unconventional and egotistical, but he was forthright. His testimony so infuriated the president that he was relieved of his command of the 7th Cavalry.

His military career had been in jeopardy a few years earlier when he was court-martialed and convicted on a number of charges, including being absent from his command and giving orders to shoot deserters without the benefit of a trial. He was relieved of his command and rank at the time and without pay for one year. It was only his national hero status as a swaggering cavalry commander during the Civil War that prevented him from being dismissed from the army altogether. And now it was due to General Sherman's close friendship with President Grant, forged during the Civil War, that Sherman's plea to reinstate Custer to his command met with success, despite Custer's humiliation of Grant by testifying against his brother. Once again, "Custer's luck" prevailed, but for the last time.

Unfortunately, this reinstatement presented Custer with the opportunity to lead his troopers to their date with destiny. His resiliency and luck dated back to his days at West Point, where his record-setting string of demerits, along with ranking at the bottom of his graduating class, almost resulted in his expulsion from the Academy. It was only because the Union army desperately needed officers for the Civil War that he had an opportunity for an army career. A few years after graduation, at the young age of twenty-two, he became a two-star general. He was, to be sure, a remarkably adaptable and fearless warrior who insisted on leading his men by example—from the front of the column.

The more I read about him and the ill-fated campaign at the Little Bighorn, the more I felt drawn into this fascinating historical mystery. Finally, I realized—I wanted to be there. Something was driving me to actually see and be a part of the experience. It became a mission, an obsession of sorts. In retrospect, I'm convinced that this was a disguised form of making some connection with my own combat experiences. The subconscious is remarkably persistent at making all sorts of internal plea bargains in an effort to bring forth its payload by whatever route may present an opening. This business of the inner life is a uniquely different matter for each one of us. In my case, some sort of compromise had to be forged that would allow me to identify with aspects of war, but from a reasonably safe emotional distance. Of course, this undertaking would also be operating at a level below my subconscious radar screen.

One of the most important Freudian concepts, if not the most important, that I learned over years is that our behavior is over-determined. That is, a certain specific behavior, feeling, or thought may well have a variety of motivating factors that are driving it into the realm of consciousness or action. Again, it is essential to remember that this matter is as individual and personal for each of us as our fingerprint or genetic makeup. My lifelong interest in history, along with having served in the air cavalry, combined to afford me a window from which to view war, albeit from a safe distance. The fact that Custer was court-martialed for military infractions also served as a point of identification for me. Even though reading about all this was very much a cerebral matter, it was one step closer to confronting the ghosts of Vietnam. Without realizing it at the time, my inner dictates were making preparations for the next phase of my campaign trail—the Little Big Horn River.

Donna and I were in the kitchen one day in the spring of 1999 and she asked me what place in the world would be on top of my list to visit. I immediately answered the Little Big Horn River, historical site of Custer's last stand. She was bewildered that of all the places one could visit, I would choose a remote hill in southern Montana. What neither one of us realized at the time was the buried emotional baggage that was involved in setting the inner compass toward a westward direction. Unlike previous vacations, we did not make any reservations or specific schedules for activities once we arrived. Other than our time off work and the kennel service for our miniature dachshund, the only thing we planned was the approximate time of our return. We simply loaded up our van and headed for Montana.

The last time I ventured that far west was in 1971, when I flew to Fort Hood to complete my hitch in the army. We drove about six hundred miles a day and then stopped at a roadside motel for the night.

There was no appreciable change in the landscape until we entered South Dakota, where a sea of grass emerged that seemed to go on forever. We were now in the Great Plains, an endless expanse of land sprinkled with small trees and knolls. For the most part it was flat land that offered a 360-degree panoramic view. It was a treat to observe small herds of antelope as they swiftly moved through the tall grass in unison. This was the heartland of America, God's country. It is so magnificent that it's a shame many people fly over it and never take in its natural beauty. As we approached the Black Hill country near Wyoming, I recalled the expedition that Custer led there in 1874 which coincided with the period when gold was discovered in the area, sealing the fate of the sacred land of the Sioux nation.

We arrived at the site of the Little Big Horn Battle in mid afternoon. The area included a few good-sized souvenir shops near the park that were managed by Indians and an administration building within the park itself. Fortunately for me, only about a dozen visitors were in the entire area on this particular day. The administration building was located near Custer Hill, the site of the last stand. It was here that the famous general was killed, along with about eighty of his troopers. Headstones marked the spots where the cavalry relief column found the bodies a few days after the battle. Reading dozens of books on the subject did little to prepare me to appreciate the unique topography that the 7th Cavalry regiment had to contend with on that fateful day.

A cavalry unit is designed to be a highly mobile offensive force used mainly to deliver a quick strike. In order to maximize these qualities, it is essential to have a 360-degree field of vision. The command has to know the exact location of the enemy forces so it can react, organize, and deploy its columns in the most expeditious manner. However, in order to accomplish the latter, it also has to know exactly where its own forces are at all times and maintain ongoing communication with them. Unfortunately for Custer and his horse soldiers, these ingredients were totally absent on June 25, 1876.

The entire battlefield, which was roughly three miles long and over a mile wide, would have been a large area for six hundred soldiers to manage, even if it were flat. But the topography of the area consisted of rolling hills and knolls, divided by deep ravines. Tall prairie grass, shrubs, and bushes provided excellent cover for the Indians for sniping and concealing their movements. Custer had his 210 soldiers spread out in five units on hilltops over most of this area while he was still in an offensive mode searching for a crossing point over the river so that he could attack the village. Meanwhile, groups of Indians were pouring across the ravines, largely undetected, and cutting off the companies trying to maintain tactical cohesion on their respective hilltops. It was a disaster in the making—a dismounted cavalry unit with a limited field of vision, separated from other units, blind to the encircling enemy forces, and situated on hilltops placing them in an ideal location to be sniped by an enemy they could not see. One would be hard-pressed to script a worse scenario for a cavalry regiment in which to find itself.

I believe I was the only person over the next few days who walked the entire course of the battlefield. People elected to slowly drive their cars along a designated route marked by key points of interest along the way. But I felt compelled to walk and feel the *spirit* of the scene. I had to read every headstone that was strewn throughout the site. After all, this is were they fell and this is where they died. I stood alone for long periods while I made the trek. It was a solemn occasion as the breeze rustled the grass and shrubs near my feet, while in my spirit I could hear the cries of the wounded emerging from that awful day so many years ago. It was at that moment I realized that, in some mysterious way, I was connected to those dead troopers. Perhaps a timeless and kindred spirit connects those who have tasted combat and death. After all, who better than they would know the sheer terror of the moment that can last a lifetime and the daily fear that has to be suppressed in order to prepare for the next battle? A soldier in the Union army said after Gettysburg, "A bunch of us went to fight that day and many never came back. And if you weren't there, you'll never understand."

There was a qualitatively different mindset in those who were about to die between the defenders of the Alamo and those of Custer's command. In the case of the former, they had all been informed of their hopeless situation for some time and were prepared to die for their cause. They were waiting for the thousands of Mexican troops to attack them. Mentally and spiritually, they had the opportunity to prepare for death the best they could. For the 7th Cavalry, it was an entirely different matter. They were only temporarily positioned in a haphazard defensive posture, while still searching for a means to unleash the unit as an attack force on the Indian village. It wasn't until the last few minutes as they realized they were surrounded and cut off from each other that they went from predator to prey in an instant. Unlike their counterparts in the Alamo, their destruction came upon them suddenly, as moments earlier they had been in a victorious mood.

Taken in total, the evidence strongly suggests that there was indeed a last stand, but it was hardly the glamorous one etched in our minds that Hollywood and history books promulgated over the years. Custer was positioned on a hill with about eighty of his troopers with full view of 130 of his men less than a mile away in separate groups. He and his men must have witnessed in horror as several thousand warriors finally overwhelmed their comrades from all different directions. A few dozen escaped and made it to the relative safety of Custer's position. They knew it was their turn next as the Indians surrounded them and continued to snipe at them until only a handful remained. It is believed that George Custer was one of the last to die. Testimonies from the surviving warriors consistently noted that some of the companies lost their tactical cohesion and broke off to bunch up in smaller groups to continue the fight; they were overwhelmed. Other troopers ran for cover, but there was none to be found and warriors ran them down on horseback. However, Custer and his band maintained their position and fought bravely until the Indians rushed in to finish them off. I replayed these scenes many times over in my mind while I walked my private procession covering the order of battle. For me, it was a spiritual experience.

Contrary to popular belief, there was at least one survivor from Custer's immediate command. While all of the 210 soldiers were killed, the relief column found a seriously wounded horse that had been shot a number of times with bullets and arrows. His name was Comanche, Captain Miles Keogh's horse, the commanding officer of I company. He was nursed back to health and a few years later was decreed the official symbol of the 7th Cavalry with all rights and privileges and was pampered for some fifteen more years until his death in 1891.

Unfortunately, Comanche was habituated to a "whiskey bran mash" administered to him by the cavalrymen while he was recovering from his battle wounds. Reportedly, he developed such a craving for alcohol that he would show up at the canteen on payday to panhandle for beer from the troopers. Since he had the freedom to roam the fort, he would often make a nuisance of himself by destroying gardens and overturning garbage cans. The regiment voted to have him preserved after his death, making him a very popular exhibit at various museums. The famous "mounted mount" even made an appearance at the 1893 World's Fair. The battle over his final resting place in the Natural History Museum at the University of Kansas continued among various departments and agencies well into the 1970s. It would appear that everything about the Battle of the Little Big Horn was filled with controversy, including its sole survivor—a wounded and traumatized horse who became a drunk.

I stood very still the last time I was surveying the beautiful landscape of rolling hills and the Little Big Horn River as it meandered lazily through the valley below. I thought how different the scene was from that day of death nearly 125 years ago. My sense is that such an observation can be made of any battlefield years after the carnage. It's also ironic that, of all the books and details I read about the event, the account that seemed to bother me the most was only indirectly related to the actual battle itself. Maybe it had something to do with a woman's insight into the mind-set of the cavalryman. Louise Barrett wrote a fascinating book entitled, *Touched by Fire: The Life, Death, and Mythic Afterlife of George Armstrong Custer.* She presented numerous illuminating insights into the life of this famous American and his devoted wife, Libbie. But her description of one particular incident stands out for me personally.

At their last camp before the battle the water was so strongly alkaline that it was undrinkable by man or beast, a circumstance that would have serious consequences during the long hot day that followed. When the Indian war veteran Henry R. Boynton enumerated the "almost unbelievable" hardships encountered in frontier service, he began with thirst. In the heat and dust of that June 25 the lack of water at the beginning of the day would both contribute to the sufferings of the men and horses who retreated to the bluffs and delay the pack train, whose thirsty mules could not be hurried out of the river and on to join the command. And a final indignity in an army that ran on coffee and hardtack was the deprivation of the former on what would be the last morning of their lives for 263 of the men, including the coffee-loving Custer. [6]

Although I'm firmly convinced that even a full-service Starbucks would not have altered the course of the battle, it still bothered me as a soldier that these men would enter eternity without having had a final cup of coffee on the morning of the day they died—with their boots on.

Memorial Day 2004

Until now, I had shared the Vietnam-related events that unfolded over the past two years with only family and a few friends. The idea of recounting my experiences with Bill Wood, Beulah, John Gmack, or Trudy in front of a group of people had not entered my mind. I was still numb from the death of an old friend's son who was killed in Iraq a few weeks earlier. Then one day, my private eulogy suddenly came to an end. It was at this juncture that my friend Bill Stott asked me if I would be willing to share my story with his congregation on Memorial Day.

Speaking in front of an audience was nothing new to me. I had taught college classes and conducted workshops and seminars for mental health professionals on various topics in psychology, psychiatry, and nursing. It was all straightforward preparation and presentation. However, the idea of sharing something that was so deeply personal was an entirely different matter. These were feelings and memories that I held sacred. They had a profound impact on me in ways I was just beginning to understand—critical events that charted the course of my life. Events that remained part of my being, try as hard as I could over time to deny, separate myself from or outright discard. I agreed to go ahead mainly because I felt that somehow Bill, John, and others would not be remembered if I declined. Remembering them in the company of others became meaningful to me.

My wife and I arrived at the First Baptist Church in East Aurora, New York, on Memorial Sunday, May 30, 2004. I carefully placed some photographs on a table in the rear of the sanctuary that people would see at the end of the service. I included photos of Bill Wood, John Gmack, and others who I served with in Vietnam. There was one particular photo that Mrs. Gmack sent me of her son, John, laid out in a military coffin. His upper torso was encased in glass, which offered a faint reflection of light. With his eyes closed, he was still and lifeless. Regrettably, his mother took the advice of the funeral director and had a closed casket to discourage curious viewers. She noted, "John would have liked to have his friends see him in full dress." She felt that, since I was his friend, I would want to see him in an open casket and sent me that photograph in particular. She couldn't have been more right. It was on Memorial Day, 1970, that John was killed in Cambodia. Honoring his sacrifice, on this of all days, was the right thing to do.

It was a somewhat unusual service, as two separate denominations that shared the building agreed to officiate at the service. Bill, a psychologist and an ordained Anglican priest, rented the building from the Baptist Church. Both ministers, Rev. Gary Moore, the Baptist pastor, and Fr. Bill Stott, took turns presiding over the service. A U.S. Marine Corps Color Guard opened the service as they presented the colors. As I sat facing the congregation, waiting my turn to speak, I noticed two familiar faces. My next-door neighbor, Paul Simon, was seated near the middle row. It was Paul, who serendipitously found a picture of his father in *Life Magazine* on a beach in the Pacific Theatre during World War II, who encouraged me to search the same magazine for articles on Vietnam. The other one was a friend, Andy Fleming, a local attorney and former Marine Corps officer, who was sitting near the back pew. I had known both of these men over the years, and our lives had become intertwined in meaningful ways. Seeing them amongst the rest of the gathering offered a welcome measure of support and reassurance.

There was the customary reading from Scripture and singing of hymns throughout the service. Frankly, I was in such a numbed state of mind that I wasn't paying much attention. Images of other soldiers who were killed or wounded were gently fading-in and fading-out in my mind. I scribbled a few items on a piece of paper along with letters I brought along to read. Then, shortly before I was to share my message, a group of four musicians came on to attend to their musical instruments. I believe they were members of the Vietnam Veterans Motorcycle Club and soon began to sing *Goodnight Saigon* by Billy Joel. It was the first time I had heard that song and it touched me deeply. Then it was my turn to be introduced and I began to share my story.

I talked about the call from Peggy, my visit to Alliance, communication with Mrs. Gmack, and how I felt God's gentle hand guiding me throughout the entire process. It was difficult to talk about what happened to Bill Wood and how John was killed on Memorial Day. I told them about John throwing his dentures into the beer and I read some of the letters from Mrs. Gmack. People especially appreciated the ones about her insisting on being called "Trudy," finding cigarette butts piled up at the doorway to her son's school, and the story about how he lost his tooth. I can't recall the sequence of the stories. However, *they were remembered*—and that's all that mattered anyway. One thing I do recall for certain and that was the last thing I shared with the congregation. I reached into my suit jacket and pulled out the letter I had received from Sharon Main, Bill Wood's sister, following her mother Beulah's death. I struggled unsuccessfully to suppress the tears that were welling up inside. I had a difficult time reading the letter and felt emotionally drained when I finished.

A few days later, my neighbor, Paul Simon, knocked on our door and presented me a copy of a newspaper clipping entitled, *Island GI's Parents Presented Silver Star.* The write up, with accompanying photograph, was about his cousin, Specialist 4 Joseph E. Muench, who was killed near An Khe on October 4, 1969. He was posthumously awarded the Silver Star for his courage following the ambush of his recon patrol, while serving as a rifleman with the 4th Infantry Division of the U.S. Army. Mortally wounded, "He returned a live grenade and kept the enemy at bay with rifle fire while his comrades escaped to safety." It's ironic, that for all the years Paul and I had known each other, this was the first time he mentioned his cousin. This is perhaps one of the reasons that Memorial Day is meaningful for those who have a photo or an obituary about someone who never returned from a war. Regardless of one's political or religious views about a war, especially the controversy that continues to surround Vietnam and now Iraq, the pain of the loss is the common denominator that all share on this special day.

Joseph was from Grand Island, an unusual piece of land that is surrounded by the Niagara River as it bifurcates and then merges again, flowing toward its destination—Niagara Falls. I drive across this island several times a week en route to the Monsignor Carr Children's Clinic. In fact, the entire distance of approximately fifty miles runs parallel to

Lake Erie and then the Niagara River. Since my drive misses the rush hour each way by several hours, I can relax and enjoy the scenic route of the meandering waterway. Preferring to be alone with my thoughts, I rarely play the radio during this nearly one-hour journey. The steady flow of the mighty Niagara reflects a quality of timelessness as I realize that it has been here long before my arrival and will continue its steady course long after I leave this earth. I have consistently found this time to be a source of inspiration for the writing of this book, as the faces of the fallen visit me during the drive. Now I have one more to envision as I cross the bridge over the Niagara River and enter Grand Island.

Dear America

A few years ago, a fellow Vietnam veteran lent me a video entitled *Dear America: Letters Home from Vietnam,* based on the book by the same title. He felt it might be of benefit when I finally got around to writing this book. It captivated my attention and stirred my emotions. Every clip of the film footage was an authentic presentation of the soldiers, marines, sailors, and airmen who were in Vietnam from 1965 to 1973. The letters that were read throughout the documentary were their original letters to their families back home. Interestingly, they were read by popular Hollywood celebrities like Tom Berenger, Robert DiNiro, Martin Sheen, Willem Dafoe, Elizabeth McGovern, and others. Many of these stars were in well-known movies about the Vietnam War like *The Deer Hunter*, *Platoon*, and *Apocalypse Now.*

The film stirred up a wellspring of memories, laced with feelings of longing just at the sight of mail being disseminated to the troops. We eagerly awaited these little envelopes from home with their precious cargo. It was like manna from heaven to partake of the magical contents that had the power to make everything better, even for just a little while. Rest assured that they would be read and reread dozens of times in jungles and firebases. My girlfriend, sister, and mother were all regular contributors to this most blessed of occasions that I relished beyond description. It was my only contact with "the world," as it seemed that we had been transported into an evil kingdom from which so many would never return. The contents within these envelopes were our main link to the land of "milk and honey" which we desperately wanted to see once again. We were cut off from the land of the living, but the letters gave us the priceless commodity of hope, which truly

239

springs eternal. Letters from home were our very life source. If one was extremely fortunate, a care package from home was a sight to gladden the heart of any recipient, not to mention his buddies who were accustomed to the practice of sharing the wealth.

Christmas Eve, 1970, is still my most memorable birthday, as I had just received a package from my mother. Although I was officially born on Christmas Day, I couldn't resist celebrating a few hours earlier. It was about 10:00 p.m. and my platoon was settled in our night defensive position in the bush on top of a hill overlooking our base camp in Duc Pho, a few miles away. Although both sides were observing a brief Christmas ceasefire, we were still on full alert. There were about twenty-five of us in the thick foliage and we were quite uneasy. I had just finished my shift at the listening post and had returned to see a group huddled around the platoon leader and radioman. He had the radio volume turned low, but just loud enough so that we could hear *Silver Bells* being broadcast from the base below. It started to rain, so I returned to my sleeping area where another soldier and I had rigged our ponchos together for cover. I opened my care package and shared some of my mother's famous Hungarian pastries and a can of Portuguese sardines for a feast from heaven. I was celebrating my twenty-first birthday and had about seven weeks left in Vietnam. I was beginning to feel that maybe, just maybe, I might make it out of there alive.

The last letter in the video, read by the actress Ellen Burstyn, touched me in ways that I will not soon forget. She was reading a letter written by a mother, Mrs. Eleanor Wimbish, who was making her pilgrimage to the Vietnam Memorial Wall to visit her son, William R. Stocks, on February 13, 1984, the fifteenth anniversary of his death. Bill served with the Americal Division's 198th Light Infantry Brigade at Chu Lai. This last letter was especially meaningful to me for several reasons. My unit, the 11th Light Infantry Brigade, also of the Americal Division, operated alongside his group around the Chu Lai area. It was my last duty station in Vietnam before I went home. Mrs. Wimbish was telling her deceased son about a surprise telephone call she received from one of his buddies who witnessed his death in Vietnam. He informed her how "after a while over there, instead of a yellow streak, the men got a mean streak down their backs." Reportedly, this "mean streak got bigger and the men became meaner" with each passing day.

Her letter described how delighted she was to discover that this was not the case for her son. His buddy shared how Bill kept his "warmth and friendliness" that helped retain a measure of humanity in their unit. She related that she loved this soldier, who called her New Year's Day, "for just being your close friend, and for sharing the last days of your life with you, and for being there with you when you died." The eternal bond she felt for her son was reflected in the closing words of her letter, "But this I know. I would rather to have had you for twenty-one years, and all the pain that goes with losing you, than never to have had you at all."

Although it had now been nearly four years since my initial telephone call to Beulah Wood, this letter provided me with a deeper appreciation of how valuable it had been for both of us. Moreover, it opened the way to contacting Trudy Gmack and allowing the healing process to continue with another mother who lost a son. It still amazes me how close I came to closing the door to a once-in-a-lifetime opportunity. I was now more convinced than ever that the hand of God was at work all the while. However, I also came to better appreciate the freeing and healing power of telling and knowing the truth, regardless of how painful it may be at either end. There is a unique bond between the one who spent the last moments with a person and the surviving loved ones that transcends time.

The letters in this documentary are very personal. For many, it will be the last words they would share with their families shortly before they were killed. I was struck by the contrast of how young the troops initially looked and how they seemed to unnaturally age before my eyes. More than anything, the film effectively communicated the visceral quality of being in Vietnam. There was no glory to be found here. Even the award of medals left one with a sick feeling, especially the recipient. It presented the human side of war, marked by the incessant longing for home and not knowing if you would come back alive. It was difficult for me to watch, but I had to see it again and again. It was important to connect with those buried feelings and images that have become an integral part of my identity. It took me back. Vietnam has a haunting beauty that can mesmerize my soul if I allow myself to drift away to its siren call. *Dear America* was truly a letter written collectively by America's finest to those who sent them there, and to those who eagerly awaited their return home. There were no e-mail or cell phones in those days, just pen and paper. But how infused with emotion was the written word. What an enduring tribute to them all.

One Week's Toll

The June 27, 1969, edition of *Life Magazine* includes a most unusual piece about the Vietnam War that had already claimed thirty-six thousand American lives. Although the magazine is noted for pictures accompanied by tersely written articles, the text was brief even by their standards. The thirteen-page layout barely contained one and a half written pages. Entitled "The Faces of the American Dead in Vietnam: One Week's Toll," it neatly displayed the photographs of 242 Americans who lost their lives during the seven days from May 28 to June 3 of that year, which included Memorial Day. Ironically, it was set up like any high school yearbook, but since many of the fallen were in uniform, it more closely resembled my graduating class from Fort Dix.

As one slowly scans the individual faces, it soon becomes apparent that some of them were the same photographs that were found in their high school yearbooks. Less than a year before many of them had been at the school dances, driving their parents' cars, dating their childhood sweethearts, playing their music too loud, wearing their hair too long, and drinking beer under age. For many parents, their main worry was focused on school grades, driving, and weekend curfews. They were from all over the land: Flint, Michigan, West Quincy, Massachusetts, Petersburg, Kentucky, Hamden, Connecticut, Queens, New York, Tyler, Texas, Napa, California, Great Falls, Montana, Bedford, Pennsylvania, Milwaukee, Wisconsin, Hato Rey, Puerto Rico, Nickerson, Nebraska, Hilliard, Ohio, Miami, Florida, Rapid City, South Dakota, Portland, Maine, Buffalo, New York, and so on. Many of these locations had a familiar name; some I had not known existed. But even more importantly, the number 242 killed was no longer just a statistic.

Having their faces to look at begins to give one an appreciation of the real toll of war—the very personal and priceless cost in individual lives.

The face is the point of focus when one is dying, especially the look in the dying person's eyes. The face is what we view when we approach the open casket. We look at photographs of their faces when we want to remember what they looked like. I would imagine that the photographs on these pages are the same ones that are frequently viewed by loved ones whenever they want to remember. In all likelihood, they are the ones that were placed on a table in the family room or on the mantle above the fireplace. They may be found in the homes of a surviving brother or sister, parents, nieces and nephews, or even grown children. They have become permanent fixtures in the homes of their loved ones. Every once in a while, perhaps during a Thanksgiving gathering, a kindergarten-age child asks about the person in the photograph for the first time. A golden opportunity is provided by a child's curiosity for the family to share the story of their hero. It is at this point that someone may even mention how the little one resembles his great uncle, perhaps something in his smile or the gleam in his eyes. A fresh connection with remembrance has been formed, signaling that he is not forgotten.

A number of these photographs are prominently displayed in the high schools they attended. Although the hallways are flooded whenever the bell signals the end of a class, I wonder how many make eye contact with the fallen alumni. It wasn't that long ago when they, too, were students responding to the same bell as they passed the photographs and memorials dedicated to the World War II and Korean casualties to whom their own youthful smiles are now added. Many schools have scholarships in their names and recognize them during school assemblies around Memorial Day. Not long after we honor them during family gatherings or school functions, we return to the business of living. This, after all, is what they would wish for us, as we have been given the gift of life. It is because of their ultimate sacrifice, and countless others before them, that we enjoy the freedom of this precious gift. We can return to greet these photographs and the cherished memories of them whenever we want. As we grow older, we will be adding many more photographs of our families and ourselves to view as well. We will also have the memories of our loved ones that span the course of a lifetime. But the memories and photos of the fallen are of a different world. Their faces will never age; their brief lives on earth are frozen in time. They will remain—forever young.

The One Boy Who Died

A color photograph of a U.S. Army soldier with a warm, radiant smile can be found on the front cover of the January 21, 1972, edition of *Life Magazine*. His boyish face bears an uncanny resemblance to another baby-faced man who made the cover over twenty-five years earlier—Audie Murphy, the most decorated soldier of World War II. The opening lines were encouraging enough, as they bore testimony that the war in Vietnam continued to wind down. Statistically speaking, the good news for America was that only one soldier was killed during that particular week in December of 1971. Compared to over one hundred dying per week a year ago and reaching over four hundred per week at times in 1968, the country as a whole could take a certain measure of comfort. The bad news for the Duffy family of Charlotte, Michigan, was that their son, SPC 4 Jerry N. Duffy, was the one who made the front cover of the popular magazine. He had been in Vietnam for over ten months and was scheduled to complete his tour early and be home for Christmas—a surprise that he was planning for his family. He even decided to try his hand at typing his last letter. Quite expectedly, it was a rough attempt, typical for a guy with no typing experience, and the fact that he was using an army typewriter didn't help matters. Nevertheless, he got his message across in the following words.

SHORT BUT SWEET

4 Dec. 71

HI!

How are you? Fine I hope! I'm doing pretty good. War is hell when you get to type A letter. We have a type-writer in tower 1. So i thought i'd try to type a letter

I received the Box of goodies yesterday and believe they are great. Today is the nicest day we've had in quite awhile.

I suppose everybody filled themselves up with turkey

Thanksgiving. did everybody show up? How is Dad feeling now? Better I hope. Wow I should' nt of // typed this letter I have ran out of things to say. Except i sure wish i could be home for Christmas this year. I hope you all have a MERRY CHRISTMAS a HAPPY_ NEW YEAR. Take-care & Be-Good.

LOVE

SP/4 JERRY N. DUFFEY

His mother related that the fact he sent a typed letter wasn't the only unusual thing she noticed. It was also the first time there was no mention of how many days he had left in Vietnam before he came home. As described in *Life Magazine*

Thirty minutes after midnight on Dec. 12—at 11:30 a.m., Dec. 11 in Charlotte, Mich.—Acting Sergeant Jerry N. Duffy pulled on his clothes, laced up his jungle boots and took his place as guard sergeant for the shift they called "the graveyard watch" on Hill 131. It was a moonless night, especially dark without the perimeter lights (skeleton support units could not deliver spare parts to the generator as more American units were operating under strength with the gradual pullout of troops). Thirty minutes later, while Jerry was in a hootch, a devastating mortar barrage pounded the lonely garrison (which itself was recently reduced from 24 to 17 soldiers). Twenty Viet Cong sappers slipped through the jagged wire and systematically blew up buildings with their satchel charges. It was over in 20 minutes. The hilltop was ablaze. Nine of the 17 GIs were wounded and Jerry Duffy was dead—three days before he was to go home for Christmas and as it turned out, just 19 days before Hill 131 was to be turned over to the South Vietnamese.

Christmas will never be the same again for the Duffy family. It is said, "The first casualty of war is truth." For the Duffys and thousands of other families around America, the empty chair during holiday dinners is *one truth* that will never be compromised.

The Wall

It was sometime in late November 2005 and I was waiting in the main room of the college library while my nursing students were in a nearby classroom receiving their orientation on how to conduct research within the library system. I had some extra time to browse around the few remaining stacks in the rather expansive, half-empty room that seemed almost barren of books. Everything is computerized nowadays, and the volumes of research journals and articles are readily accessed from the privacy and convenience of one's personal computer. As I was browsing through some of the books, I recalled the endless stacks of books in the library during my days at the University of Buffalo, some thirty years earlier, when books were books. There was a sense of awe as one was confronted by the beauty and enormity of the endless volumes, each with a title and personality of its own.

On this day, however, I managed to be standing near the rather limited selection of books about the Vietnam War. I came across a book entitled *Offerings at the Wall*, a most unusual piece of literature. I did not know what to expect as I opened it and began to thumb through the pages. It was simply and profoundly a collection of photographs of various items that were left at the Vietnam Veterans Memorial by people who had visited the site over the years. But to end with such a generic description would be missing the essence of the entire healing process, for healing is, as it has always been, an intensely personal matter. It all started in 1982 when a U.S. Naval officer stood over the trench of the foundation where the concrete was being poured. He was observed to have tossed an object into it and then offered a salute. He informed a worker that he was offering his dead brother's Purple Heart to the Wall.

As I continued leafing through the pages, I soon found myself mesmerized by the gravitational pull of its contents. Some had brief captions near the bottom of the page explaining the significance of the item(s), but most just stood alone, like the name they were there to accompany. There was a full page of several dozen Purple Hearts all lined up, much like the recipients in their graves. There was even a Medal of Honor that a soldier was returning in protest for U.S. government support of the Contras. Many personal items like photographs, boots, even a can of Spam and sardines with personal notes attached, were included. Then, all of a sudden, I came to page 159 and there she was, again—Eleanor Grace Alexander—the same person I met as I read her memorial plaque near the elevator door at D'Youville College nearly sixteen months earlier. Here we met again, a few weeks before the end of the semester, as I was concluding my brief tenure as a nursing professor. The longer I live, the less inclined I am to believe that such encounters with others are coincidental. I became lost in thought as I gazed upon her photograph and reflected on my nursing students in the next room. I wondered if any one of them would be compelled to join the military in the manner that led Eleanor Grace on her mission of mercy for which she ended up making the ultimate sacrifice. Already, we have had several visits from recruiters expressing their growing need for nursing personnel to treat the casualties of our present war, again, half a world away from home.

Over 2.5 million people visit *The Wall* each year; many of whom are Vietnam veterans. While I visited *The Moving Wall* when it passed through the area in the 90s, I have never been to the permanent site in Washington DC. I am not alone in this regard, as I come across fellow veterans who, like myself, plan to go "someday." Then there are those who never want to go at all. We all march to a different timetable relative to our inner healing as we approach various junctures along the way. Judging by many of the personal writings on the offerings at the wall, these individuals waited a long time to make the trek. Yet, the inner dictates for their eventual journey were never far off. Maybe it wasn't a daily event, but the persuasive urgings began to undertake a spiritual character that required a pilgrimage to this sacred place. With each passing year we came to realize just how young they were, those who paid the ultimate price. We continued with our own daily struggles and personal setbacks, but we knew we were alive and in the fight. We also got to enjoy the many gifts and blessings that life has to offer along the way.

It is also here that the humanity of our adversary is revealed. The photo of a North Vietnamese soldier with his daughter is left at the wall, one that an American soldier from the 101st Airborne Division had been carrying since he shot and killed him decades ago. I remembered when his story and personal interview were on TV. Accompanying the photograph, the soldier left a brief letter commending the NVA for being a brave soldier defending his homeland. He was still confused why the North Vietnamese soldier didn't shoot him first when they met on the trail that day. He ended the letter with the following words, "Above all else, I can now respect the importance that life held for you. I suppose that is why I am able to be here today…it is time for me to continue the life process and release my pain and guilt. Forgive me, sir."

It's the same story again. The guy in the trenches, regardless of which side, is afraid and would rather be elsewhere, like home with his friends and loved ones. It is the mothers, wives, brothers, sisters, children, and friends who will be left with the void for the remainder of their lives. It is they who have to continue grieving long after the war is over. It is they who make the journey to our nation's capital to seek some sort of closure with the deceased. Some offer an artifact with a deeply personal meaning, many known only to the visitor and the name etched on the wall. I looked at a photograph of a package that was returned because the soldier was killed on October 31, 1972. The attached note reads, "Mom and Dad want you to have these cookies and Kool Aid. It's time they gave these to you. They send all their love. Peace, Gary B." I remember how happy I was to receive such care packages wrapped in brown paper from my own mother. Each one was consistently filled with precious cargo—her homemade cookies and pastries. I am grateful that she was spared such a scene as this family had to endure. It was fitting, painful as it was, that I got to bury her a few years ago. The natural order was not reversed like it had been for the tens of thousands on this wall.

Then there was the plaque and photograph of a two-star general with the following inscription:

> One of the general's remarks to me back in October 1967, "My heart goes out to the mothers who bore these young fighting men and had to nurse them growing up, feed them, educate them, and had to see them come to this foolish war. My heart bleeds for the mothers. These young men are the bravest men I have ever seen in my life time."

> Maj. Gen. Bruno A. Hochmuth was the commander of the Third Marine Division Headquarters "Hue." The general was killed in a helicopter explosion November 14, 1967.

Many of the Vietnam veterans struggle with the guilt of having survived. In an instant, their buddies qualified to be listed on that marble wall. And here they are, staring at the name and wondering why it wasn't theirs, as they gently caress the letters on this cold, inanimate structure. For some reason, trying to convince yourself that it was not your turn to die will not suffice, but all too often it will just have to do. But I need something much more substantial to sustain me as I envision Bill Wood's dead body slowly being hoisted into a hovering helicopter just above the thick jungle canopy. The *enduring image* of his head hanging limp to one side is a stark reminder of One who was crucified and hanged on a tree many years before, fulfilling His own words, "Greater love has no one than this, that he lay down his life for his friends." War, after all, is an outward manifestation of a spiritual disease that resides within individual souls. Someone, somewhere and sometime, had to effect a radical cure in order that there may be hope for a better life both here and in the world to come. It is on a daily basis that I continue to learn what that historical sacrificial act means to me in time and eternity. My only hope is in Jesus' own words of comfort to Martha, who was grieving the death of her brother Lazarus, "I am the resurrection and the life. He who believes in me will live, even though he dies; and whoever lives and believes in me will never die."

Epilogue (Life 101)

And God said, "Let the water teem with living creatures, and let the birds fly above the earth across the expanse of the sky." So God created the great creatures of the sea and every living and moving thing with which the water teems, according to their kinds, and every winged bird according to its kind. And God saw that it was good. God blessed them and said, "Be fruitful and increase in number and fill the seas, and let the birds increase on the earth." And there was evening, and there was morning—the fifth day (Gen. 1:20–23).

The ongoing struggle with life and death includes all living things, be they plants, insects, fish, birds, or mammals. The instinct for survival is built into every living creature, regardless of its relative position on the phylogenetic scale of development. We live in a world full of creatures that God designed to share our planet. Perhaps because they can fly, while I start to get anxious at the mere thought of becoming airborne, birds have always held a particular fascination for me. Their infinite variety of shapes, sizes, colors, and flight patterns is nothing less than amazing. I have a number of bird feeders in my front yard that are visited by year-round as well as seasonal feathered friends. Robins, cardinals, woodpeckers, and the bold little chickadees are always welcome. Cowbirds and the ever-vociferous grackles are barely tolerated. But I guess they have their reason for being here, just like all the other more desirable types. Therefore, it's no surprise that God in His infinite wisdom has used the birds of the air to teach me about the sanctity of life and the necessity of death.

My previous office bordered a 150-acre wetland and sat back about fifty yards from the main road. A grass lawn of only about thirty feet separated our building from the wood line of the preserve. Deer, wild turkey, raccoons, and a host of other wildlife frequented that stretch of land to feed on the goodies we placed there for them, especially during the cold, snowy winter months. The bird feeders were also very popular, and I often scrambled to my *Audubon Bird Book* to try to identify the visitors before they flew away.

It was business as usual in the wild when, one day, Barb, my secretary, called my attention to a mother Mallard Duck leading her brood across the lawn to feed. Barb had been observing them for a few days and noticed that one of the ducklings displayed an unusually awkward gait—even for a duck. Upon closer observation, it became quite obvious that he was considerably smaller than his siblings and had only one leg. More than likely, it was lost in an encounter with a snapping turtle while swimming in the pond. These submariner hunters take their toll on young aquatic birds each year. They have to eat, too.

The little guy was lucky to be alive. But he was a fighter, to be sure. He would use his one leg to propel himself forward in a gliding fashion, stand up, and repeat the same motion as he struggled to keep pace at the rear of the procession. I named him "Rocky" because his main goal each day seemed to be that he "just wanted to go the distance." On some days the family of ducks would have company, as a group of Canada Geese and their offspring would feed nearby. One day, a goose inadvertently waddled too close to the ducklings. The much smaller mother duck suddenly positioned herself between the goose and her precious brood, as she spread her wings and lunged forward, quacking loudly at the bewildered goose that immediately backed off and returned to her own group some twenty feet away.

As the weeks went by, we would watch with concern for Rocky to make his entrance from the wood line, lagging far behind the group. By now he was even further behind in physical development compared to the others. Nevertheless, his mother patiently waited and watched for him to join them for daily meals of the grains that we scattered on the lawn near the birdfeeder. A wildlife rehabilitation specialist informed me that it was doubtful he'd survive. Some predator would probably get him during the night. Besides, if by some miracle he survived until adulthood, he would need both legs for a proper takeoff in order to become airborne. Any way one considered it, the deck was definitely stacked against him.

But this little guy would not give up. Every day he would make the thirty-foot trek across the lawn, lagging well behind the others. I was conflicted watching this all too familiar daily event. On some occasions the rest of the family was already well under way to the feeding area and he was nowhere to be seen. I almost breathed a sigh of relief that perhaps some predator finally ended his misery the preceding night. But this was short-lived, as he again emerged from the bushes to shimmy and slide his way for yet another day. Although I am not a hunter, I even had some Kevorkian-type thoughts of purchasing a pellet gun and putting him out of his misery, but quickly dismissed them. Then, all of a sudden, it dawned on me—he wasn't suffering. Quite the contrary, he was fully involved in doing the best he could with his handicap. He seemed to be relishing every moment that he was alive and showed absolutely no lack of enthusiasm and zest for life. Although he was the runt of the litter, he had the heartiest appetite. I was the one who was miserable watching him struggle. The whole problem resided with me, not him.

But then again, life is a struggle. I recalled learning such a lesson from Dr. James D. Lowe Jr., chairman of the psychology department at the University of Southern Mississippi. Bearing an uncanny resemblance to distinguished actor Vincent Price, he had a commanding presence. I was with a group of doctoral students in the psychology laboratory observing a goose egg hatching in an incubator. The temperature and humidity were carefully controlled in order to make conditions as conducive as possible for the emerging gosling. We were all watching in amazement at the new life emerging right before our eyes. That poor little gosling struggled mightily to break free from the shell. It seemed like it took the better part of the day for him to complete the exhausting task. All the while he strained and pushed, stopped and started, and labored to free himself from what was once his protection and home, but which now was taking on the character of a personal tomb. Some of us wanted to immediately jump in and rescue the poor struggling creature before he just gave up altogether and expired before our eyes. But our professor cautioned us against interfering in this necessary struggle for life because it is during this critical period that the creature gains the strength to survive after he is freed from the shell. In short, doing the work for him would diminish his chances of survival. God in His infinite wisdom designed it so. The only contact the professor had with the exhausted little creature was to gently remove the eggshell on his head after he emerged from the shell.

As the summer slowly faded and fall was around the corner, I was beset with new worries. Rocky had grown to an almost full-sized duck but still lagged behind the rest of his siblings. He had miraculously survived predation. The question now looming on my horizon was his survival over the winter months ahead. I finally decided to trap him somehow when his family flew away and left him behind and then turn him over to a wildlife specialist. But apparently he had other plans.

The day came when, instead of waddling back to the woods or to the small pond, the entire family, minus Rocky, suddenly took to the sky. As I watched to see his reaction, I got the surprise of my life—he made a perfectly executed vertical takeoff, every bit as impressive as one made by a Harrier Jump Jet from a British aircraft carrier. So much for all of my well intentioned plans and misguided ruminations over the past six months. I continued to feed the deer, turkeys, and other wildlife over the course of the cold winter months. To my delight, Rocky and his entire family flew back from Lake Erie to join in the feast on a regular basis. This pattern continued for the next few years. Although I know that he has been dead for some time, the mere sighting of a brightly colored male Mallard never fails to generate a warm feeling and a smile.

Acknowledgements

Donna Fazekas, LCSW-R, my wife and soul mate, who knows first hand that the war is far from over after the soldier returns home. Her love and support were essential as we healed together over the years. Her background as an English teacher came in quite handy for editing and proofreading. She was on her way to Woodstock five years before we met, while I was shipping off to Fort Dix that same week in the Summer of '69. We were meant to be together.

Mr. & Mrs. (Jerome & Betty) Fingerhut, my father-in-law and mother-in-law, who both proudly served with the U.S. Marine Corps during WWII. They were very supportive and always made me feel welcome, despite the fact that I was one of the few Army veterans who was consistently outnumbered by the Marines during family gatherings.

Very Rev. Dr. Michael W. R. "Bill" Stott for his close friendship dating back to my early college years and return to civilian life. His encouragement and guidance were key ingredients in writing this book.

Larry Toczek, Ray Cage, Ed Dillihunt, Larry Tax, and other Vietnam veterans of the First Cavalry Division (Airmobile) who helped fill in the gaps of our tour during the flurry of telephone calls and email exchanges following the "rude awakening."

Peggy Barstow for the telephone call that ushered in the "rude awakening" and set everything in motion. She provided much-needed support during those early, difficult months when Vietnam became all too real, again.

Mr. & Mrs. (Robert & Trudy) Gmack and family for sharing their memories about their beloved John.

Mr. & Mrs. (Sam & Bonnie) Rhodes for being sensitive to the needs of grieving mother, Mrs. Beulah Wood, and setting up the arrangements for our meeting in Alliance, Ohio.

Larry Wood for sharing your memories about your big brother, Bill, and meeting with us. Sharon Maines for the letter you wrote to Donna and me following your mother's death. I will cherish it for the rest of my life.

David McKeever, Sr. friend and fellow Vietnam veteran who allowed me to enter his grief during the tragic loss of his son, Sgt. David Mckeever, who was killed in Iraq.

Linda Pike, my sister-in-law, and Amy Moebius for their review of the rough draft of the manuscript; and providing me with insightful comments about the overall formulation of the work. Patricia Lane for her editing and proofreading assistance. Gary Wolfe for the design of the book cover and restoration of old photographs. Most of all, I'm grateful for his friendship over the past thirty plus years.

A Special Acknowledgement to my deceased parents, Mr. & Mrs. (Paul & Valerie) Fazekas, who lived through the horror and hardship of World War II that ravaged their homeland. I am most grateful that they immigrated to the United States of America during the Hungarian Revolution of 1956 so that we may have hope for a better life. Thank you both for giving me two essential ingredients for life—a sense of humor and endurance.

The author may be contacted at **PFazekasPHDNP@verizon.net**

Bibliography

1 G. Livingston, *Too Soon Old, Too Late Smart: Thirty True Things You Need to Know Now* (New York: Marlow & Company, 2004) 38.

2 Ibid., 116.

3 C. Sherman, Interview with S. Greenspan in *Clinical Psychiatry News* 3 (2006) 1.

4 A. Tozer, *The Pursuit of God* (Camp Hill, PA: Christian Publications Inc., 1982) 46.

5 B. Rooney, *Testimony before the U.S. Senate Committee on Energy and Natural Resources* (Washington, D.C., 2004).

6 L. Barnett, *Touched by Fire: The Life, Death, and Mythic Afterlife of George Armstrong Custer* (New York: Henry Holt and Company, 1996)

LaVergne, TN USA
17 June 2010
186535LV00002B/22/P